The

WORLD WITHIN

The WORLD WITHIN

Writers Talk Ambition, Angst, Aesthetics, Bones, Books, Beautiful Bodies, Censorship, Cheats, Comics, Darkness, Democracy, Death, Exile, Failure, Guns, Misery, Muses, Movies, Old Boys' Network, Oprah, Outcasts, Sex, Suicide, Smoking, Strippers, Torture, Vietnam, VD, Violence, and More

TinHouseBooks

Published by Tin House Books, Portland, Oregon, and New York, New York
Distributed to the trade by Publishers Group West, 1700 Fourth St., Berkeley,
CA 94710, www.pgw.com

ISBN 10: 0-9776989-6-3
ISBN 13: 978-09776989-6-7

First U.S. edition 2007

Interior design by Laura Shaw Design, Inc.

www.tinhouse.com

Printed in Canada

Contents

A CONVERSATION WITH
CLARIBEL ALEGRÍA

Abbie Fields

Claribel Alegría is a Nicaraguan-born Salvadoran writer best known for her poetry and novellas about her homeland. She gained prominence during the 1980s as her country was torn apart by a civil war that the Reagan Administration fueled as part of its strategy to bring down the Sandinistas in neighboring Nicaragua, and which left more than 75,000 Salvadorans dead.

The first of five children, she grew up in a home filled with books and culture in the western Salvadoran city of Santa Ana, living with the comforts and privileges of the Central American upper class. In 1943, at the age of eighteen, she moved to the United States to attend George Washington University. There she met her husband, Darwin "Bud" Flakoll, who worked as a journalist first in Washington DC and then in Mexico City. He later served at U.S. diplomatic posts in Latin America.

Alegría came of age as a writer in the 1950s, during the years she and Flakoll (and their four children) lived in Mexico and South America, their lives intersecting with some of the region's most dynamic writers. By the early sixties they were living in Paris, again keeping company with many of the writers who would soon gain a foothold in Europe and the United States. Not long after the Bay of Pigs invasion, Flakoll resigned from the State Department and the family moved to the small village of Deyá in Majorca, Spain, where they would spend most of the next twenty years.

When the Sandinistas overthrew the Somoza dictatorship in Nicaragua in July 1979, Alegría and Flakoll shifted their focus entirely to Central America, and by the mid-1980s had installed themselves permanently in Managua, Nicaragua. Alegría has lived there ever since. Following the death of her husband in 1995, Alegría reached a new crescendo with her poetry.

Though she defines herself mostly as a poet, Alegría's work also includes stories, novellas, testimonials, and anthologies. With her son Erik, she is currently translating the Chinese *Tao* into Spanish. Her work has been translated into at least fourteen languages, and she has received numerous awards in Europe and Latin America, including the Casa de las Américas prize for her collection of poems *Sobrevivo* (*I Survive*) in 1978. In October 2006, she was selected as the recipient of the Neustadt International Prize for Literature.

I met with Alegría in the lush garden of her Managua home. After a strong cup of Nicaraguan coffee, we sat down to talk about the roads she's traveled, her friendships with other writers, and her work.

Abbie Fields: You lived in Mexico, Chile, Uruguay, Argentina, and Paris during the 1950s and early 1960s, which was where many of the writers who would become the most critically acclaimed of the Latin "boom" were living at that time. Writers such as Cortázar, Fuentes, Vargas Llosa, García Márquez, Benedetti, and, of course, Neruda. Why do you think this was such a key moment for young Latin American writers?

Claribel Alegría: I think the Cuban Revolution had a lot to do with it, because when the Cuban Revolution won, lots of people from the United States, from Europe, from all over suddenly focused their eyes on Latin America. They were wonderful writers, but nobody had paid much attention to many of them. And there was a publishing house called Seix Barral in Barcelona, Spain, that had started publishing these writers, and that caused a sort of "boom." So these writers were very well known in Spain and the rest of the countries of Latin America.

AF: Were they writing something new that caused this "boom"?

CA: It was not new; they were writing years earlier. Julio Cortázar had been writing his beautiful fantastic stories and nobody had paid attention to them at all. And yes, Vargas Llosa had won a prize and was published by Seix Barral, and then the editor of Seix Barral was very clever and he saw all of this talent, and he thought it was the right time to start making Latin America known in Spain. But they had been writing for a long time.

AF: Do you think the interest in these writers had something to do with political repression in their countries, or with living as political refugees or exiles? For instance, the writers who were in Paris in the early sixties?

CA: Yes, many of them were in exile because they couldn't go back to their countries. Julio Cortázar, for instance, wasn't in forced exile but he chose exile because he didn't like the *Peronistas* [in Argentina], and so he went to Paris. When I met Vargas Llosa he was working at the Agence France-Presse. It was dangerous for him in Peru at that time, I think. And for Mario Benedetti, it was far too dangerous to go back to Uruguay. So they were living in exile. I am talking about 1962 to 1966, before we went to Majorca.

AF: Who were the writers of that period with whom you most identify, to whom you were closest?

CA: I always felt very close to Julio Cortázar, although our ways of expressing ourselves are completely different. And also I loved the book *The Death of Artemio Cruz* and Carlos Fuentes very, very much.

AF: It's interesting that you keep mentioning Julio Cortázar. *Hopscotch* has always seemed to me a seminal work of that period, and one of the most creative and self-searching books I've ever read.

CA: I agree.

AF: How did you first meet Cortázar, and why do you think you became so close to him?

CA: It's because of the anthology. When we were living in Mexico, Tito [Augusto] Monterroso was a very close friend of ours. He introduced us to Mexican writers, especially Rulfo, who became a very good friend, and Juan Jose Arreola, who knew lots of writers, and he's the one who introduced Bud and me to Cortázar. And we became fascinated with him. We met lots of people, and Bud said to me, "These are really some great writers." Cortázar wasn't even known in Mexico, and in the U.S. and Spain even less. So Bud started thinking that we should do an anthology of young—at that time—poets and short story writers. When we were living in Buenos Aires, some friends invited us to an asado and that is where we met Julio and his first wife, Aurora, in 1962. It was beautiful—we felt like we had been friends for many years. It was fantastic.

You know, *Hopscotch* is a book that I have read about three times, and I always love it. Somebody once asked me which book I would take to a deserted island, and I said *Hopscotch*, because it's always new to me. I discover new things each time.

AF: You and Cortázar also shared a love of the Nicaraguan Revolution, didn't you? I know he came here in the early years of the revolution and spent time writing a book.

CA: In 1979. We came in September and he and his second wife, Carol, first came in November of '79. He adored Nicaragua and he loved the revolution. They were contemplating living between Paris and Nicaragua. But he died in 1984. So he didn't see the Sandinistas losing and all of that. He never became disenchanted, as many of us are.

AF: Maybe he was lucky that way?

CA: Yes, lucky, I think.

AF: You have been defined as—I'm quoting from Smith College here—"a formidable champion for Central America, continuing the region's tradition of revolutionary poetry," and Margorie Agosín has said that your "ideological and literary tendencies are a reflection of a literary current that gained momentum in Central America during the 1950s and 1960s known as '*la generación comprometida*' [the committed generation]." Some of your writing refers directly to political events, such as *Ashes of Izalco* and the massacre of 30,000 peasants in El Salvador in 1932. But much of your writing, especially in this last decade, is more personal, and not overtly political. I know you do not consider your writing "political" as such—you have said that your political poems are not really political, but are rather poems of love to your country. Do you think that political events have motivated your writing?

CA: Let me tell you something. Before the Cuban Revolution—there's that Cuban Revolution again!—I didn't care about politics. I thought that writers couldn't do anything about these dictators in Central America. I thought, What can we do with these military dictators and the U.S. government always helping them? Then the Cuban Revolution happened and I marveled at that. I thought if the Cubans could do it, why not Central Americans? At that time I was living in Paris, and I started thinking about 1932 in El Salvador. I was only a child in '32; I was seven years old, but I remember—a child's memory is really something. And then I started talking about this, and it was Carlos Fuentes who told me I needed to write about it. But I had been a disciple of Juan Ramón Jiménez, who had taught me to work very hard in poetry—that was my genre—and I had no experience with prose. I'd always worked with poetry, all my life. And then Bud, who was a newspaperman, suggested we write it together. And that's how *Cenizas de Izalco* (*Ashes of Izalco*) came about. And, yes, in *Cenizas* I was very focused on the fact that the people who would read the book would find out what had happened in Central America. The love story is incidental. We mostly wanted to transmit the historical event.

But when I said that my poems are poems of love, that is true too, because I never sit down to write a poem in order to denounce something. For that, I have prose, or the testimonials, or historical novels. However, I was hit really hard by the things that were happening in Central America, and those things filtered into my poetry, and so some people think they are political poems. I don't care; it's okay, whatever they think. I never wanted to commit my poetry in that way.

AF: What do you mean by "commit"?

CA: That the poems should be free. That I'm not going to use poetry, but instead let the poetry use me. Do you know what I mean? The poetry is using me to let me express myself. But I am not going to use poetry to denounce something for political purposes. There are other ways to do that.

AF: I'm not sure you've convinced me. What about a poem like "La Mujer del Río Sumpul" ("The Woman of Sumpul River")? Doesn't it refer to a massacre that took place in May 1980, in which hundreds of civilians were killed by government soldiers as they tried to flee across the Sumpul River into Honduras? And don't you quite directly finger the "Yankee strategist and his armed vultures"? Isn't that a pretty clear denunciation?

CA: Yes, but that is something very different for me, because that is something that really shook my emotions. Like the death of someone you love very much. It shakes you. And so all of that filters into my poetry. I had read a short story in the newspaper that recounted what had happened at Sumpul. And it mentioned this woman who was there with two children, one that was not her own. It shook me, and then I invented all of that. But I didn't sit down to denounce something. That episode shook me to my roots, and I started writing about mother earth, and imagining it all, all of the helicopters, and what that poor woman would be saying. That's why people say that my poems are political, and in a way they are right, because when something shakes my emotions, it filters in.

AF: It would also seem that your testimonial books have been extremely politically driven, such as the book in which you and Bud interviewed Somoza's assassins [*Death of Somoza*], or the story of the spectacular prison breakout by the MRTA rebels in Peru [*Tunnel to Canto Grande*].

CA: In those, yes, we set out to say something. That is why we loved testimony, because something real is happening. We are listening to the people who not only witnessed these events but actually made them happen. That is something else. Poetry and testimonials are very different, completely different. Poetry and journalism are very different. And for me poetry comes from pure emotion, an emotion in you that transforms you. I am not going to write a poem about all of the horrible things that Somoza did, because it's not for poetry.

AF: Is that because poetry is more abstract?

CA: Well, I'm not generalizing. I'm just talking about me. For me, poetry is something sacred.

AF: Many of your closest friends—like Cortázar, Mario Benedetti, Eduardo Galeano, and others—shared your commitment to the Nicaraguan Revolution, in both their writing and publicly expressed views, but some of your closest friends, such as Mario Vargas Llosa, held very opposite, and at times very public, positions. I remember a night at your home in the late 1980s, Mario Vargas Llosa was there and Tomás Borge—who was then Minister of the Interior and known as one of the most ideologically strident members of the Sandinista Government—showed up, more or less uninvited, to confront him. I remember how uncomfortable you felt, because Mario was your friend. Yet the stakes at that time were so high. The Nicaraguan revolution was floundering, becoming very frayed at the edges, and tens of thousands of people had died. Did political positions ever come to define your relationships, or sever them?

CA: No, actually. I consider myself a very good friend of Mario Vargas Llosa. We have discussions, and he laughs at me because he thinks I don't understand politics . . . But no, that has never marred our relationship.

AF: But what I mean by the stakes being high is that the opinions of somebody like Vargas Llosa could have been used against the revolution, in other words, could have added fuel to Reagan's fire. Couldn't his words have been used to attack this revolution you loved so dearly? Didn't that bother you?

CA: Yes, it bothered me very much, but I could still discuss things with him. I would argue with him, and we never agreed in any way. I would get furious with him, and he also would get furious with me, he would say I was naïve. But our friendship was strong enough, thank goodness. And I don't think his words gave any fuel to Reagan. I don't think Mario allowed himself to be used that way. He was too intelligent.

AF: Carolyn Forché said in the *Los Angeles Times*, "Julio Cortázar was among the many who urged [you] to bottle *Luisa in Realityland*, cork it, and throw it in the sea." She went on to say that he would have been pleased with the results. What do you think she meant by putting it in a bottle and throwing it in the sea?

CA: That is what one does with a book: you put it in a bottle and cork it and throw it out to sea for whoever finds it. He was really the one who urged me to write that book, he and Carol, and also his first wife, Aurora. I had started writing my vignettes, remembering things that had happened in my childhood. But it was only for me, and Bud, and my children. And one night, Julio said I had to make them into a book. And there was something very curious that Bud pointed out to me. I had named the book *Luisa en el país de la realidad* (*Luisa in Realityland*), inspired, of course, by *Alice in Wonderland*. And I don't know why the name "Luisa" came to me, but it did. I thought it was because of a dream I'd had, where I saw myself with a great friend who was called Luisa. And so I used the name Luisa, which was me. But he said, "Look, Claribel, Luisa is Lewis and also Carol, from Lewis Carroll who wrote *Alice in Wonderland*, and this is just amazing," and so I dedicated the book to Carol, who was Julio's wife and a very good friend of mine and a wonderful woman. And we all laughed about the coincidence, but Julio said, "There is no coincidence, and this book is going to be very well received."

AF: I know your family in El Salvador is for the most part very politically conservative. Were they disturbed by the publication of this book?

CA: No, not by *Luisa*. But they were very bothered by *Cenizas*. They were very upset because in the book I invented a love affair. I based the characters in my book on real people, everybody does that, but then you lie and lie and lie. My father's character is Dr. Rojas, and my mother's character is Doña Isabel, but then we lied, and I invented a love affair between my mother and a gringo who was passing through town. And before we sent the book to Seix Barral to compete for publication, I sent the manuscript to my parents and asked them to please read it, and if they didn't like it I wasn't going to submit it. I was especially worried that my father would be mad, my mother too. And they said, "Don't be silly, go ahead and send it." But the rest of my family was very conservative and furious about the book; they said it showed a lack of respect toward my mother, and that I'd abused my grandfather and all of my relatives. And what they did was buy up all the books—because the book was published in Spain and the bookstores in El Salvador were selling it—and they would burn them. And the owners of the bookstores were very happy because they had to keep ordering more. Until my relatives finally got tired of that.

AF: So you did suffer some fallout, though not from the publication of Luisa, but from your political involvement here in Nicaragua.

CA: Very much.

AF: One of the poems in *Saudade* that really moved me is about how haunted you are by your mother's death.

CA: Yes. It was 1984, and we were already living in Nicaragua. I had a cousin who was the Minister of Defense of El Salvador, and he was terrible. General Vides Casanova. He hated me, hated my politics. At that time it was very dangerous for me to go to El Salvador. So my brother or somebody asked him what would happen if I came, and he said, "I won't protect her at all. She shouldn't come." My mother was dying, she was calling for me, since we were very close to each other, and I was desperate and wanted to go. And my brother called and said, "If you come, there will be two funerals." So Bud hid my passport because he didn't want me to go. And I didn't go. I wasn't with my mother when she died, and that has haunted me all my life, it will haunt me for the rest of my life.

AF: Although you left El Salvador when you were around eighteen, your writing has remained firmly grounded there. What are the things that seem to make Central Americans so strongly identified with their origins?

CA: I think that where you spend your childhood and adolescence— because I didn't leave El Salvador until I was eighteen—is what marks you. Your first flavors. Your first smells. Scenes, the people who surround you . . . so El Salvador marked me.

AF: And do you think that moving around so much over the years has affected your writing?

CA: Living in exile has two sides. First, I was in exile because I went to study in the U.S. Later, I was in a forced exile, the years when I could not return to El Salvador. But I think exile helps, too, because then you see your country in another light, completely, in a way you wouldn't have if you had just stayed there. For instance, when I wrote *Luisa*, I had another perspective, since I was living in Majorca when I was remembering all of these things that had happened to me as a child. So it enriches you, as long as the exile doesn't last too long. Now I can come and go to El Salvador as I want.

AF: It may be enriching on some levels, but exile does mean tremendous loss at times. Like not being able to be with your mother when she was dying. There is great pain in exile as well.

CA: Very great pain. That was one of the greatest sorrows in my life, not to be able to be with my mother. What you say is true. Exile is horrible. Not just when your mother dies. It's a longing to go home . . . to smell certain things, to see things. Of course there is pain.

AF: Much of *Luisa in Realityland* is clearly autobiographical. It's a very unusual collection of short stories, bits of prose, and poetry. Can you tell me why this book is so significant for you?

CA: You know, it has to do with the other question that you asked me about El Salvador, why I'm so strongly identified with El Salvador. I hadn't lived in El Salvador since I was eighteen—I would go to visit my parents, but would only stay for a short time. And living in Deyá, I had a great deal of solitude. It was a very small village without much to do. And then I started thinking of my childhood, and how it had marked me so much, and wondering why was I involved in these revolutions in Nicaragua and El Salvador, how this was linked to my childhood. Because my family was very well-to-do, and as a child I wondered why so many people had nothing, and why I was so privileged. If I hadn't had those experiences, I wouldn't have become a revolutionary. My parents were wonderful, they would say, "Look at that, it is terrible." In *Luisa*, I was trying to understand why I was reacting the way I was now. I had to go back.

AF: I wonder if people who have never lived here can imagine the extremity of the poverty, this terrible impoverishment that you're talking about, which is something that tears you apart from the inside out?

CA: Completely. For instance, I could never forget something that happened when I was about six years old. I was with my nana, and we went past the house of a very rich lady who had lots of dogs—they were Great Danes—and a truck pulled up filled with so much meat for the dogs, and there were two little boys my age, maybe a little older, watching this meat being unloaded—like a whole cow—for the dogs. And some little bits fell on the ground, and the children scrambled to get those little bits. I remember I came home crying. It marks you, a lot.

Or Carmen Bomba. There was a man who would carry heavy things on his shoulders, what do you call that, a *cargador*? I would be taking my piano lesson in the living room—I was very young—and he would come to the window after having worked so long and so hard, and he would stand outside the window telling me what we call "*bombas*" in Spanish, or rhymes, in order to make me laugh. Imagine that. That is so beautiful. I have that in *Luisa*, Carmen Bomba. And it was my mother who said to me, "Can you see this man, who works so hard and yet he comes and wants to make you smile?" Imagine. We don't think of that. Such humanity. And after a hard day, bothering to make a child smile.

AF: You also lived for almost twenty years in Europe, first in Paris and then settling in Deyá, Majorca. You had a very close relationship with Robert Graves, who also lived in Deyá. Can you tell me something about that?

CA: We were remodeling a very old house and we were up on the second floor in what was going to be our bedroom. And all of a sudden—I didn't even know that Robert Graves lived there—I saw him passing by, in shorts and a big hat, playing with a little Ping-Pong ball in his hand, and I just shouted out, "You are Robert Graves!" He looked up and said, "Yes, who are you?" And so I explained and we invited him in for a glass of wine, and it was truly wonderful. Like with Julio Cortázar, we immediately took to each other. And from then on, he would come by two or three times a week, and we always had a glass of wine and Bud and he would talk about UFOs. Then he wanted me to be his translator, because he said he was very well known in Spain and Latin America for his mythology and for books like *I, Claudius*, but not for his poetry, and he said that above all he felt himself a poet. He already had an offer from a publishing house in Spain to publish his poetry, but the condition was that I translate his poems. And I told him no, that I wasn't going to do it, because, I said, "I adore your poetry but it's very different from mine. It's of a very classical cut, and mine is not." He said, "All right, then I won't publish it," and so Bud offered to help me. They finally convinced me, but my condition was that I choose which poems to include. I chose one hundred poems. And when I couldn't grasp the exact sense of something, Bud would help, and Robert too. It took me three years, and I still remember it. First I would translate a poem literally, then I would pace up and down listening to the music, then putting it to the same music as Robert's, or trying to, since I believe poetry is very hard to translate. No matter how wonderful the translator, it loses its aroma, some of its aroma.

AF: Why do you think that some Latin American writers are so appealing to European and American audiences? Why do certain Latin writers speak to these cultures?

CA: I think that both Europeans and North Americans look for things that are unfamiliar and strange to them, and they are curious. They have a great curiosity about the way we see things. It's the same thing that happens to me when I read the work of someone from Poland or Hungary. I am deeply interested in what touches their sensibilities.

AF: And why do you think that certain writers, such as García Márquez, touch them more deeply?

CA: Well, in the first place because they're great writers! He's a beautiful writer. Also, I think because of the fantasy. For instance, in *One Hundred Years of Solitude*, it's this magical realism that they don't have in the United States. They don't see it. So a writer like García Marquez helps them discover that. Here in Latin America, magical realism is always right in front of you. We just have to be observant and there it is!

AF: You wrote the collection of poems entitled *Saudade*, which is translated as "sorrow" in English, shortly after Bud's death. Can you tell me something about the process you went through writing these, where you started from and where you ended up?

CA: When Bud died, it was such a horrible blow, because we weren't only man and wife, we were everything—friends, companions, we were together continuously. When he died, I felt like I had lost my legs or my arms, and I was desperate and I wanted to be alone. So I took a trip by myself to Asia and that trip was very good for me, but I thought I would never write again. Then, suddenly the muse came to me, like a butterfly, and it helped me accept Bud's death. The first poem in the book is "Salí a Buscarte" ("Searching for You"), but it was useless to look for him because I realized he was inside of me.

AF: And did the process take you somewhere?

CA: I just wrote whatever I felt, but mostly I was trying to understand this thing that had happened. When I had enough, I arranged the poems for the book. And by the end, when I had finished putting it together, I was so much better emotionally that I added a small poem called "No Puede" ("It Cannot") that says, "Sadness / can't cope with me. / I lead it toward life / and it evaporates."

AF: Although "saudade" is translated into English as "sorrow," it seems to me that in Portuguese the word has a slightly different meaning that seems to encompass nostalgia, homesickness. Would you agree?

CA: I agree completely. That's why I used the word *saudade*. It's Portuguese but the Spanish Academy has adopted it, because it's such a wonderful word, because, as you said, it expresses not only sadness but also nostalgia, and we don't have a word like that in Spanish or in English.

AF: It's true. "Sorrow" is not a full enough word to transmit what you're saying. Do you think that languages are really interchangeable? Do you feel that your writing is as fully expressed in English as in Spanish?

CA: I have been very lucky, because my first translator was Bud, and he knew Spanish and English very well, and he knew me very well, and I worked with him. And if the music wasn't there for me—music is very important in a poem—we would discuss it until we agreed on the translation. Later, Carolyn Forché's translations were very good, and my daughter Maya also worked with her, and now Margaret Sayers Peden is just wonderful. She loves my poetry and that helps a lot, and she sends me her drafts and I indicate where I have problems. I've really been very lucky.

AF: You are completely bilingual. Obviously this helps your translations as well because of your ease in English, yet I know that you are most yourself in Spanish. Would you say that you have sort of two different personas, depending on the language you're speaking? Could you ever write poetry in English?

CA: I don't feel like I have different personas. I learned English when I was young, and then I went to university in English and then I married Bud. But I would never write in English. It has to do with your mother tongue. For instance, when Bud and I fought, I never fought in English, only in Spanish. And when I was very tender, it was also in Spanish. And poetry is something that comes from the soul. Once in a while I have translated a poem of mine into English, but I cannot imagine writing a poem in English.

AF: And as you say, poetry loses some of its "aroma" when translated. Do you think English speakers can truly appreciate the brilliance of, say, Nicaraguan poet Rubén Darío, considered one of the greatest in Latin America?

CA: I don't know. Darío is one of the greatest poets in the world. His rhythm and the music in his poems are so fantastic that I don't think an English speaker can really and truly appreciate his genius. There are other poets, for instance Pablo Neruda, who are easier than Darío, even though Neruda also has his own music. I don't know how to describe it. I think somebody like Neruda translates better to English than Darío, even though both of them are musical. The music of Neruda is more accessible.

AF: I suppose the greatest benefit of speaking so many languages is that it's given you access to writers from all over the world. I wanted to mention Harold Pinter's recent Nobel Laureate speech, in which he said:

> Everyone knows what happened in the Soviet Union and throughout Eastern Europe during the post-war period: the systematic brutality, the widespread atrocities, the ruthless suppression of independent thought . . . . But the U.S. crimes in the same period have only been superficially recorded, let alone documented, let alone acknowledged, let alone recognised as crimes at all. . . . Direct invasion of a sovereign state has never in fact been America's favoured method. In the main, it has preferred what it has described as 'low intensity conflict.' Low intensity conflict means that thousands of people die but slower than if you dropped a bomb on them in one fell swoop. It means that you infect the heart of the country, that you establish a malignant growth and watch the gangrene bloom.

And then he speaks at length about how the U.S. pursued this strategy, and committed this crime, in Nicaragua. Have you read the speech?

CA: His assistant sent it to me, saying Harold Pinter wanted me to see it, and I wrote to him, thanking him for that truly beautiful piece of work. Marvelous. I met him in London. Luisa Valenzuela and I were doing readings and we opened at Royal Albert Hall in London. And Harold Pinter was there. And he liked some poem that I read, and he just rose up, so everybody else did too!

AF: You have said that love and death have been recurring themes in your poetry over the years. Has the meaning of death changed for you over time?

CA: Yes, very much so. I always had a strange fascination with death. When I was about five years old, I saw my best friend die, and I was so horrified. I touched her and she was cold, kind of blue, and since then I've had a strange fascination. But death was very far away. And I wondered why children died; it was so wrong. My last book is called *Soltando Amarras* (*Casting Off*). It's about cutting ties, even with those I most love, seeing them at more of a distance, but still adoring them of course. You see, now I think that death is very near and I want to be prepared. I don't want to protest that I am dying. I want to accept it. That's why this is a period in which I am cutting ties. But don't misinterpret me. I always adore my children, but I don't feel that we have to be completely enmeshed, so close. I am leaving, and that is fine, and I have to accept that. They have to.

AF: Is it more for you or for them?

CA: For both. I don't want them to suffer too much.

A CONVERSATION WITH
SHERMAN ALEXIE

Rob Spillman

Sherman Alexie, a Spokane/Coeur d'Alene Indian, is currently one of the fiercest practitioners of the English language. The self-proclaimed "ticked-off Indian" has published eleven widely acclaimed collections of poems, three collections of stories, and three novels, *Flights*, *Reservation Blues*, and *Indian Killer*. Alexie also wrote the script, based on his short stories, for *Smoke Signals*, the first major movie release directed, produced, and written by Native Americans. In 1996 he was chosen by *Granta* as one of America's best twenty writers under forty and in 1999 by the *New Yorker* as one of twenty writers for the twenty-first century. Among his many other accolades are the mantels of first Heavyweight Champion of the People's Poetry Gathering in New York City and the reigning Heavyweight Champion of the Taos Poetry Circus, the two largest slam poetry gatherings to date.

We spoke just before the publication of his story collection *The Toughest Indian in the World*. While maintaining his uncompromising political rage at the mistreatment of Native Americans, Alexie ventures into new territory with this book—the land of the middle- and upper-class Indian. Alexie still fearlessly pokes fun at white and Indian hypocrisy, yet at the same time he has written emotionally resonant stories about a group of people one rarely hears about: sober, successful Indians with happy marriages. Himself married with a son, Alexie now lives in Seattle, across the state from the Spokane Indian Reservation in Wellpinit, Washington, where he grew up in what he has called "the basement of the skyscraper called poverty." I caught up with Alexie before he headed out on his first book tour in three years.

Rob Spillman: When you first started touring, you used to short-circuit Q&As by answering the dumb questions before they were asked, like "Yes, this is my real hair; yes, I grew up on a reservation; no, I do not drink." Post-*Smoke Signals*, do you still find audiences steeped in stereotypes?

Sherman Alexie: I don't do that anymore. By now it would take too long. There's an endless number of dumb questions. *Smoke Signals* brings people who never read my books, expecting to see Thomas, which they sort of get. It's just the number of people that's changed; a lot more come. The movie hasn't changed anyone's perceptions. It is very Catholic. I'm Catholic, as well as Spokane. The people are generally disappointed when they hear that. They want the image of Father Sun, Brother Moon.

RS: Robert Bly, at the recent People's Poetry Gathering in New York City, said, "When mythology is completely gone, what you've got is slam."

SA: That is really stupid—elitist and arrogant. What the slams are all about is an attempt to create an oral tradition. The real issue is that

I don't think there is a lot of critical distinction in the slams. They are more interested in the quantity of expression versus the quality of expression. When I was at a slam in Boston I got in trouble for saying that a lot of the poetry was terrible. I got in trouble for making a critical distinction. But, damn, it's poems. I'm happy any time someone gets up and gets poetic. Bly should talk—the whole *Iron John* bullshit—talk about making your mythology commercial.

RS: Do you find yourself being infected and influenced by the myriad voices you hear at slams?

SA: No, not really. My influences were all white guys from the forties and fifties: Lowell, Ginsberg, Wright. I was really influenced by Ginsberg. But I love poetry of all kinds. My approach has been more traditional. The thing is that the poems I read at slams are not necessarily my best poems. There are two kinds of poems: ones that sound good out loud, and ones that are better on the page. Most of what I read there is the stuff that's better out loud. What I'm most interested in is the line. I can tell you exactly why I have broken every line. People at the slams tend to confuse formalism with conservatism.

RS: Who would you want to take on in the ultimate steel-cage grudge match?

SA: Jayne Cortez and me versus Walt Whitman and Dylan Thomas.

RS: What do you think of Richard Howard coming out against National Poetry Month, arguing that poetry should be "ours every minute of every night and day, all the year round, insubordinately, insatiably, in secret"?

SA: He's probably against the printing press. What is the point of art? For Bly and Howard, it's to maintain privilege.

RS: William Gass, when asked why he wrote, replied, "I hate. A lot." Is anger your main inspiration?

SA: It used to be. But you can't sustain it. You become bitter. Nothing is going to change. Anger leads to resentment, then to spiking your orange juice, then to martyrdom. Certainly I am angered, by politics, by racism, sexism, all these "isms." A lot of my image was a misperception, sarcasm mistaken for rage. A white guy could say the same things and get away with it. The hostile Indian is still an icon. It's what people expect.

RS: Do you feel a need to live up to your image as a "ticked-off Indian"?

SA: In public forums I like to create drama. I don't take it seriously. Nothing changes in an hour. At a book festival, in a classroom, over the course of an evening, those aren't effective forums. It's not like Ollie North's devotees are showing up. I'm also slamming liberals, especially liberals, and they don't like that. They want to be congratulated. The real value of art is a long promise, no one book is going to do it. I don't want to sit up onstage and be profound. I'm just a writer trying to sell my book. I try not to be seen as too self-important. I just want to have fun. My hard-core political life is outside of the writing.

RS: Do you worry that people might wonder if you're growing soft by writing beautiful stories like "Saint Junior" and "One Good Man"?

SA: That was part of my inspiration for this book—changing the expectation people have of me. You never read about middle-class or upper-class Indians. It's all about poverty. I'm now in the top ten percent of income in the country. My needs are met. My concerns have stayed. But writing about a real marriage is real revolutionary. We live our lives. I wanted to write domesticity. A friend of mine read these stories and said they sounded like Rick Moody, Rick Moody with braids. It's a combination of going to a powwow, then coming home and watching Michael Jordan on the TV. It's about the romance of the ordinary. I tried to be really ordinary. I wanted to avoid what people were expecting of me, avoid flights of magical realism.

RS: You did have a burning basketball.

SA: I worried about that. Took it out, kept it in, took it out, until I finally rationalized that the ball *could* have caught fire from the kerosene used to burn off the snow from the court. In the collection I wanted to point out how we all worry about the same damn things.

RS: In "Indian Country," Low Man is searching for his battle, saying, "There it was, the central dilemma of his warrior life: repetitive stress. In his day, Crazy Horse had to worry about Custer and the sociopaths of the Seventh Army." Do you feel like you are at war? What is your battle?

SA: When I was writing that story I got repetitive stress syndrome. I had to ergonomic everything. It was utterly demeaning; I couldn't do what I do. In a sense it was one of those moments when I realized that this is not a real life. It's become increasingly surreal. You plan and dream about being successful, and then it happens. Because of the movie I am recognized. I am recognized because I'm Indian, because I'm a writer, because I'm an Indian writer. That war, that struggle, fighting being Indian in the dominant culture; part of being successful is that I am an Indian. Awhile back I was on tour, on this flight was me and ninety-seven white Willy Lomans, and I suddenly realized I am Willy Loman, I am a traveling salesman, selling my product, then going back to the hotel to watch bad porn.

RS: In "Dear John Wayne," you write about the "brain drain" of bright kids leaving the reservation, plus the fear of Indians "disappearing by halves" through having children with non-Indians. What happens to the tribe's secrets when there are no purebloods left?

SA: It falls into the hands of people who have no vested interest in keeping the secrets. Indian secrets are easily commodified. People with one-sixty-fourth Cherokee blood, or even one-eighth, feel a need to have public demonstration of their Indianness. It is tradition placed in the hands of the insecure. I'm not denying their Indianness, just the way they prove it. You don't have a lot of full-bloods doing this, going around with dream-catcher earrings or running smoke lodges.

RS: In "Saint Junior," you write, "There were Indians who belonged on the reservation and there were Indians who belonged in the city, and then there were those rare few could live successfully in either place." What about you?

SA: I'm a city boy. I can imagine living back on the reservation when I'm old. Looking around in my office, at the DVDs, CDs, over here short stories by Lorrie Moore, a book of essays by Pauline Kael, this wouldn't have shown up on the rez. I'm urban. But with my son, my wife and I have to work extra hard for our culture, expose our son to as many other Indians as possible. But I like the diversity of my friends. I don't want to deny my son the liberalism of the city.

RS: Is it more important for you to be read on the reservation or off? By Indians or by whites?

SA: Indian kids specifically. When I was a kid I felt so alone and weird. I wish an Indian writer had shown up on the rez. That's why I try to get to as many reservations as possible. I want them to see that it is a good thing to be weird, eccentric. I tell them, and at all schools, you better make an investment in the geeks, 'cause they're going to be the interesting ones. The popular ones are not going to do anything. Buy cheap, buy geek. I tell them, all those things that are eccentric will bring you power. For me, I want to be seen and heard. It's not that necessary that they read me. I don't think of myself as a role model, but I do present myself as, this is what I've done.

RS: You have gone after non-Indians like Barbara Kingsolver and Tony Hillerman for writing about Indians. Can non-Indians ever get it right? What about Ian Frazier's *On the Rez*?

SA: Sure, some can get it right. But I slammed Frazier in the LA *Times*. Not for the reasons you'd think. The whole phenomenon is what gets to me, that these writers become experts. The reviews are all by white guys saying they're such experts, that they are so authentic, he knows this or that. But they haven't written one original word. Everything they have written has been written by Indians before. The Frazier book was real sloppy, putting Sacagawea in the wrong tribe, getting the dates wrong. But what got me was that it was why he likes the Oglala; it's about Ian Frazier. Also, the title is insulting. For a non-Indian to write something like that is insulting. What if a white guy did that about a black area? Imagine George Will writing *In the Hood*? I didn't have a beef with Tony Hillerman until I saw a book about the Navajo territory called *Hillerman Country*. It's Navajo land and he's claiming it for himself. I didn't have anything against Barbara Kingsolver until I read an interview where she said she felt "Indian in her bones." She claimed Indian feelings. Frazier claims the Oglala. For a non-Indian to say, "It is my tribe" is wrong. It is not the same as when an Indian claims a tribe. Frazier is claiming ownership. It's amazing to me. The U.S. is a colony. How is it different than South Africa? Barbara Kingsolver, Tony Hillerman, and Ian Frazier are all writing colonial literature. They think just because they are writing from liberalism that it will make a difference. Liberalism does not spare them.

RS: Again, in "Saint Junior," my favorite story in the collection, you write, "Having fun is very serious." Do you still have fun writing?

SA: I do. Once it's outside of my hands it's different. But I'm excited by this book, excited to be back out in the literary world. I've been doing film stuff and there are positives, but film negatives are so huge. Nothing happens. And I have so little power. With publishing it is different. By now I could get my grocery list published. The immediacy of expression is wonderful. I love it, I miss it. I haven't published a book in three years, and for me that is a long time.

RS: What happened to the *Indian Killer* project?

SA: The option died. If I had done one about a white woman being butchered it wouldn't have been a problem. We couldn't find a coproducer. Now I'm working on adapting *Reservation Blues*.

RS: You've written poetry, short stories, novels, and films. Is there any form of storytelling that you hold most sacred?

SA: Poetry and short stories are what I enjoy most. I write them all the time. It's my natural mode of expression. I have to really work on a novel. I can be driving and poems will come to me. Poems and stories are an avocation, novels take evocation.

RS: Have you considered switching allegiances and rooting for the Trail Blazers? They're a lot more fun than the Sonics this year.

SA: I've never lived and died for a basketball team before. I feel like a battered wife. A few weeks ago it looked like Gary Payton had really messed up his knee. I was crying when he was carried off the floor and I didn't realize it until my wife, Diane, pointed it out. At that moment I realized I'm in love with that little shit. The Sonics are like an Indian tribe—sacred and traditional, capable of absolute beauty and then total idiocy.

RS: In the poem "Defending Walt Whitman," you write, "God, there is nothing as beautiful as a jump shot on a reservation summer basketball court." Still true?

SA: I think so. They don't play like we used to. We'd play sunrise to sunset. We'd stop when someone got a bloody nose from not seeing the ball coming, or when the bats started swooping—we'd call it "the bat quota." We were all young and skinny and beautiful as long as we were on the court. Off the court everything was messed up. But on, we were little indigenous gods. It's my most beautiful memory of the rez.

A CONVERSATION WITH
TRACY CHEVALIER

Ellen Fagg

With the publication of her second book, *Girl with a Pearl Earring*, Tracy Chevalier enjoyed the kind of breakout success that some writers spend entire careers dreaming about. Reviewers lauded *Girl*, about a servant of the painter Johannes Vermeer, as "a jewel of a novel." Readers and booksellers were even more enthusiastic, passing the novel along hand to hand, book club to book club. In 1999, Dutton issued a first printing of 17,500 copies. At the time of this interview in 2002, the book had sold more than one million copies.

Instead of returning to the familiar ground of the art world for her third novel, Chevalier chose a more ambitious path, setting the story in a milieu closer to home than *Girl*'s seventeenth-century Netherlands. *Falling Angels*, anchored at the turn of the twentieth century, revolves around two families who meet at adjoining family plots in a fashionable London cemetery. Young wife and mother

Kitty Coleman is the telltale beating heart at the center of the story, which is told through the eyes of nearly a dozen characters. The novel, which unfolds with a charming wit, darkens and accelerates as Kitty is swept up in the rush of history, striking out for her own freedom by joining the suffragette cause.

Chevalier is a Washington DC native who graduated from Oberlin College before settling in London. She worked in publishing and went on to earn a graduate degree in creative writing from the University of East Anglia. She is also the author of the novels *The Virgin Blue* (1999), *The Lady and the Unicorn* (2003), and *Burning Bright* (2007). While touring the United States to support the paperback release of *Falling Angels*, Chevalier talked to *Tin House* about finding her voice as a writer of historical fiction, the white male school of contemporary fiction, the recent furor surrounding Jonathan Franzen's hesitancy at joining the Oprah Book Club picks, and the sweet tooth of twenty-first-century readers.

Ellen Fagg: Your books seem to be about women who are trying to discover their own voices. Kaye Gibbons once said she writes "around the house and out in the yard" fiction. How do you describe your brand of historical fiction?

Tracy Chevalier: I suppose it's sort of domestic historical fiction, but I'm uncomfortable with labels. I almost feel as if I've stumbled into writing historical novels and I feel comfortable here, but it wasn't by design. For me, "historical novel" tends to be a label that I associate with a kind of genre that's not very fashionable anymore, like Georgette Heyer—you know, set in the eighteenth century, with kings and queens and romance and heaving bosoms. But when you look on a table in a bookstore and you look at all the novels that have come out, you'd be surprised at how many are historical novels.

EF: Is there another label that you might feel more comfortable with?

TC: I suppose "literary fiction." But I also feel very ambivalent about that label, because it sounds too exclusive to me. Also, the college student in me thinks, Literary fiction, oh, that's experimental, that's about style, that's about structure, that doesn't care about the plot too much, but it's very rewarding at the end; you could write a good paper from it. And I don't like that, either, because I really like story. I like plot. I like it when people say to me, "Oh, God, I had to stay up until three in the morning finishing your book because I wanted to know how it ended."

EF: You've said that after reading the first draft of *Falling Angels*, you cried, because you thought the writing was really flat. Then you found a new way of telling the story, through multiple points of view. How did you regain confidence in the story?

TC: It was very hard.

EF: Particularly after the big success of your second book. If you had been writing to a smaller audience, there might not have been so much pressure.

TC: The success put a lot of pressure on me. The first draft wasn't a complete failure. Basically I had the idea to write it using the three children. When I finished a draft and I hated it, I did hold on to the fact that I had really enjoyed writing Simon's voice, and I really enjoyed writing Lavinia's voice. So then I thought, Maybe it's just the way I'm telling it that's bothering me, not so much the story itself. Maybe I just need more voices. That was my lesson: if you're bored writing it, then nobody's going to be reading it.

EF: I think writers are often overoptimistic about first drafts.

TC: I only had one draft of *Girl with a Pearl Earring*, but it's hard to talk about drafts when you use a computer. I mean I write longhand, and then I type it in at the end of the day, but I'm constantly reworking it. But the first time I read a draft all the way through, of course I went back and made changes—yes, there was another draft, but there was nothing major.

EF: It sounds like that was a story that—

TC: Came out fully formed. Whereas this one, I was kind of finding my way as I was writing it.

EF: Most of the reviews for *Falling Angels* have been very positive, but a few contain some criticism: "Children too wise for their years and men who seem incidental." "A page-turning Edwardian soap opera." The book jolts from a "comedy of manners sans jokes," to paraphrase another reviewer, and becomes something of a political morality tale. How do you respond to such criticism?

TC: I'm so much my own worst critic. Nothing anybody else writes is harsher than what I've already told myself. It's hard to describe: I think in some ways *Falling Angels* is a more ambitious book than *Girl*, in terms of the points of view, how it's told, and issues it is dealing with.

EF: A greater cultural story, too.

TC: *Girl* is quite narrow in its scope whereas *Angels* uses a bigger canvas. And both approaches have their advantages and their disadvantages. I can certainly see why people have felt it has not been as successful a read for them.

EF: It's done very well in the marketplace; it climbed higher than *Girl* on the best-seller list.

TC: Did it? Yeah, I think it was on for a week or so.

EF: *Girl* got to twelve on the *New York Times* best-seller list, according to the publicist at Dutton, and *Angels* got to ten. So what did you learn from that criticism in thinking about your next project?

TC: I think that this story got out of control a little bit for me. Although, I think the best part about *Falling Angels* is the way it's told. But I'm not sure that I succeeded in making it clear why the story needed to be told that way, why what happened happened.

EF: Are you talking about linking the story and the telling of it together so that readers don't even question the structure? I have to say the book was a page-turner for me. I stayed up very late reading it one night.

TC: I think it's the kind of thing where you really want to find out what happens, but then afterward you might feel vaguely disappointed, that you're not quite certain what the point is. And some people say to me, "Why did you make Ivy May die?" And I don't have a good answer to that, except that she's a silent witness. And, in a way, this is a book about change, and there's always going to be a victim of that change. There's a knowing victim, who is Kitty, and then there's an innocent victim, the one who doesn't have a voice.

EF: Well, that's dark. It's a book about change and there's always going to be a victim when you write about change.

TC: I know, I know. Actually, my husband said the same thing. He and my son tuned in to one of my interviews, and he said, "You have to be clearer about what this book is about." It seems like this mélange and it's not. Actually, a lot of it is funny. A lot of it is about misunderstandings between classes. The thing is, you can play a lot when you have these different points of view, as the different ways that people see the same event is very funny. And then, about halfway through, the tone changes.

EF: Both *Girl* and *Falling Angels* are bleaker than the reviews or even the book club audience might imagine. You know, in *Girl*, Griet chooses one of eight paths, and we're not led to believe that choosing to marry the butcher is a path she thinks is particularly good.

TC: He's good-looking, though.

EF: But none of the descriptions make the reader think she is in love with him. She's always conflicted. Her big love, of course, is the master's eye. So the ending is . . .

TC: Very bittersweet. But it's real, too. I didn't want to sweeten it because we have a sweeter tooth in the twenty-first century than they did back then. People read a book like this and they want that romantic Hollywood ending. I think the power of the book is that they don't consummate or even express their love for each other, except in the most indirect ways. That's the reason for the exchange of the earrings at the end. He's left her the earrings, and it's a kind of token that he did feel something for her, and that he owes her something. But he's dead already, you know.

EF: But she has to sell them.

TC: And yes, she sells them. She can't even keep them. So there's this feeling of them never quite being able to *say* it, or being able to show it in any way. And I think that we are so used to having it all, to getting it all, to getting the full frontal, in books and in films, that now, when you don't actually get it, it's incredibly powerful. People say, "God, this book is so erotic," and I say, yes, but he only touches her twice: once accidentally on the hand, and once he touches her ear, and people think that is more erotic than actually reading about a full sexual act.

EF: So she winds up with the steady choice.

TC: This is the ending that has to be because that's what her circumstances are, and it's very hard for us to swallow, because we're twenty-first-century women. We feel like we just want her to have it. Actually, as her parents very pragmatically point out, she married a butcher, she's going to eat well, and he's a good man, he has never beaten her, he's good-looking, he's a catch. That's the irony, and I was very deliberate about that. It would have been too easy to make him ugly or boring or unkind.

EF: What about the ending of *Falling Angels*? It has a very different flair than the rest of the book, in that so much happens in just a short period of time. It seems very different than the ending of *Girl*.

TC: Yes. It's a much less controlled book. It feels a lot looser; it felt a lot looser writing it. It's really Kitty Coleman's story, and it's the story of her losing her way and becoming more and more unhinged. Even though she thinks that she's fighting for a good cause, joining the suffragettes, she really joins so that she can let out some energy. I don't think she actually cares all that much about women getting the vote. And as she's losing her way, the story takes on its own momentum, and it speeds up, in a way that reflects her losing her bearings.

EF: The beginning of the book foreshadows that, with that amazing first line: "I woke this morning with a stranger in my bed."

TC: I started the book that way very deliberately as a way of reminding us that our preconceptions of Victorian life are just that: preconceptions. Certainly, by the end of the Victorian period, people were looking outward, becoming more modern. But this beginning was a way of taking our stereotypes of Victorian values and just sort of cracking them open. But it was also, in a way, symbolic of Kitty Coleman cracking apart and trying to emerge as a modern woman but not being able to find her way.

EF: What are the artistic concerns about writing for an audience of post-Freudian readers—an audience whose members are much more aware of their own psychologies than characters from a previous time were?

TC: It's very hard. It's a constant struggle not to make characters have twentieth-century thoughts. Or not even twentieth-century thoughts, but twentieth-century thought patterns, like self-analysis and self-consciousness. I write about women because I'm a woman—it's easier. I choose women who, in one way or another, don't quite fit what's expected of them in that particular time. For instance, Griet has an artistic eye and she has no means to express it. If she lived now, she'd just go to art school. And Kitty Coleman is an intelligent woman who is not expected or allowed to do anything apart from run a house or have a child. If she lived now, she would probably be a lawyer.

People have often said to me, "Why did *Girl* have to end like that? Couldn't she have run off to become a painter?" And I say, "Look, you want a twentieth-century ending. This is a seventeenth-century girl. She did what was expected of her in that time." You have to maintain a level of authenticity within what the characters are thinking, but you also have to present it to the reader so that the reader can see the difference. You know, the characters aren't self-analytical, but the reader needs to be able to analyze them and feel comfortable with that.

EF: That's a difficult challenge, that of not speaking down to a modern-day audience and yet consciously having to leave out elements, such as the analysis or self-knowledge, that readers might expect in contemporary fiction.

TC: I feel more comfortable writing sparely, and that is very deliberate. It started when I wrote my first novel, *The Virgin Blue*, which is part contemporary and part historical. I had to reread it recently because it's coming out in England, and the editor said, "Is there anything you want to change?" I didn't change the plot and I didn't change the majority of the style, but there were some awkward clunker sentences that I changed. The sections that I did still like and still stand by are the historical sections, and I think that's when I realized that was my calling, more so than trying to do contemporary stuff.

EF: It seems like a list of American writers who might be your contemporaries, in terms of how much they've sold out of the gate, might include David Foster Wallace and Jonathan Franzen. They're writing about contemporary culture and they have the authority of speaking as a commentator on a culture in which they're living. And that seems very different than the path you've chosen.

TC: In some ways, it's harder to actually write something with authority that's set in the past. On the other hand, ninety-five percent of readers know a lot less about what I'm writing about than I do. And if I write clearly, with authority, and with a style that goes hand in hand with the story, then a lot of people really give me the benefit of the doubt. Now I'm not saying I don't research or that I make it all up.

EF: The research is very apparent.

TC: Oooh. That's always the biggest danger for a historical writer, that you wear your research on your sleeve.

EF: No, no, no. I meant I trust the details.

TC: In a way, it's easier for me to write about the past. I sometimes find when I read stuff that is set in contemporary London or contemporary America, I find myself disagreeing with the writer, more than I would when I read something set in the past.

EF: In contemporary fiction, it seems like male writers have the ability—or are allowed the ability—to speak for all people. Do you believe it's possible for women to write with that kind of authority?

TC: I'm sure it's possible, I'm just not sure that women have taken up the gauntlet. And I'm not sure why. It's true that there's a whole genre of men. You named David Foster Wallace and Jonathan Franzen, but the older generation, as well—Saul Bellow, Philip Roth, John Updike, Joseph Heller—it's all men. Where are the women in there? Maybe I shouldn't admit this in print, but I don't read those writers very much.

EF: Why not?

TC: They just don't interest me. I'm not interested in the big sweep. Maybe it's partly because I live in Europe now so I think the great sweeping American novel doesn't necessarily appeal to me. Maybe if I were living in the middle of American culture it would interest me. I suppose there's a part of me that's irritated by the arrogance of these men who feel they can make a big sweeping statement about American culture. On the other hand, why not? Why shouldn't they? Tolstoy did it, and we all love it. I don't know why it is that I'm so critical. Or, not critical exactly, because they're clearly good writers.

I mean, I read *The Corrections* and there's some brilliant writing in there, but it's too long.

EF: I think he is amazing at writing dialogue.

TC: Yes, and family dynamics—fantastic. But I just grew impatient with the sweep of it. You know, I have Don Delillo's *Underworld* and I just can't even begin to crack it. It's just too long. I see it as this big mountain, and other novels, particularly by women, I don't see them as mountains. I think it's like a nice comfortable bed to get into and sit and read. It's reading for pleasure rather than for edification. It's not pure pleasure—it's not a bubble bath. Like Margaret Atwood—she's one of the authors I admire the most, and she's probably one of the few who could kind of stand in among all those guys, except she's not American, so it does make it harder to make the comparison—she doesn't do sweeping things. And yet she does, she does a sweeping of the psyche. She doesn't write the huge sprawling Canadian novel; she writes about people and relations and important things, and it's all there, it's more organic or something. I don't know. I just feel the men's books are like big skyscrapers, and her writing is like a horizontal art gallery. You know?

EF: That's an interesting metaphor to describe the difference.

TC: Yeah, like the great penis in the sky.

EF: It's interesting because so many readers are women, and yet the publishing establishment is having a problem reaching those readers.

TC: This brings up the whole Oprah thing, of course, and Jonathan Franzen. Franzen is an interesting case because of the question of whether it's actually there already—this school of white, male American writers who write against a great sweeping canvas. When Franzen was published, I think his publisher took a very deliberate step to market it that way. Wasn't there a quote from Don DeLillo on the cover?

EF: Yes.

TC: It's like, "C'mon, buddy, join the club," and people see that. He talked about how much he admired these writers—which is a completely legitimate thing to say, but it's very much like joining the club.

EF: I want your perspective on this because much of your success, it seems, has been really fueled by book clubs rather than by the publishing establishment.

TC: Yes, very much so. It has not been led by the publisher. And that, to me, is one of the great joys of this whole writing trip, that *Girl* did well because people genuinely respond to it as a book, as a piece of writing. I mean, they published it beautifully, and it has a great cover.

EF: You've mentioned that cover a lot in press interviews.

TC: It is a great cover. It's beautiful. And it's not just sort of shoving a beautiful painting on there; it's used for a purpose, because this is what the book is about. And so many people have told me they've flipped back and forth reading and then looking at the cover. It really is part of the work, of the book. I think it's a pure kind of success, as opposed to one that has been sculpted by the publisher. And, yes, of course the publisher jumped on it and enforced its success. I feel like the purity of its success will affect all of my other books; they can't be pure successes because now my name has become like a marketing name.

EF: I want to ask you about that. Some literary writers are dismissive of the book club world. Do you feel like you are marginalized because you are read by book clubbers? Is there a downside to the pure success that you talked about?

TC: Well, I know that Jonathan Franzen has lived to regret all that between him and Oprah, and he has had a very hard time extracting himself from it. And part of it is his fault and part of it isn't. The media machine got him and it won't let go. And I kind of feel sorry for the guy.

EF: It certainly helped sell books. There would be some people who might claim, cynically, that it didn't serve him poorly.

TC: To be honest, I heard the interview he did with Terry Gross and at the time I thought it was interesting, but I didn't think, Oh, he has really dissed Oprah. It was only afterwards when people mentioned it that I realized how it could be interpreted. What I was going to say is that the difference between him and me is it sounds like he has his ideal readership in his mind—and that readership is primarily male. For me, I just write, and it never occurs to me that I'm thinking of the fifty-year-old woman sitting in her armchair in Duluth or the teenage boy on his skateboard. It never occurs to me to think of it that way. I'm just grateful to whoever does read it.

One of the surprising bonuses of the success of *Girl with a Pearl Earring* is how many teenagers have come to it on their own or been assigned at school to read it and then have given it to their mothers, or their mothers have given it to them. That was something I never, ever anticipated. I mean, a book about a seventeenth-century Dutch artist? What teenager is ever going to touch that with a ten-foot pole? But the thing is if I had had in my mind a readership—"Oh, I'm going to write this, and I'm going to want teenagers to enjoy this, so I'm going to write it in a certain way"—I just don't do that. The day I start doing that I guess I better set down my pen. I don't ever want to become that cynical.

EF: But how does a writer write and then market and not have the two start to affect each other in bad ways? How do you sell your book at readings and not cynically tell the same stories over and over again?

TC: It's really hard because everybody asks the same questions—but they don't know that they ask the same questions, do they? It's tough.

EF: I guess it's the big marketing question. Every beginning writer feels like he or she won't have a chance. And then once one has a chance, as you have had, how do you deal with something that takes on a life of its own?

TC: I think, ideally, you want to keep the two as separate as you can. Of course, I have general readers in mind. The reader matters more than anything, but it's a generalized thing, it's not got an age, it's not got a sex, it's not got a geographical location, it's not people wearing black in New York cafés. It's not that specific. I want the reader to be entertained. I always try to be true to myself in my writing; I write about what I'm interested in, and I write to tell a story. I have to hold on to that and not allow what people are expecting of me to dictate. For instance, even my husband was saying, "Oh, why don't you write about the Mona Lisa next?" and I thought, The day I start writing a formula, forget it, I've got to stop.

EF: You worked in publishing before quitting to write full time. What did you learn from your day job that has helped in your writing?

TC: I learned very specifically about editing myself. I write sparingly, and I leave a lot of gaps, deliberately, because I want to draw the reader in. It works with the historical setting and keeping the writing visual, so that the reader reads it and can transfer the story to a film in his or her head. But the readers do have to work on it a bit. I think that's partly why *Girl with a Pearl Earring* was such a success as a book club choice, because there are a lot of unanswered questions in that book.

People ask me which of my books is going to last, which I like the best, and I say it's like asking a mother to choose between her children. But I think the one that is going to last the longest is *Girl*, because it's a rare instance, for me anyway, that the story I was telling and the way I was telling it were absolutely interlocked. I started it knowing I was writing about a Vermeer painting and I needed to write in the style of a Vermeer painting. It was a cheat for me, because Vermeer had already done a lot of the work. He had already established the look, and as far as I was concerned, he had already established the story of the book within that painting, and he had also given me the style and I just had to copy. I mean, it's not as simple as that, I'm being a bit simplistic, but when you don't even notice that the style is feeding the story and vice versa, that's the sign of a good book, and it's pretty rare.

EF: You used the word "cheat," and maybe that's not fair, but it's true that you didn't have to make decisions about what color the girl's headscarf was. Some of the details of a climactic moment were already provided by the imaginative work of selecting the painting.

TC: I suppose it isn't a cheat, because you could say that people who write about contemporary life have that life in front of them. We all copy from nature, so to speak.

EF: Which is what makes fiction truthful.

TC: But I do tend to use an element of reality to create verisimilitude. I often ask this of people, "If Vermeer hadn't actually existed as a painter, and that painting didn't actually exist except as something that a graphic designer came up with for the cover, would the book have the same impact on you? The same power?"

EF: What's the answer?

TC: People don't know. They're not sure. Because the painting exists, it's very hard to make it not exist in your head.

EF: To take us in another direction—in some ways, historical fiction seems to share relevance with science fiction, in the way that historical record is bent through imagination. If science fiction is about the future, and bending contemporary life to fit a future view, then historical record has to be bent too. Are there some rules that you think about in your imaginings of history? Are there some things you won't do that you could get away with?

TC: I think I just do it by feel a lot. I do have a rule that the story always comes first—story, characters, setting—because I don't want it to be a history lesson. You need to do your research so well that you actually feel it naturally. So that you may not know what a character would eat for dinner in fifteenth-century France—which is what I'm writing about now—but if you've read enough, if you've absorbed it enough, looked at enough pictures, thought about it enough, you just write the scene and it will come naturally to you.

A CONVERSATION WITH
CHARLES D'AMBROSIO

Heather Larimer

Driving east from Oregon to Montana, the terrain shifts abruptly. Lush stands of conifers break apart to reveal desiccated high plains and an enormous red-rocked gorge. Gently undulating farmland becomes snowy mountains. After two days on the road, the effect is disorienting; with each abrupt change, reality disintegrates further.

To drive was extravagant, maybe foolish, but it seemed necessary to watch the landscape morph, to observe, physically, how Charles D'Ambrosio got from his hometown of Seattle, where he had been living and teaching for several years, to the middle of nowhere—Philipsburg, Montana.

Directions come by e-mail: "I don't know which way you'll be coming, but I guess I-90. After Missoula take Hwy 1 for about 25 miles until you start feeling lonely as hell; then just when you're feeling downright suicidal, there will be a gas station on your left."

These directions might seem alarming coming from anyone other than D'Ambrosio, but because he is so adept at describing emotional landscape, a visitor trusts their accuracy, even while sensing the levity buried in them. He has also assigned a poem to prepare for our visit, "Degrees of Gray in Philipsburg," by Richard Hugo. It begins: "You might come here Sunday on a whim / Say your life broke down. The last good kiss / you had was years ago. You walk these streets / laid out by the insane, past hotels / that didn't last, bars that did, the tortured try / of local drivers to accelerate their lives."

D'Ambrosio emerged as a writer in 1991, when his story "The Point" was published in the *New Yorker* and was also selected as a Best American Short Story. He came out with a short story collection by the same name in 1995. Then, by his own description, he "checked out," spending the last several years working but keeping a low profile and moving to Philipsburg.

After *The Point*, D'Ambrosio held several teaching engagements, but his publications were scant until the *New Yorker* published his essay "Documents" in its Summer Family Issue in 2002. "Documents" juxtaposes a family correspondence—letters from D'Ambrosio's schizophrenic brother and his father and his youngest brother's suicide note—with descriptions of the author's self-imposed exile in Montana, where he combs the hills for animal bones and sleeps in giant holes made by long-dead miners. In 2005, he published the essay collection *Orphans* (Clear Cut Press) and in 2006 the short story collection *The Dead Fish Museum* (Knopf).

Other than his directions, the poem, and a brief e-mail assurance that he is "feeling pretty good actually," he gives me no sense of what to expect. The strange town, D'Ambrosio's place in it, his life—these are potential sources for trepidation. Having heard from mutual acquaintances that he is hard to reach and possibly crazy, I also fear unearthing another cautionary tale about writers' penchant for self-destruction.

D'Ambrosio meets me at a run-down gas station with football game dates posted on the marquee, driving the old Bronco he's had since I met him a few years ago, when he was my teacher at the University of Washington. This element of consistency is a relief. He looks all-around functional—shaven, nails trimmed—both embarrassed and amused I've driven so far for such a vague purpose.

I follow his truck past the narrow turn-of-the-century storefronts along the main street of town. On the hills above the street sit old Victorian houses from the mining heyday, interspersed with a few quaint churches. The first resident I spot is a boy of eight or so, trying to launch his bike off a makeshift plywood ramp. He fails to gain enough momentum and just rolls defeatedly backward down the ramp again. As I watch him I think this earnest, futile act might summarize Philipsburg somehow. I am wrong. The failure in this place is more sweeping, far older, and final.

Philipsburg, a mining town that reached its economic and cultural apex in the late 1800s, is a living ghost town barely breathing. Its close neighbor and rival, Granite, is truly abandoned, reduced to various stages of rubble and leaning timber, which makes Philipsburg look kind of mediocre in comparison, as if both its heyday and its collapse were halfhearted.

D'Ambrosio's truck veers off the main street, and then the pavement ends. As we wind up an endless succession of hills toward the woods, I scan the few houses in the distance, trying to pick out D'Ambrosio's house, one that emanates "lost-ness." Then D'Ambrosio parks in front of a plain, square house, so simple it resists contemplation.

Inside, the front room is packed with artifacts. Photos, scraps of paper, odd objects, an impressive collection of old typewriters, and heaps of bones are arranged in deliberate patterns on shelves made of scrap wood and metal—themselves artifacts of abandoned work that D'Ambrosio has dragged from the woods.

D'Ambrosio asks what I want to do, and I reply I want to do whatever he normally does, so we decide to take a tour of the backcountry and then go shoot his gun. After we pack up a few things for the day—sunscreen, flashlights, water, bullets—we stop by a thrift store to find targets. D'Ambrosio chooses some plates and a giant plush mouse. I grab a few LPs. We then drive up a steep gravel road into the hills. First, D'Ambrosio wants to show me a specific mine he likes. I assume the challenge will be finding the lone mine, hidden like a secret, but I quickly realize the problem is locating the one he intended. The hills are infested with these holes, dark shadows perforating the green of the trees. The timber structures built around them are all weathered the same deep brown. Many are cordoned off with barbed wire or deliberately caved in by the government. Others have been kicked open again.

We find D'Ambrosio's mine, one he has slept in several times, and park the truck. The fence blocking the entrance has been pried open, and so we walk in, armed with several flashlights in our packs, in case one or two die at once. The temperature drops abruptly at the mouth; the light changes just as quickly. The mine is cold and dark and smells faintly metallic. We move farther down the tunnel, giggling nervously, playing an undeclared game of chicken. After a few minutes, I discover water dripping from the rock ceiling and, below, an ominous pile of collapsed timber supports. D'Ambrosio says, "Okay, let's go," and we are both relieved to have a reason to turn around.

We drive through miles of relentless trees, stopping at various mines, collecting things—a rusted cigarette machine, boots so weathered they've shrunk to half their size. Finally, we find a mine that's perfect for target practice. We wedge the targets from the thrift store in a barbed-wire fence and take turns with the old Marlin bolt action .22, noting which targets we like—china, a carton of soy milk from the car—and don't like—the stuffed mouse, who absorbs bullets too stoically.

Later, we wander some more, up and down the hills on winding dirt roads. Everywhere we go, even in town, we are alone. In Granite, the main ghost town, we find a vast graveyard of some abandoned industry. Huge turbines and other work objects lie dismantled and on their sides. In the middle, five old Cadillacs are lined up neatly, as if in an executives' parking lot. "I wonder who decided to call the whole thing off," D'Ambrosio says. The question hangs everywhere in Philipsburg. The immutable fact of abandonment and, with it, the idea of a mistake, is as pervasive as the weather.

When the sun goes down, D'Ambrosio makes a fire. We sit outside, behind his house, and talk about isolation and purpose, his work and family, and his impending comeback, while the changing light moves shadows across our faces. I watch the lights in the valley below and remember what D'Ambrosio wrote in his essay "The Lighted Window" about this spot where we sit:

> It's fall now and I live on a mountainside overlooking the Flint Valley and the town of Philipsburg. At night it's so quiet I can hear men and women fighting in their homes. When the bars close wrecked trucks rattle off in a brigade of drunks and then the silence returns and after a minute or two I can see the stream of headlamps grope their way across the valley floor. Each light seeks out another light, a home miles distant, and from where I live I can watch them connect. I often feel enclosed and trapped in my house and grab a sleeping bag and sleep outside, at the bottom of what seems like a huge black bowl. The stars are cold in their vast Pascalian spaces but rather than fear I find comfort in their indifference. The lights in the valley are seamless with the stars in the sky and only slightly dimmer and we are all here together, alone.

Heather Larimer: You have said you moved here because of Richard Hugo's poem "Degrees of Gray in Philipsburg." In one of your essays you mention that Hugo calls himself a "wrong thing in a right world" and that the idea defined your ambitions as a writer. Might this be the antithesis of how most artists conceive of themselves, which is as a right thing in a perverted world?

Charles D'Ambrosio: I have to say I side with Hugo on this one. From the writing point of view, it's important to think the world matters, and to place it before yourself. You can't say the world's bullshit. Hugo was the first person to articulate something about Seattle, as a particular place—the colors, the moods, the temperature. What it's like being from nowhere, looking out on the ocean, which is also sort of nowhere, being sandwiched between nowheres. He laid out some territory and felt it and wrote about it. Also, for me, as a man, Hugo got better in life. He didn't splash at twenty-four and drink himself to death later. He actually grew and became better and better as a poet and a person. He interests me biographically because I don't have any models for going forward.

HL: How did you discover him?

CD: He's sort of in the air. Like drizzle. Hugo falls on your head. I knew he was a supposedly good poet who was actually from Seattle. It's like, kids my age, we worshipped Jimi Hendrix. His music is like reveille; I still put on Jimi Hendrix when I go for walks. Hugo's the same way, if you're writerly. He's just there. Of course, that's all gone, because now there are other laurels in Seattle. But it was such a culturally impoverished place. Hugo earned the position, though. As a poet, he's terrific. Very friendly. I would call him for advice. Most of those poets, I would never call any of them for anything. But I feel like Hugo would know what to do. His poem put Philipsburg on the map for me.

HL: You seem to be not content with just being in a place; you tend to commune with it—sleeping on the beach, in mine shafts. Is that what you need to do in order to write about a place?

CD: "Commune." It's an odd word because behind it you have Rousseau and something more optimistic and salutary about nature than my deal might suggest. I'm obviously not drawn to Paradise. When I was doing a piece on the Makah Indians of Washington for *The Stranger* about their decision to hunt whale, I was sleeping on the beach—the exposed, ocean side, not the sheltered side in the strait—and I had this idea of myself as the antijournalist. There are motels you can stay in but they were packed with media people who I thought were saps and who, I knew in advance, were going to tell the exact same story. They were staying warm and dry and would eventually just swap clichés. But not me. I was going to take on some of the exact same exposure—to cold, to wind, to isolation and loneliness—that a bunch of boys in a cedar log out on the ocean might feel chasing a whale. I don't think you could really write about the Makah and whaling without a feel for the horror of irrelevance, because ultimately this project—whaling—is about a need for meaning. That land out there is the end of America and what the fuck is it all about?

On a personal level, my family lived out one of the central American stories—emigrants and westward-ho!—and we just turned out stupid and tragic; nothing added up, we never got it. I kept thinking of the Makah story in terms of having gone west of the West, out beyond the last story. It wouldn't pay to flinch, to step back, into cliché, so then what? I was also baby-obsessed at the time and realized that not only had the land run out but also that our family name was pretty much kaput. My brothers weren't going to have kids, so I was like a walking dead end. Out on the beach, alone, I was getting a taste of nothing, a healthy helping, and it was all very spooky and strange and okay.

HL: You liked it?

CD: I liked it. I liked cooking salmon using my dipstick as a skewer. And then for the Makah, they had the same project, but were looking in a different direction, into the past. They weren't just killing a whale for the fuck of it; they needed meaning, bad. This was about an entire civilization. In the sense that all thinking is a kind of homesickness, I was out there and so were the Makah and we were all homesick. What could we do with our intense longing? Anyway, I'm probably also the son or grandson of Gonzo and I don't believe in removing myself from the story, the falsity of it. And there's some lurking Rimbaud thing of deranged senses, and out there you don't need drugs or whatever— ~~the surf and the cold and the rain blast your~~ ~~idea of self just fine~~.

HL: What about sleeping in mine shafts?

CD: Walking in the freezing cold in Philipsburg and then finding old mine shafts or abandoned cabins or buildings to sleep in was partly just an uninteresting thing that's been addressed by my mood stabilizers. But of course I like to spin out a romance around the hard dull facts. Landscape is like putting on a jacket; it keeps me warm. First I felt like shit and thought I'd just go out and match an inner deadness with an outer one. I'd see who was better, mano a mano, ruin against ruin, and cold against cold. It was the only kind of homeostasis I could imagine. I was letting everything cold and lonely squeeze me so hard I'd find a core of warmth and feeling I could live with. This may all sound like bullshit and I won't deny it; my life was bullshit. Nonetheless I wanted to feel something, just like anyone else

HL: You were writing mostly essays during this time. What different conception do they have from fiction?

CD: An essay you can lean against reality, sort of take it off your back and rest a bit; fiction you haul without relief. It takes an enormous amount of human generosity to write a story; it takes a lot of extra emotion, an overflow, a love and kindness I just didn't have. In fiction you give and you give and you give. In my checked-out state I couldn't do that, not in writing, not in life; I treated real people and fictional ones like shit. Also myself—I was indiscriminate. I couldn't organize narrative, and I just went with stuff that would let me muck around in confusion. I thought of myself as a poison I could stir into any situation to ruin totally. I was doing that in life and doing that in essays. It's strange I'm thinking, I hate to make too much of my own emptiness, yet I do want to stay alive, so I needed to pull stuff—pull something—out of my empty black hat. Instead of rabbits or doves it was like, voilà, gargoyles and grotesques. It's madness of course, mangling the world that way. I knew beauty and love and goodness, I knew that was all out there, even though I didn't have any personally; that vague sad awareness was probably saving me.

HL: Now you're writing fiction again?

CD: I'm back to writing fiction. That kind of writing is egoless, and there's nothing better than spending four, five, six hours, indifferent to yourself, caring, engaged, et cetera. Now I can ask characters what they need, I can love the narrative enough. I have enough compassion for the story's destiny to write; I can respond to the needs of fiction and people alike and it's pleasant not to be a shithead.

HL: When you went to Russia to do a piece on an orphanage for *Nest*, it took you three days to begin to pack a duffle bag. How can you be unable to pack and yet able to write an essay?

CD: The duffle bag had me baffled. It was black and it was in the middle of my room and I was mystified about how clothes were going to get in it. I wasn't writing then. Even the essay thing had shut down. All I could do was read Ann Rule books and eat black licorice. I love Ann Rule—I do, I admire her enormously—but the thing about her books about serial murderers and rapists is that the plot's easy to follow. You kind of always know what's going to happen next. My pathetic daddy wound was aching pretty badly at this time, too, and he shares just about everything with the cretinous shits in Rule's books—the loathing of women, the cowardice, the brutality—except the actual fact—and even there, I consider him a killer. But really he's like a serial murderer manqué. And his favorite candy was black licorice and the duffle bag was black and I couldn't get any clothes in it and the point is: Who needs dreams?

HL: That essay is one in a collection published by Clear Cut Press. What else is included?

CD: There's an essay about Mary Kay LeTourneau, the Makah whaling, Richard Hugo, Seattle and writing, my uncle's bar in Chicago and gambling, a few other things, all of which, boiled long enough, are about me—surprise.

HL: You were also talking about a thing you want to do for *Harper's*.

CD: I haven't laid this one on Lewis Lapham at *Harper's* yet but I'm optimistic. My brother-in-law was childhood buddies with the Mitchell brothers, who made, most famously, *Behind the Green Door*. I want to go down into the gone world of San Francisco porn. I don't like the story; I like the back story. When I approach a thing I want somebody to say, "I'm sorry, I can't tell you the story," because my response is like, "Fuck you, I don't want your story, I want the story about how you won't tell me the story." Back story is where the fecundity is before everything cools and hardens and dies into cliché. It's where life is. It's where contradiction is. If somebody offers me the story, I immediately look for the back door and the room where all the props are stored.

HL: So what's your take on porn?

CD: The porn thing is particular and amazing. I suspect it began with hippie chicks who'd fuck on camera for fifty bucks and then like so much of the sixties—the glories of sex, drugs, and rock 'n' roll—everything turned to shit. Porn is where free love had to start paying for Vietnam, maybe. Anyway, I'm always interested in this kind of black de Sade underside, what happens when the civil barriers between people are removed. In Piero Pasolini's brilliant movie of *120 Days of Sodom*, one of the characters says something like, "The only problem with sex is the need for another person." Woody Allen has an answer for this, but forget it. The point is, once you pose that extreme question the next step is the elimination of the other, the annihilation of that other who frustrates, who pollutes your need. We live in muck and I'm not big on purity as an answer; more muck, I say. But the consciousness fascinates me. And I want to sink down into it. It's gone but I've got a tour guide, a great one. Then there's this lingering fifties thing, this strange Sandra Dee world. A lot of the guys making porn in this particular heyday were maybe jocks in hot cars whose main sexual ambition was to get a hand up a girl's skirt; then they did, and more, and what happened after—after, the aftermath of an innocence, the horror and despair of what was initially a victory—that's the shit.

HL: Last time we saw each other, you were reading your essay from the Salinger anthology, *With Love and Squalor: 14 Writers Respond to the Work of J. D. Salinger.* I think the essay was really instructive to me as a reader of your work. It encompasses a thematic repertoire, or gives a map somehow.

CD: You think I can just shut up now then?

HL: Probably not.

CD: For that anthology, I had written something in my isolation that had a weight about it. And I wasn't trying to be weighty; I never am. If I can, I always try to leaven it somehow. The smallest jokes are precious to me. I wrote something a lot more serious. I knew it had to be compelling but I ended up with something more beefy than a reminiscence. The content was challenging, and the place I was in made everything a challenge. I was just about to get black as hell.

HL: You raise some really interesting ideas about the acts of reading and writing: you think of Salinger as part of a socially atavistic prep school tradition and you like Joyce better. You say you read fiction as a source of moral-free advice, that "stories looked squarely and bravely at lives without criticizing or condemning them."

CD: It's a reverse process of what I grew up with. I grew up very much in the Catholic Church and I'm not quite out of the Catholic Church. I still like going to mass and still feel a sort of intellectual Catholicism and an existential Catholicism. The process of the Church is very different from the process of writing fiction; they move in opposite directions. In the Church and its schools, you went from the story into the moral. And very often for me, life is getting out of the moral world and going into the more vibrant world of the story. Where can you go if every story leads to a moral? I have to fight that in myself, that wrapping up and needing to get it to summarize.

HL: Are you seeking your own morals through writing?

CD: It's more like the freedom that lies outside of morals. I feel like the moral life is too simplistic. So what's the complicated, real life? The life that's lived, not ideally presented. That's the life that's contained inside a story, the sympathy it evokes. In the Church, the moral is structured right into the mass. You read from the Bible, and then you get the homily. You arrive at an idea of things that is specific, narrow, fixed. I try to work in the opposite direction.

HL: When I read something of yours, it's hard to distinguish if it's the topic or if it's the language that feels weighty. It feels so different to me than what other people are doing. The language is so precise and then you'll break from it. Have you noticed you use the word *thing* a lot?

CD: What, "thing"? "Thing" in writing? I believe I probably do.

HL: It's such an imprecise word, something you're told in composition class not to use. But in your writing it's a relief. It feels precise, substantial instead of a blank.

CD: I am aware that I do it. I was thinking about it when I was preparing the collection of essays. They were written in a weird time, and I wondered if they had any integrity, if the language had any integrity. When I was writing them, I was doing insane stuff. Not like stunts or anything, but I was behaving bizarrely. Like sleeping on the beach.

HL: Were the last couple of years the weirdest period of your life?

CD: Well, one of them. It's kind of like a bad movie with a lot of sequels. That was number five. Anyway, language-wise I was obsessed with this idea of having garbage in the language and leaving that garbage in. I have had what you would call an amazing education. I have gone to very good schools. I've had all this opportunity and have never had anything but bullshit jobs. I've never had a job anything near responsible. I have never had a nine-to-five job. So it's like hypertrophy. I've had this education that's made me a bulbhead, but a reality that's, in terms of work, pathetic. So what kind of language am I allowed to use? I'm going to go with my education. Fuck it that all my education is leading to a moronic life. I'll use my education in this moronic life. I've always kept vocabulary lists. Often, when you keep a vocabulary list, you never end up using any of the words, because who wants to hear them? But in these essays I started using them. I thought, This is a newspaper, and I am going to use language that no one ever sees in a newspaper. It's a challenge: you either get off your ass, put down your bagel, and look it up, or you won't know what I'm talking about. But along with that high diction is using things like "thing."

HL: It's a weird high/low mix. You're one of the only people for whom I have to use my dictionary. There's this echelon of vocabulary words that people with a certain degree of education recycle. It's a sort of in-speak. There's a little list we all keep under our pillows, but you're off the radar screen. I'm having to haul out the dictionary. It's like, okay, you win, here comes the OED. But then I realize that it has an etymological precision—this is absolutely why this word was created. It's the right word. When other people use these sorts of words, it's often like a Mad Lib, fill in the blank with an expensive word, even when it's not particularly precise.

CD: Yeah, I use language exactly. And never rhetorically. Despite using a word like *revanchist*.

HL: I just had to look that one up yesterday.

CD: I do believe Orwell's right. Prose-wise, he's amazing. Simple words, simple rhythms, never using rhetorical language. I would never use a word like *parameter*, unless I'm making a joke.

HL: I don't get it. What's the difference?

CD: That part of the language, the in-speak, is culturally acceptable, but it's a rhetorical thing. It's not about anything. It's about the kind of people who are in the position to use words like *parameter*. It's not about the thing itself. Whereas *revanchist* is very specific to what I am talking about. I would never use a word for fancy's sake. It's testy, though. It's my little version of Dada, taking on the audience. As private a joke as it is.

HL: What about in "Documents?"

CD: "Documents" was simple.

HL: But you still throw in the tricky shit.

CD: I was trying, but sometimes they threw it right back out.

HL: Was it heavily edited?

CD: Well, the *New Yorker* has a style, a house style. The rhythm, more than anything, was evened out. Comma placement. In the essay, along with the tense diction I was working with, I was very interested in off-balance sentences that weren't pretty, that didn't soothe, that gave kind of a grating music. I'd extend them out one clause too many, or write a really short sentence, even using slightly bad grammar. I can play the instrument. It's not like I am making mistakes because I just picked the fucker up. So the noise that I'm making is noise that I want to hear. Antimellifluous. The pretty sound all the time seems to put people to sleep. Saying, 'Don't worry, don't worry, everything's going to be fine. This won't affect you. Your coffee is nice. This won't upset you." But I think the content of that piece resisted that sort of editing process.

I think people were silenced by the content a little. You can object to writing, but it's hard to object to the topic as a writing event, because it's such a heavy life event. But I mean, fuck it. If it's not good writing, I don't care what kind of shitty life you've had. If you can't turn out a good sentence, then I don't care. It's weird to hear people say that was a great piece. Yeah, well, that's my shitty life!

HL: After rereading "Open House" from *The Point*, I wondered how much of the language you use, especially the high diction, is not from your formal education, as you say, but from your dad.

CD: Yeah, a lot of it comes from him. I guess I kind of overlook that part.

HL: I also saw it in his letters in "Documents."

CD: Yeah, you didn't even get the half of it. He is so insane. He's got this faux, elevated Latin diction. I love mocking him.

HL: You don't ever think he's brilliant?

CD: No. Well, he is in other ways. He's brilliant like Hannibal Lecter is brilliant. It's like, "What's the point, Dad?" He is brilliant in his way, but it's this phony elevation, like he's above life. And he's using language to establish that elevation.

HL: Didn't he keep citing the OED in his letters?

CD: Oh, yeah. The *New Yorker* needed to verify it. The fact-checkers needed to see the entire letters. I was so embarrassed.

HL: Why?

CD: He's my dad! And he's saying this shit about *me!* I was trying to be a good son. That was my project. How did this person who I at some point respected more than anybody in the universe, and for whom I probably will never summon an equal type of respect again, turn out to be a lunatic? What does that say about my judgment? The letters were embarrassing to me. I'm not one of those people who think it's interesting to be a fucking freak.

HL: What did he do for a living?

CD: He was a professor of finance at the University of Washington. An economist. He gave us a sense-of-humor allowance. You get forty smiles and three laughs this month. Don't spend it all in one place.

HL: How has the response to "Documents" been?

CD: I haven't heard much. How would I? I mean, I'm here. My mother called. Well, I called my mother. I told her. She's never read my brother's suicide note.

HL: She knows nothing about it?

CD: Well, no, she knows he's dead. But she's never read it and so I called her and said, "I'm quoting it, I'm talking about it, and you don't have to read this." I actually called everyone in my family, except for my dad, of course, and I said, "I write what I write but I don't think it's a test of loyalty whether you read this or not." And so everyone made his or her own choice. Of course my mother read it because she's such a fan of mine.

HL: As she should be.

CD: But my sister Kath works in a big international bank—swishy— and they get the *New Yorker* and all the fancy magazines and so she stole their issue because she didn't want anyone to read it. Someone else brought in another copy and she couldn't get rid of it; it was like a nightmare. Finally, someone came up to her and said, "Is he your brother?" and she said no. You know, I understand. You don't want to be at the bank and having people saying, "Gosh, your family's fucked up." So, that's what I heard, from my family, not from anyone else.

HL: That surprises me.

CD: Well, I've gotten letters. I've heard from the people I would expect to, but as far as jibber jabber . . . See this vast immense valley? I can guarantee you no one out there has read it. Not one person.

HL: I just thought you might be getting a lot of annoying "Are you okay?" calls from people who aren't necessarily your friends.

CD: Fair amount of those. I heard from cousins I hadn't heard from in a while. And the usual lunatics.

HL: I feel like there's a grotesque interest in you: "Oh, that guy . . . What's he like?"

CD: I'm nice.

HL: When you sit down to write, are you thinking about what it means thematically or about what's going to happen?

CD: It's hard for me to talk generally. But take, for example, "Drummond and Son," which was also in the *New Yorker*: I saw a father working at his bench and his son was sitting in this brown chair and that was it. I just wondered, What are they doing there? I mean, I knew something was fucked up. And I knew that in the last line, the father was going to tell the son, "I love you." And the story was going to justify that. The story was going to be written so that it isn't pathetic or disgusting or ironic. That one man could say to another, in this case his son, "I love you," without it being a ridiculous joke, which in my life it always has been. I was going to correct that and create a world in which it could happen. I think I did it!

HL: So that's what got you going on the story?

CD: Those were the guideposts. It didn't all just tumble out. For instance, typewriters. I like typewriters.

HL: I've noticed.

CD: The typewriter is like a genie in a bottle. There's something in there. It's not in me, it's in the typewriter: "I know you're in there!" The guy in that story is in difficult straits. He can't express himself. He's surrounded by typewriter keys, words invisibly coiled inside these things. It became this whole thing about how difficult it is to say, "I love you." Language stuff running counter to this simple thing. This guy was into old things. He restored old machines. I was thinking that with old things that have been touched and handled, they have love in them. There are reasons why you have old things around, not because they're objets d'art or aesthetically pleasing, but because they've been touched and cared for. And it teaches you something about how you're going to have a relationship. This guy isn't educated. He knows love through objects. They survive the wreckage of everything.

HL: Old objects are about perseverance.

CD: Persistence through time, independent of the vicissitudes that visit everyone. The objects endure.

HL: There was something else in the Salinger essay that I recognized from your other work. You were talking about your younger brother and the buddy system in your family, being paired off with someone. I noticed it in your stories, like "Her Real Name" and "The Point," and I was fascinated by it because it seems to be an antiquated notion, something that doesn't really survive into adulthood.

CD: But I haven't gone into adulthood. I refuse, so that notion has survived in me. Really, I think that sometimes.

HL: That you haven't gone into adulthood?

CD: Yeah, because I'm so stuck in a tribal mentality.

HL: But how can you be tribal out here?

CD: I can't tell if people like me. That mechanism is broken. But I trust my sisters. I take vitamins. I don't know what is in those things; my sisters tell me what to take. I trust them. It's tribal. In this world where I have no instinct for what other people are thinking, they could tell me, stick this piece of seaweed up your ass, you'll feel better, and I would do it. They're tied together. That I trust. It's a weird hesitation about what other people are thinking.

HL: Why would you move so far away then?

CD: Why would I move out here? Well, I was . . . fucked up. Estranged from my own mind. To be honest, I think I came out here to die. I don't like to be dramatic, but that's what I think.

HL: Really?

CD: In my mind, everything was dead, and I'd get away from the last few people I cared about and that would be it. Everything would implode.

HL: When we were up at the mine, you said you thought moving here was fated, and that you had no volition. You meant your sense of dying was fated?

CD: I thought that if I removed the last remaining obstacles, that that would be the conclusion my life had arrived at. I didn't want to be around people I cared about. Things were collapsing neatly, like an arrangement of dominoes, but the people were in the way. So I got away from them, and therefore away from the pain of having to *feel* when everything else was really deathly. I wish this was grand and metaphysical, but it's probably biological. And pharmaceutical.

HL: Mundane, in other words?

CD: Right. Take a multiple vitamin and an aspirin and everything will be better in the morning. Which I'm actually glad of. Because the other way was never going to deliver me from that kind of thinking.

HL: We were talking about the buddy system. People's relationships, in your work, are often involuntary relationships. They're assignments. I didn't recognize it until I read the Salinger essay, but I think it's strange. Adult relationships, especially in the age of therapy, are supposed to be elaborate choices.

CD: I have never chosen a relationship.

HL: Really? Even in love?

CD: I'm very passive. I never had the idea that I could. Any shitty thing I will stick with. The tenacity and loyalty in those stories, where people just stick with the situation. I'll do that. I've only recently realized that.

HL: That people choose relationships and you don't?

CD: Yeah, and that they should be an interesting part of your life and blah blah blah. It should be at least as interesting as going to McDonald's and selecting off that menu. I had no idea that you could even make a choice, even though it might be a circumscribed choice.

HL: Many people write relationship stories and they're about making choices. But in your work, these adult relationships feel more like family ones, which you obviously don't choose. If you reject your family, especially when it's the only context you have, tribal or whatever, then you've essentially fallen off the earth. ~~So you have to stick with the shitty hand.~~

CD: I never conceived it that way, but it's definitely true. It's true in the stories and it's true in life. Take the other story the *New Yorker* took, "The High Divide." I wrote it twelve years ago, the first twenty drafts. I was always trying to knock it out and I couldn't get it, and then about four years ago I wrote another ten or so drafts. And then I just took it out and wrote another seven or eight drafts, and I finally got it.

HL: What was the challenge?

CD: It ended up being an enormously angry story that could never find any shape, because anger places a coil or spring in something, but it doesn't envelop or shape or surround; it pushes away. It became another story about the quest for the language for love—at least some ability to express it. But it was interesting how that evolved over time. For me as a writer, imagination, exposure are very difficult. And I suppose, like for everyone, love is very difficult. But they're both based on exposure. And the anger was preventing that risk. Once I risked in the story, everything took shape and lived without me. Out of the willingness to be exposed. You have to love your stories. And this was a thing about hate, and I hated hating and I hated the story and once I got outside of the sorrow and anger . . . I feel bad for people who can't figure out meaning.

HL: Is that what you think suicide is about? An inability to find meaning?

CD: No. But ~~there are people who can't figure out reasons for living.~~ I think what's really sad is ~~they don't understand why they're killing themselves,~~ either. It's the ultimate gesture but it's the ultimate, deepest mistake. They don't know why they're doing it. Or why they're doing anything. Why am I out here? Why am I even talking? You never know why you're doing anything. Certainly suicides don't.

HL: Do you think that because of Danny's suicide note?

CD: It's not just that. I've read collections of suicide notes. Edwin Shneidman, who is the grandfather of suicidology, began by studying suicide notes. He was hired by the LAPD because you have to classify a death and a lot of times it's ambiguous.

HL: Would he agree that suicides don't know what they're doing? You think it's the ultimate confused stance? It seems such a resolute thing to do. The most resolute thing.

CD: It does. It's certainly final. But it's not resolute. It's not articulate, it's not . . . my brother was an amazingly sensitive, beautiful, intelligent person whose life should not have been leading to that. You add all those things together, and it doesn't go there. It goes somewhere else. Why there? He was on a bad track, but it was not who he was. One thread was taking him down there. He knew nothing about himself. He's like me.

HL: When you say you came out here to die, do you mean die as he did? Or curl up and die?

CD: Well, last winter resembled death. What is death? I'm out here, I have no friends, I have no relations, I have no bookstore. What could be more hellish? I was stripping away all the things you think of as life. I was removing myself from everything I understood because they were painful tethers pulling me back into something I couldn't live. I didn't know what would happen. I didn't have a fully articulated idea, but I was really gone in my mind. I was gone. Of course, you never really want to end up there, and I have lots of reasons not to.

HL: Like what?

CD: Oh, I can't remember any of them right now. But I remember that there are some.

The weird thing about me, maybe everyone, is that I have a bodily optimism, despite how disgusted I am. It's in my veins, my bones, and I don't know why. It's always been there and I hope always will be. It's sustaining. It's where the energy comes from.

HL: When you're writing, why are you doing it? Who are you talking to?

CD: I don't know. To me, it's what I love doing, but I don't know that that's enough. I don't really love doing other things in the same way. As a child, I was paralyzingly shy. Outside of my family, I hardly talked to anyone. In college, I didn't speak until I was about to graduate. I had to make huge efforts to be a person who spoke. I took a job bartending, not because I needed it but because I wanted to have to talk to people. I practiced conversation with other people. Writing is somehow tied to that. To the extent that I'm writing about something that matters, I never feel like I'm talking to myself. I'm having a conversation.

HL: In one of your essays, you talk about writing as a way to justify being alone. Doing perfunctory scrawling in a notebook so it would be okay not to have friends.

CD: It's more like, you find yourself in a bad situation, what do you do? Writing is one of the things you do. Especially if you are an introvert like myself. The words on a piece of paper inside your notebook, they're like pets. For me, very early on I found myself alone with nowhere to go. So I scribbled. It made it okay to sit where I sat. You're like sixteen, seventeen, eighteen, nineteen. You don't have any power or place to go. How do you make an excuse for yourself? If you're a man, you're dangerous. A man untethered at that age is extremely dangerous. The IRA stops watching young men as soon as they get married. They change their status and dial them down because they're no longer that interesting. As long as you're single and free, you're dangerous.

HL: To whom? Yourself?

CD: Socially dangerous. I think that's the perception, and I think it's the truth. At that time, you feel the need for an excuse for yourself. What's your excuse? The universe is asking.

HL: Do you think you have a "mission" or purpose as a writer?

CD: Nothing too large. It's intense and specific. The only place as a child I talked a lot was at home, to amuse my brothers and sisters in a dark situation, and I feel that. I love when I am working and I start cracking myself up. It may not actually be funny, but I'm measuring it against some reaction they may have. It's a conversation. Kids down in the basement talking. I'm trying to replicate that mood. Sharing secrets. Telling the story. Or what we knew was the story but wasn't allowed public airing. And then there are the people who write and read. I love all of it. I really do. It's one thing that makes teaching interesting. I don't know that teaching is effective, I don't know that I am effective as a teacher, but I do like walking in and having a group of equals with a shared interest. I don't get that a lot otherwise. It means more and more to me. I like people who care about things that aren't worth caring about. Money is worth caring about, everyone agrees, right?

HL: In terms of efficiency, yes.

CD: It's the people who care about things that are worthless. Who love even though it's pointless. The people who give, who think, who act as if there were meaning, or purpose, that's who I care most about. Not the people who say, "Ah, fuck it." Those dark little nihilists. They're pussies. The people who persist when there's no reason to persist, that's who I care about. Writing's the same way. There's no reason to write.

HL: So then I'm surprised to hear you think nihilists are pussies.

CD: I do. It's too easy to acquire the thinking of a nihilist. It's obvious, it's no longer adventurous thinking. It's like Freshman 101. Every freshman is a nihilist. What do you do after that? It's already been established. It's been established there's no meaning, there's no nothing. What do you do the next day? ~~You have to cook, you have to eat, you have to love, to invent again and again.~~ Plus, it's a phase, no one follows it to its conclusion. ~~You go on and you live.~~

HL: Some people do. Others don't. But if one believes what you've said in your work, you think you're a total failure. How does that fit with building anything? In that Salinger essay you say you're a shitty friend, you've never loved anybody—

CD: I think that's true. But I don't matter that much. It doesn't mean I've lost sight of what those things are. I would wish them on everyone I knew.

HL: Have you ever been aware of your career? The things you supposedly have to do to be a successful writer?

CD: Obviously, I haven't thought about it. I'm trying to! For the first time in my life I'm trying to. I'm ready to kiss anyone's ass . . .

HL: I'll drink to that. I'm out here kissing yours!

CD: No, I am actually. I don't exactly know what it means. I've made some bad choices. I just wrote a long e-mail to my agent telling her I'm considering my career, telling her to think that way because I obviously don't. I never read an issue of the *New Yorker* until I was in it. But when the *Paris Review* called me recently, I could barely stand up. I was shaking.

Anyway, I'm trying to elaborate the idea of a career. It's important to me, after being so fucked up for so long, to get my name out there.

HL: It's important all of a sudden?

CD: Yes. I never considered it, I never cared. I think to an extent I disregarded and did not further an idea of my own integrity. I think I thought I was, but actually I was doing the opposite. I have to believe I matter. To myself at least.

HL: But when you say you didn't observe your own integrity, it seems like you mean you whored yourself out. But it's the opposite. You just didn't jump through the hoops you were supposed to. Except going to the Iowa Writers' Workshop.

CD: I think the idea of a career is important; I don't think Iowa has anything to do with it.

HL: Well, as a matter of fact, I have a hard time imagining you at Iowa. It's so "legitimate."

CD: Really?

HL: Well, I can't really think of anything more legitimate in terms of writing. I mean, to exist outside of it is to be a pariah, if you're into that grad school tradition. You being there seems incongruous with what I think about you.

CD: I sort of kept my distance at Iowa. Writing was new to me. I didn't know what it was about. I had a Best American Short Story before I left, but I was embarrassed by it. My first year, I had no friends. Or one friend. Tom. I never talked to anyone, or hung out or went to the bar. I was terrified of contact. I learned something about shutting myself down. I felt apologetic for something. It's hard to get comfortable with having an imagination and using it.

HL: Why? Don't you think it's just a human impulse? I don't think you need to be entitled to it. It's like having opposable thumbs.

CD: I thought it was like breaking into the universe's vault, stealing something that didn't belong to me. I now understand more, but I felt like I was trespassing. I still do in some way.

HL: How'd you get there?

CD: I just applied. I got in on the first story I ever wrote. I stayed up one night. I spent thirteen hours writing a story. That was eventually my application. No wonder I didn't trust anyone.

HL: Well, Iowa just seems so sanctioned, your career choices have not been.

CD: If I had been susceptible to that, I might have gotten a boost from it. I think maybe now I'm feeling sanctioned. I feel virile toward my own work in a way I never have. I have mostly apologized for it. Not now. I'm self-sanctioned, though. Nothing's going to calm your uncertainty. Writers are uncertain people. That doubt is part of the territory. If you're feeling it, you're feeling what there is to feel. I don't know how much of it goes away. It goes away by being in the middle of something.

HL: So, these Iowa stories got made into a collection, *The Point*, and then what?

CD: I was working on a novel.

HL: What happened?

CD: What really happened was story stuff, book tour, and then I was supposed to move to London, and things went haywire . . .

HL: What were you doing before Iowa?

CD: Being a moron.

HL: What do you mean?

CD: I worked in construction. I tended bar. I met this guy who owned the newspaper. They'd let you write. Really write. I was doing construction twelve hours a day and then I'd write at night, these pieces. I hated my job; I loved doing that. Then I ended up moving to the Catskills.

HL: And then you went to Iowa, wrote *The Point*, started a novel. What happened to the novel?

CD: The vast disarray of that novel is all loaded up and ready to go. It's going to take me a little while to pull it together but I've now got—knock wood—the inner consistency to give myself to it and bring it off, I think. I hope. I had a contract on it, pulled it, et cetera, so the whole wobbling mess is something I'd like to finish, just to prove something to—probably to God. For writing it helps to feel fated, fated word by word, fated to stories, fated period—like what you do, and when you do it, and every stray thing, every little accident, is absolutely necessary. You finish something, you were fated to finish; you don't complete something, that's fate too. And you have a trust that you'll always meet up with fate. It's Panglossian, maybe, but there it is: my only form of optimism.

HL: You have another unfinished novel. What is it?

CD: It's partway done, about a Catholic priest out on the coast, presiding over the end of everything and stopping nothing. I've got things to do, obviously.

A CONVERSATION WITH
LYDIA DAVIS

Rick Moody

Lydia Davis is well known and fervently admired as a writer, but she is equally adept, and successful, as a translator. The following discussion concerns both vocations. As a writer, Davis is the author of a novel, *The End of the Story*, and four collections of short stories, *Break It Down, Almost No Memory, Samuel Johnson Is Indignant*, and, most recently, *Varieties of Disturbance*. Her translations have included works by Maurice Blanchot, Pierre Jean Jouve, Michel Leiris, and Michel Butor, as well as Marcel Proust's *Swann's Way*.

Among Davis's prizes are the Whiting Writers Award, the French-American Foundation Translation Prize, a Guggenheim Fellowship, the Lannan Literary Award, and a MacArthur Fellowship. Most recently she was honored for her translation work with the French insignia of the Order of Arts and Letters.

This interview was conducted by e-mail, in several discrete layers, in September and October of 2005.

Rick Moody: Can you talk a little about the effect of international literature on your development as a writer and reader? I assume because you grew up in a family devoted to literature that your tastes in your youth were pretty polymathic, but were there specific books from Europe that affected how you thought about literature?

Lydia Davis: My family was, yes, very involved with literature, particularly contemporary literature. Both my parents were writers, though my father abandoned fiction writing early on and concentrated on criticism and teaching. Their friends were writers, critics, and teachers. My father taught modern American literature, and many of my parents' friends were . . . modern American writers. (One of my father's students was Sylvia Plath; another, before that, was Norman Mailer, who remained a friend.) But as for international literature, which for me was pretty much limited to European literature, it depends how far back you want to go into my childhood. The first "grown-up" book that made a strong impression on me (aged thirteen) was Beckett's *Malone Dies*. Another early one, though, was John Dos Passos's *Orient Express*. The Beckett for the strangeness of the vision and the narrowness of the range of action. The Dos Passos for the lushness of the prose.

My family did also travel as much as we could, though we were always strapped for cash. My father took a teaching sabbatical when I was seven, and we stayed briefly in France and spent most of the year in Austria; we went back to Austria for the summer when I was eleven. I think that had the effect of turning me toward Europe early on. In the first visit, we lived in Graz and Salzburg for most of a year, and I was speaking German by the end of it, so the influence was not superficial.

Later, the writers I studied most closely during my "apprenticeship"—when I was in my twenties and actually living in France and

Ireland—were Beckett, Joyce, Kafka, Nabokov, and Dickens, Europeans all.

RM: Can you contrast how literature from abroad affected you with the literature of the United States?

LD: I would be tempted to generalize wildly and wonder if the European writers seemed to me more restrained, more cerebral, than the Americans, which would feel comfortable to me because this was more or less the style of my family (if you mix in a good dose of humor). But as soon as I say that, I think of Henry James, who seemed to me overly confined within his tight, balanced syntax and whom I didn't appreciate until relatively recently (this semicolon is in his honor); and I also remember how much I relished Saul Bellow's *Herzog*. So I'm not sure I can generalize. I deeply appreciated individual qualities in these writers: Beckett's wit and doggedness, and the beauty of his sentences; Joyce's specific vocabulary; Nabokov's specific vocabulary; Dickens's characters and economy; Kafka's variety of forms. And so on. But I know that part of the attraction, also, was being transported away from home—by Isaac Babel, for instance, to Odessa.

RM: When did you begin translating? Was that interest coincident with your fiction writing?

LD: Yes, I think it was, since I imagined the possibility of translation as a career even back in high school, when I was also beginning to feel a vocation as a writer. The early year in Austria definitely hooked me on foreign languages—I was put cold turkey into a classroom in which all the teaching was in German, and over the weeks I witnessed the miracle of the impenetrable wall of meaningless sound gradually becoming penetrable and meaningful. I truly haven't gotten over that, and still like to plunge occasionally into a language I don't know—such as Swedish—and try to decipher it. I began translating the occasional poem from French in college, and then lived in France and earned an extremely meager living translating art catalogs and film scripts and eventually a mediocre book or two and then a good book. This was happening alongside those first stories that I worked over so painstakingly (and sometimes painfully).

RM: Do you experience translating as a deep kind of engagement with the text, or is it a more mechanical operation? Do you select the material you translate accordingly? Because it offers a deep engagement?

LD: It depends on the project. For a long time I had to earn my living almost entirely from translating, so I had to accept books that were not very good or well written, which actually made them harder to translate. The work became a chore. (I have rarely been in the position of selecting something I wanted to translate; publishers were more likely to come to me with a proposal.) But when it comes to the good or great authors, such as Butor, Jouve, Leiris, Blanchot, Proust, I do have a deep engagement with the work, and with the author himself.

There is a strange self-effacement that goes on in the act of translation, which I rather welcome. I leave myself for a while, disappear, enter this other prose, assume the guise of this other writer. In the case of Proust's *Swann's Way*, I tried to stay closer to the original than I have with any other writer except perhaps for Maurice Blanchot, though I'd have to go back and check that. (I suspect that at the time, I *thought* I was staying very close, but might not think so now.) I suppose you do become intensely loyal to the author you are working on, as day by day you take such care not to misrepresent him. At the same time, I had the great pleasure of composing Proust's sentences in English. I could feel, with *Swann's Way*, that no effort was too much, and I went to great lengths to look into the history of, often, a single word in my search for a good equivalent. But I thoroughly enjoyed all that. So to get back to your question, in the best projects there is nothing mechanical about it.

RM: You refer to the work as *Swann's Way* here, but in the English edition, at least, you make explicit an argument for referring to the work by a different name. Considering the importance of "le mot juste" in translation, does the proliferation of names of this project create difficulties for you? Or is it just part of how Proust has been rendered in English?

LD: *Swann's Way* is a very good title in itself but is not as close to Proust's title in rhythm and meaning as I thought it should be. So I spent a great deal of time trying to find the ideal title—one whose sound and sense would be true to Proust and also strong in itself. The best candidate, in the end, was "By Way of Swann's." The English publisher (Penguin UK), however, nixed this and we arrived at a compromise that probably no one liked much, *The Way by Swann's*. The American publisher (Viking Penguin) was at first willing to let me have the title I wanted, but then the marketing people said that under that title the book wouldn't sell, as they had discovered when they tried to sell Kafka's *The Transformation*—readers were looking for *The Metamorphosis*. In the end, I accepted this—*Swann's Way* under that title has a long and interesting history in the last century and, also, keeping this title avoids involved explanations such as the one I have just given!

RM: After I'd read the Proust translation, I wrote to you once about it, and I said that it sounded very French to me. You replied that this was *not* supposed to be the case. If not, then what is your aim for the English versions of these texts?

LD: This of course brings up the eternally debated basic questions about what a translation should sound like. One camp—to which, incidentally, the translator of the second volume of the Proust, James Grieve, belongs—believes that the translation should strive to read as though it had been written originally in English. Another camp believes that the translation should retain a flavor of foreignness—a flavor of its original diction and structure and culture—so that it is not entirely assimilated into English and the reader remains aware that it is a translation from another language.

I can't say I belong fully in either camp. I wanted my translation of *Swann's Way* to read comfortably and naturally in English (though necessarily in a rather formal or Latinate English)—or at least no less comfortably than Proust reads in French—while at the same time following the original so exactly and closely that one could look right "through" the English to the French. I wanted students of this book, for instance, to be able to study not only the content of the book but also Proust's own style as nearly as possible. Often this was beautifully, neatly, possible. (I won't dwell on my state of mind when I couldn't achieve it!)

RM: Does Nabokov's translation of *Eugene Onegin* fall into one side or the other of the eternal debate about the mission of translation? As someone who is both a translator and a producer of literature, how do you understand the controversy surrounding that particular translation of Pushkin?

LD: Well, it's interesting. I've discovered that all these years, without reading the translation itself, or the negative reviews, or Nabokov's replies, I had quite unfairly accepted prevailing negative views of Nabokov's translation as being—because it was so literal—hopelessly bad, clumsy, a failure. What I did not know, what I've been finding out lately, first from reading the very good biography of Nabokov by Brian Boyd and then from reading Edmund Wilson's review and Nabokov's replies, is that Nabokov never intended his translation to have the grace and music of the Pushkin original, but simply to be an extremely close "trot" for the use of Anglophones who wanted to know what the original actually said. He hoped, in fact, to lead them to read the original. It is nearly impossible in a translation to reproduce both the meter and the rhyme scheme of an original poem without somewhat skewing the meaning or at least padding the translation. This was what Nabokov wanted to avoid at all costs—he wanted to be as close and as literal as possible, even if the result was awkward and included unfamiliar or rare words. He was so angered by the misapprehensions of the reviewers that he threatened to make the next edition of his translation even uglier.

RM: When I last saw you, you were working on revising the American edition of the Proust. You said that you thought you might be correcting it for the rest of your life. Is that still the way you feel?

LD: The editor at Viking Penguin was generous enough to allow me to make hundreds of changes for the American version. These were not major changes, but, say, a comma in or out, two words switched, syntax altered slightly—the changes a writer would make rereading a 430-page book. Sometimes the changes allowed me to continue bringing even the punctuation of the translation closer to Proust's. I also called on dedicated readers, such as my aged mother and her Proust-reading companion, or the "close-reading" Proust group at the Mercantile Library in New York City, for their comments on the translation, and incorporated any suggested changes that made sense to me.

Yes, I do still feel that I might be continuing to make changes for the foreseeable future. I am distracted from the translation for months at a time, necessarily, by many other projects, but I like the idea of a text that continues to evolve. I would like this translation to be as definitive as possible—so any part of it that can be improved will be improved.

RM: Can you talk a little bit about the specific challenges of the Proust translation? I gather you did not know the Proust well when you began to translate it. What did you find along the way? How did the process change you?

LD: I was studying Proust in French quite closely many years ago, just after college, when I lived in Paris. I was reading *Du Côté de chez Swann* and writing tidy, penciled vocabulary words in the top and bottom margins of my nice little two-volume Gallimard edition. And I was evidently learning from Proust as I served my own apprenticeship in writing. But I was distracted from finishing the book at that time—by my own writing, by the study of other writers, by translation work for money—and although I later acquired different editions of the English versions of *Swann's Way*, I never read the whole book. (There are other large classics I still haven't read. It took three attempts and several months of living in Ireland for me to read *Ulysses*; it took months of isolation in another countryside for me to read *War and Peace*.)

When I was invited to translate *Swann's Way* I immediately decided that I wouldn't finish or reread the book and that I wouldn't "read up" on Proust for background. I preferred to approach each page as unknown territory, full of surprises, and to translate as I read my way through it, because there would be more excitement in the translating and the work would be fresher as a result. This was how I proceeded with the first draft, which for me is a very important draft since it establishes the tone, the diction, the character of the translation. Then, in the second and later drafts, I compared the other translations and also consulted a book that closely analyzed Proust's style (discussing his alliteration, parallel structures, embedded alexandrines, et cetera) so that I would not miss anything, even if I could not match it.

So I suppose that is one thing I discovered—how much was actually going on stylistically in each of Proust's complex sentences. As for how I myself was changed—I'm not sure I was changed, but my way of working on this translation was different from any previous translations in that I felt I could go to any lengths to achieve a faithful and pleasing text, that I was justified in immersing myself as deeply as possible in the work, to the extent of regularly consulting seven dictionaries, any number of other reference works, and various trusted friends, and spending the morning or even the day finding out what kind of ivy might have been turning red on the trees in the Bois de Boulogne in the coda of the book; debating whether I could follow Proust in distinguishing between different stages of the dawn's changing light; deciding to make a rhythmical improvement and move closer to the original (but also into less familiar English) by changing "catastrophic deluge" to "diluvian catastrophe."

RM: Are you fluent, or conversational, in any other languages besides English and French?

LD: No, I'm not fluent in any other languages, but I always seem to be dabbling. I have a fair reading knowledge of Spanish and German (must have dictionary at hand); I am currently struggling with a Latin text that I can decipher only with the French version next to me; I have done an eccentric translation of a Swedish children's book—in this case deliberately retaining the foreignness by keeping some of the Swedish syntax and idioms for the sake of the weird and pleasing English that resulted.

RM: Do you read French literature in the original for pleasure?

LD: I read a little in French from time to time—a poem now and then. The last non-English books I tackled were German (Peter Handke) and Spanish (*Tom Sawyer* in translation). I have to admit that English always gives me the most pleasure.

RM: At one point, some years ago, you planned to write a sort of French-language primer, or a novel structured after a French primer. Is that still in the works for you? And what is it that intrigues you about the structure of the primer?

LD: My first French primer, from which I began learning French in the fifth grade, was a sort of "Rosebud" for me—I looked and looked for a copy of it, finally found one, and reentered that perfect world with all its strange simplicity. I suppose it is the oddly vacuous characters, meaningless dialogue, and truncated plots of the primers that I like so much. The project is proceeding, though at a rather leisurely pace because others come along continually to compete and draw me away from it; for instance, I recently finished a two-part essay about Abraham Lincoln (as respectively sighted and interviewed by two of my ancestors); a mock-sociological analysis of a group of get-well letters from (actual) fourth-graders; and three letters of complaint (about peppermints, frozen-peas packaging, and the spelling of *scrod*).

RM: *Samuel Johnson Is Indignant* has a number of stories that are extremely fragmentary. In fact, these are in my view the most exciting stories in that particular volume. They seem manifestly engaged with French fiction, in particular Beckett, Pinget, perhaps Barthes. Do you think the fragment is still a useful form for fiction?

LD: I'm impressed that those smallest possible pieces make you think of three such interesting writers, though I did not think "French" at all when I was writing them or afterward, probably because they, even more than the longer pieces, are for me so located in American venues—with exceptions of course, like the title piece. I also did not stop to think, as I broached them, whether the fragmentary form was "useful." (Perhaps you could expand on your question, in particular the word *still*?) I was in the midst of translating *Swann's Way* and because of that—in response to Proust's long sentences and also because I had so little time—I wanted to see how very brief a piece of writing could be and still be finished, have some impact, be more than a mere joke. Oddly enough, they seem to me to operate all in different ways—all they really have in common is their brevity.

RM: I suppose I say "useful" because the fragment is so arresting in the context of American naturalist fiction. It runs counterclockwise to the "good storytelling" modality that undergirds so much of what happens in our national literature. Is it the case that you didn't think about how these fragmentary pieces would look when read in the context of everything else that happens here? Are you free from that particular kind of compositional anxiety?

LD: Yes, quite free, which is nice. I rarely, rarely think, But what will people make of this? If I do, it's a minor echo somewhere off in the distance—pretty irrelevant. What is always more important to me is: What do I feel like doing, what would be interesting to do? I'll try it and see if it works, rework it till I think it does work, though after even a lot of effort sometimes it's just competent.

RM: Here's a related question. Many of your stories are so realistic that you have a slightly erroneous reputation for writing a sort of crypto-nonfiction fiction. That is, some people believe the stories are entirely true. To me, this has always been a secondary issue, if an issue at all, because when I'm reading your work I'm engaged with how you use rhythm and sentence length to convey emotional and psychological states. Do you worry about the question of genre with respect to what you do? Or is that taxonomic approach too narrow?

LD: I like your formulation there—"use rhythm and sentence length to convey emotional and psychological states." I certainly don't worry about the question of genre—not with a furrowed brow anyway. But it interests me a lot. In fact, I like the idea that one could write entirely true stories that are just as shaped and manipulated as entirely fictional ones. The shaping and selecting would distance the story, would move it back to the same distance (from the writer) as the entirely fictional story, it seems to me.

Many poems, after all, are entirely "true," yet they have the distance—the good ones anyway—of "made" things. But that being said, my stories are usually not entirely true; they have patches of true things in them, and then good doses of the untrue. Though it's hard to generalize—since nowadays I am writing things that don't even pretend to be narrative, or not very. What would you call a letter of complaint that is, yes, entirely true but told in an adopted voice, the voice of a slightly manic version of one aspect of my personality, so that to me it becomes fictional? Or what about a "sociological study" of two old women I know? Again, it is the voice of the narrator that is fictional.

RM: The publishers in this country now translate something like less than five percent of the volumes they publish, and that includes all the engineering and computer manuals that are imported from nations abroad. Do you see your work as a translator as part of a noble effort to bring American readers closer to the literature of Europe?

LD: Well, my noble effort really is a result of happenstance. I began translating because I was happy working with languages and I needed to earn a living. I can say I'm glad to be part of that effort, and I am certainly embarrassed at the cultural parochialism of my native country. One of the regular bus drivers on the Adirondack Trailways line that I take up to Albany came here from Eastern Europe and speaks no less than seven languages.

RM: How much time do you devote to translating as opposed to writing fiction? Has that changed since the advent of your MacArthur Fellowship? Has the MacArthur had an impact on your ambitions for your new work?

LD: I more or less stopped translating after the years-long work of *Swann's Way*. I expected that—it felt like a culmination as I was doing it. Although it is true that immediately afterward I translated a short story from Spanish into English—and thought maybe I would simply switch languages. But I haven't done that. The MacArthur Fellowship came at the right moment, about a year and a half after I had sent the manuscript of the translation to England and six months after I had sent Viking the changes for the American edition. So I was relatively clear of the Proust translation and soon freed myself of the heaviest of my teaching obligations. The MacArthur has been very important, of course—I was always scrambling to squeeze in a bit of writing time. Now my perspective has widened, opened out, changed in ways I am still trying to understand.

RM: A couple of last questions on the work of translation. For example, is there anything untranslatable for you?

LD: Certain sentences in Blanchot's essays were impenetrable. Certain moments in Proust I was never quite satisfied with—and since I can't believe there isn't a solution I still go back and wrestle with them now and then. I'd say that one of the hardest challenges in translation is slang or colloquial speech, because it has to be local, natural, and lively, and you can't use one piece of local speech—like "blimey"—to stand in for another, though some translators do. Luckily, that isn't a big problem in *Swann's Way*. I thought the ideal solution would be to come up with an invented slang, one that would sound natural and inevitable and yet not be local, of course, to any English-speaking area. In the end, I didn't really need to do that, though.

RM: When you translate do you think in French, English, or French/ English? If the third, is it possible for you to communicate in this hybrid tongue?

LD: I nearly always think in English, though an occasional word will come along in French, whether I'm translating or not, or even German—*dunkel* when something is especially dark. When I'm reading a Proust sentence, I am entirely in French, of course; there is no English present, and the French itself sometimes becomes transparent.

A CONVERSATION WITH
ANITA DESAI

Ben George

Few writers have been at it as long or with as much perseverance as Anita Desai. She is the author of two story collections and twelve novels, including *In Custody*, *Baumgartner's Bombay*, and *Fasting, Feasting*. She has taught at such distinguished universities as MIT and England's Girton College, Cambridge. She is also a member of both the American Academy of Arts and Letters and the Royal Society of Literature. Yet it wasn't until her sixth book, *Fire on the Mountain*, that she was published in the United States, and not until her seventh, *Clear Light of Day*, in 1980, that she came to international attention with a Booker Prize nomination. She was the first Indian woman to be recognized in this manner, and with two subsequent Booker nominations and a host of other honors and awards, her writing career has been nothing if not ascendant. Although Desai might demur to hear you say it, the truth is that she, along with her friend Salman

Rushdie, is largely responsible for the explosion of interest in Indian literature during the last couple of decades. Without her, it's hard to imagine the universal success of the younger generation of Indian writers like Arundhati Roy, Jhumpa Lahiri, and Chitra Divakaruni.

For the last several years Desai has been dividing her time between New York, India, and Mexico, where her most recent novel, *The Zigzag Way*, is set. One late afternoon in November 2005 I met with her in Cold Spring, New York, at her 1840s home—the former parsonage for the town's Baptist church, which we could see out her back window—as she was preparing to leave the cold behind and head to Mexico for what she hoped would be a productive couple of months. With true British hospitality she brewed us a pot of tea and brought out a basket of cookies (or biscuits, depending on which side of the pond you're from), and we sat down in the living room to chat. Though she is a very quiet and very still woman, she possesses a daunting elegance. When she speaks, it is with almost no wasted words or motion and with a fierce and unassailable intelligence that belies her humility.

Ben George: With an Indian father and a German mother, you must have had an interesting childhood, culturally speaking. What was it like for your mother in India? What was your upbringing like?

Anita Desai: My mother lived most of her life in India. She only went back to Germany once, just before the war. Yet at heart she remained very European in her thinking and her feeling, though she would wear Indian clothes and cook Indian food and speak the language. And she was very determined to bring us all up as Indians. She never gave us the idea that we were partly European or partly German. She didn't want us torn between two worlds: she thought that would be an awful thing to do to her children. So when she talked about Germany to us, it was almost as if she were telling us fairy stories.

BG: Was it a joy to grow up with so many languages—German, Hindi, Bengali, and English? To be able to choose among them for the best word or phrase for what you wanted to express at the moment?

AD: Yes, very much so. Not that I thought it unusual, because everybody in India has at least two, if not three or four, languages that they dip into and use in the course of an ordinary day. The only thing unusual was the combination of languages in my home, the fact that we spoke German too. In a way, the German language was like a secret family code, although I believe that during the war my older siblings told my mother to please not speak German in public. They were conscious of it not being a safe thing to do at a time when India was a British territory.

My chief memory of wartime is helping my mother pack boxes full of coffee, tea, cocoa, sugar, wrapping them up, taking them to the post office, sending them off. We were constantly sending off these parcels without ever learning if they reached their destination. I didn't realize then—I do now—how my mother must have lived in a constant state of anxiety, because there was no mail, there were no letters coming through, she had no idea what was happening in Germany. I can remember waking up the morning we heard that the war was over and Germany had surrendered, and my mother must have just read the newspaper, and I don't think I'll ever forget the expression on her face. She was silent, she didn't give anything away. But I imagine it was both relief and also tremendous sadness.

Much closer to our feelings and our way of thinking was the Freedom Movement in India. My father's family was very involved in that. The talk was constantly about Nehru and Gandhi and whether or not the British were packing up and leaving, whether or not India would join them in fighting the war. My mother must have had very few people she could talk to at all about Germany.

BG: For the culmination of the Freedom Movement, the Partition of India, you were a little older—about ten. Do you have distinct memories of this time? For instance, in *Clear Light of Day*, when Hyder Ali and his family disappear in the middle of the night—was it really like that in your neighborhood?

AD: Yes, it was. Partition was the most significant event in my life, because Old Delhi, which was where we lived, was changed utterly by it. Before Partition many of our neighbors were Muslims; half the girls in the school I went to were Muslim. And during that summer, they all vanished. Hardly anyone stayed. There were just a few who refused to go to Pakistan, and one was always very afraid for them and ready to hide them if necessary, take them into safety. The whole neighborhood was involved in that. At night you would see the fires all along the horizon. The Muslim households were being looted and burned. There was an enormous amount of violence and killing.

BG: In *Baumgartner's Bombay* you address the internment of Germans in prisoner-of-war camps in British-controlled India during World War II. German Jews in India, who were actually refugees from Nazi Germany, were not exempted from the camps by the British army. Was this well known in India?

AD: It wasn't. In fact, to most people it came as a surprise that there were internment camps in India at all during the war. They hadn't been written about. When I started doing research for the book, I hunted for books and papers on the subject, because I knew there *had* been Germans in these internment camps. Several of them were my mother's acquaintances and friends. She herself didn't have to go to one, because she had become an Indian citizen. By the time I started doing my research, her old friends had either died or moved away, and one whom I did find didn't want to speak about it at all. In the end I had to turn to people outside India for information. I was introduced to a Jewish Israeli professor who had been in such an internment camp, and he was very helpful. Later on I met a Jewish German, by birth, who had been born in an internment camp. His parents were Jewish—they had been doctors or dentists—and they spent the entire war years in an internment camp. It was a time of great muddle and confusion. I think the British simply put them in there because their passports were German and therefore they were enemies. The people in charge of the camps weren't always well informed or educated, and really couldn't understand the enormous complications of the situation. It's ironic, but there was so much confusion at those times.

BG: Baumgartner is in a unique position at the end of the war. He's both a winner and a loser. Hitler and Nazism have been defeated, and so as a Jew, Baumgartner has won. Yet he's also forever lost his homeland. This seems a truly poignant contradiction.

AD: That scene, when he realizes what he's lost in gaining his survival, is based entirely on my mother and the expression I remember on her face, which was so complicated that it's impossible to describe or sum up in a few words. Possibly I've been trying for many years to fathom those feelings of loss and relief, how they might go together. For instance, my mother refusing to ever go back to Germany—what could that be based on? If we ever suggested to her that enough years had gone by and perhaps she should go back and meet the last few survivors in her family, then her eyes would fill with tears. She would be so upset and terrified by the thought that we could never pursue it. Yet when I first went to Germany, when I was about twenty-five, she was excited for *my* sake, making up lists and telling me what to see and where to go. The terrible thing was that of course it wasn't anything like she remembered. It had all changed completely.

BG: You've said that your work as a writer was always "utterly subservient to that of being a wife." When your children were growing up, you even hid your writing life from them, afraid that it would trouble them to learn that you had this life apart from them. Did you resent that situation?

AD: It became much easier once my children grew up. When they were little I think they would have seen it as some kind of competition, and I noticed that they grew very tense if they ever saw a book of mine lying around. I couldn't write openly. It would have created a great deal of resentment in the family, and I wouldn't have been able to write under those circumstances. So I used to do it secretly. I didn't *mind* that; it worked perfectly all right. I was left to myself to do the writing. No one stopped me from writing. But I used to resent it very much when it was somehow seen as nothing but a nice little hobby that she has. It keeps her quiet and occupied. I didn't know other people who understood my way of living or working, and I felt myself resenting that, that there was no one in my circle who understood the work I was doing. The only time I finally did have that was when I discovered that my neighbor who lived just up the road was the writer Ruth Jhabvala. That was my first experience of having a friend who really was the same as yourself, who did the same work and had the same opinion of it. We could talk about books and they seemed the most important thing in the world to us. That was a wonderful experience.

BG: Elsewhere, you say that the beginning of *Baumgartner's Bombay* in your mind was seeing an Austrian Jew in Bombay walking around and picking up scraps for his cats. Is there a pattern for your imaginative jumping-off points? How has it worked with other books?

AD: In *Fasting, Feasting* I knew this family extremely well over the years. I had seen exactly what had happened to their relationships, so that was based on observation over a long period of time and very intimate knowledge of that situation. In *The Zigzag Way* it had entirely to do with place. I never got to know any Mexican family or individual well enough to be able to write about them, so it had to be based on something else. I chose to do it about place because I found that going into an empty, abandoned place like a ghost town asks of you that you conjure up the past—try to picture what went on in these ruins when they were very grand houses in another period of history. With each book it's really quite different. Baumgartner was this figure I used to see in the streets. But I never met him. When I used him as my central character, I had to invent a whole history for him, because I knew nothing about him. I knew of course that this was the last year of his life and he was going to die that day, but to the last chapter I didn't know who was going to kill him. I had two characters who had motives and could have killed him. I played with the two of them for a long time, wondering who was the more likely murderer, before I chose one.

BG: There's a real reticence or trepidation toward sex among your protagonists. Two examples: Bimla in *Clear Light of Day* and Baumgartner in *Baumgartner's Bombay* are both at least virginal, and perhaps actual virgins. For Bimla it seems positive; it's about female independence. But for Baumgartner it seems about fear and about closing himself off. He's uncomfortable with the way his friend Lotte flaunts her sexuality. Is sex dangerous in your fictional world?

AD: It really has to do with my feeling of how far you can intrude upon other people's lives. As a novelist you are intruding, even if they're imagined lives. You are the narrator and are therefore outside. I've had great reticence about that. I feel I can only go so far into their lives, a barrier that any observer, any acquaintance or friend, might come across. I'm aware that there's so much which I couldn't possibly step into. It's probably something a lot of readers have noticed is lacking in my books, but it's due to the feeling that at a certain point your characters shut the door and vanish. You can't follow them.

BG: There seems to always be a high level of decorum in your narratives in general. Do you think it's important for a writer to avoid obscenity if possible?

AD: No, I don't. If you are living in a world where it's part of the texture of your life—and I know for many people it is—then it doesn't offend me at all. It seems to me an essential part of their work, which would be falsified if they were to cut it out. I have simply chosen to write about the kind of society in which I have been brought up and have lived, for the most part, of which obscenity isn't a part. For me it would be a falsehood to bring it in simply because it has a certain power.

BG: Virtually all of your books use the third-person omniscient point of view. We even enter the perspective of dogs and cats. Do you think this sprawling, authoritative narration and the kind of playful exuberance of your language are a result of being influenced by older English writers like Austen and Dickens?

AD: There's no denying that they were the earliest and the most important influences on my writing, what I was reading at the time I started to write. I used them as models, as inspiration, as the ideal I was hoping to move toward. It's a long time before you can get away from those influences and write something in your own voice, out of your own word. Perhaps a few writers do it straightaway, but that's the exception. I was in my twenties when I first started publishing books. I certainly didn't have an individual voice of my own at that time.

BG: Over the years, your style has changed somewhat. How conscious has the decision been to pare?

AD: I grew very impatient with the earlier style, which began to strike me as verbose, and I was embarrassed by it. I didn't want to continue writing like that. I had grown old enough to step back and read it as though it had been written by someone else, and by then I *was* someone else. After that point, I was interested in cutting and paring and reducing rather than expanding. Perhaps, again, it was a literary influence. Whereas earlier I had been reading Dostoyevsky and Dickens, now I was reading a lot more poetry, especially modern and contemporary poetry, and was learning from the poets and envying them their ability to reduce to the barest essence and yet be able to convey exactly what they wanted to convey. My literary models changed.

BG: Another thing that changed slightly was the move from a more formalized, literary dialogue to an effort at capturing the accuracy and rhythm of Indian English as it's actually spoken by, say, the café owner, Farrokh, in *Baumgartner's Bombay*. Did you find this move liberating?

AD: Yes, I did. That's one of the things one gradually learns through a lot of practice. I realized that in my early books, which I now am so impatient of, it was always the same voice that you were hearing. It was always the same person who was talking, even if I farmed the conversation out between several characters. One thing you learn as you continue with your craft is this: Listen to other people's voices. Try to replicate the individuality of those voices. And yes, it is in a way liberating. You realize you can inhabit many different characters, present many different points of view.

BG: While your narration is often all-encompassing, the books themselves are quite compact. Do you find yourself cutting a good deal in revision, or do you intend from the beginning to keep your narratives brief?

AD: What has happened to me is that I found the books coming to a halt. Perhaps I had imagined they would go further, but then for some reason they came to a halt. Either I ran out of energy, or the story had already been told and there was really nothing left to tell. For instance, a lot of readers did complain that *The Zigzag Way* was a very small book to address a big subject. My editors at both my American and my British publishing houses had suggested that I expand and add another chapter. They said, "Well, perhaps it's come to an end for *you*, but what about the characters Eric and his girlfriend? Do they get back together? What happens to Doña Vera? You've left us all hanging in the air, you haven't concluded their stories." But the story that *I* wanted to tell had come to its conclusion. Eric *had* stepped into the past. He *had* made a kind of circle for his family story. And yes, their stories will continue but those stories didn't interest me. In that sense, the book had come to a halt. There was nothing more for me to add.

Similarly, with *Clear Light of Day* I had wanted it to be like an excavation, going further and further and further back in time, starting with the present time and then going back into the youth of my characters and then into their childhood. I had considered adding a section about their parents, their ancestry, but by the time I had come to the end that I do, I found I had really told the story I wanted to tell. It would have taken another book to go further back in time.

BG: A number of your books use the technique of beginning with a present story and then tunneling backward through time to illuminate the story. What does this way of writing reveal about what you believe about storytelling and the function of time in storytelling?

AD: When you introduce your characters or a place to your reader, you can only do it by imagining you've just met them, you've just stepped into this place, because you can't grasp anyone's character or history or story immediately, all in one go. You gradually learn about people, a little at a time. That's part of the technique of a novelist.

When I used to teach writing, I would ask my students not to tell me everything at once, because that's not how life is. You only learn a little at a time. Start with a minimal amount and then gradually reveal the rest. Of course that does mean covering a certain amount of space. Not necessarily their whole history, maybe just an episode. In a short story that's all you can really grasp. But even a short story has to convey a sense of time passing.

BG: One thing you do incredibly well in your books is to take the broad canvas of a huge sociopolitical event—the Partition of India, the Holocaust, the Mexican Revolution—and then overlay a very individual story. Do you think it's important for writers to address these more monumental shared experiences of history?

AD: No, I don't. One can make a story, and even a great book, out of a very limited, very restricted life, if you're able to uncover all the richness within it. It's just that growing up in India, one has such a sense of history. One can't avoid it. You stumble upon it all the time. Its stones are lying under your feet. One therefore has a sense of what made the present. It's always been an effort of mine to bring in that sense of the background, the depths of the story I'm telling, but I think one can do it on a very small canvas as well. There are brilliant books written about nothing very much.

BG: You've said, "It's not for us to reject history, but it is for us to transform it." How does the writer go about doing this? Who are the writers who have done it powerfully?

AD: Dickens set out to write about all the ills of his society, about all the bad times that his people were living through, so I think he had a powerful effect. In our own times, Salman Rushdie brought about a great transformation of the writing being done in India. I'm not so sure he did it about the way people live their lives or the way they think in India, but he certainly had an enormous influence on the writing, because he was taking up not the formal English language that we had been taught in school but the language that Indians speak and use on the streets among themselves in their everyday, informal lives. Rushdie was saying, "Well, you can tell your story in this language too. It's a perfect vehicle for what you have to say and think, and you can even express very important ideas in it." So he had a huge influence on all the writers who succeeded him.

BG: The detail of setting and place in your work is always remarkable, whether it's a Bombay bazaar or a middle-class Delhi neighborhood or an old mining community in Mexico. Is this level of observation something that comes easily to you?

AD: It's quite natural for me. An accumulation of detail is really what one builds a book with. Before I start a book, I need a huge amount of detail to go on, and when I have an idea in my head, I start making notes, which I scribble down on little bits and pieces of paper. It's only when I feel I've got a sufficiently large body of detail that I even think of starting work on the book. The story comes about by your finally seeing a link or an association between all these details. You're scribbling them down all the time, and then you wonder, Why did you do it? What's so important about them? What's their significance? And each, individually, probably has no significance, but when you begin to link them together and say, "Oh, this is attached to that, this leads to the other"—then a story comes about.

BG: You've said that engaging in the work of writing at least offers a semblance of ordering the world. But is that all it is, a semblance? Are we ultimately like Lotte at the close of *Baumgartner's Bombay*, left with fragments that we unsuccessfully try to organize in order to give "meaning to the meaningless"?

AD: That episode and those lines reflect a sense of powerlessness which many of my characters do suffer from. They feel in the grip of events of history, powerless to alter them to make them kinder or more amenable. Most of my characters struggle to do so but are overpowered by events. At least in India, I think a lot of us suffer from the sense of not being in control of our lives, of our lives being controlled by forces that are much greater than ourselves, of struggling to get some kind of control over them, usually failing, and finding that you're controlled by your family or your financial situation or the lack of education or whatever it is that holds you back. That's the great difference between our two worlds and two cultures. You come to America and you suddenly find yourself among people who are completely confident that they can do what they wish with their lives. That comes as a very startling revelation to an Indian. How can anyone think that? How can that be true? But here one meets a lot of people who have taken over their own lives and made of them exactly what they wanted to. You rarely come across that in India, and I think that would be true even today.

BG: *In Custody* was the first book in which you broke away somewhat from the world of your previous books in order to write more about male characters. The book doesn't really have any truly sympathetic female characters, and we're even confronted with things like Deven's belief that his position of power over his wife is as important to her as it is to him. Was it a difficult book to write in this respect?

AD: Yes, it was. But I had set myself to doing it as a kind of challenge. I wanted to break out of the women's world I had been writing about so much that it had become repetitive, and I wanted to step into a male mind and a male world. I had originally thought of it as a book which was going to have no female characters at all, because the people I was writing about inhabited a very male world in which women mattered very little. Women took care of the family and they ran the kitchen, but they didn't really intrude upon the male world, which the men thought of as being lofty and above these women who weren't very well educated. So I really meant to have no female characters, other than the men addressing women as being on the fringes. Then I found myself thinking, That's simply not realistic. They have to at least step in. Even if they're only serving a meal or taking care of the children, they have to exist in the margins of the book. I realized that if I shut them out, of course they would be screaming in fury and rage and anger behind those closed doors, which made them seem very shrill and very unpleasant. I did sit back and say, "Why have I created these awful women? Nobody can possibly sympathize with them, they're so awful." That's why I had one of them—the poet Nur's younger wife—write a letter in which she explains herself. In fact, that turned out to be quite interesting in the film, because of course I couldn't have her write a letter and have Deven read the letter. It's hardly cinematic to do that. So I had her confront him and speak her mind, and that becomes a very dramatic moment in the film.

BG: Let's talk about that angry tirade that the poet's wife delivers to Deven. It comes near the end of the book and, as you mentioned, is in the form of a letter. In it, she berates Deven and all men for not taking her own work seriously. To what extent is she speaking for you there?

AD: This is unconscious. It's not that I create a character who will then present my ideas and speak for me. But unconsciously one is feeding such speech and ideas into one's characters, probably distributing them through a whole cast of characters. Quite unconsciously that's a moment in which she is expressing some of the feelings and ideas I would have had but had suppressed. I didn't think of her as being a representative of my own ideas, but possibly I was speaking for a lot of artists who've been neglected or not supported.

She also presented me with quite a dilemma. I didn't really like her very much. [laughs] Even though I had a feeling that she was not a great artist, I still wanted her to have her individuality. She should at least be able to speak for herself, and no one had heard her.

BG: You wrote the screenplay for the film adaptation of In Custody. What's different for you about the challenge of writing a screenplay as opposed to a novel? Did you find it rewarding?

AD: It's utterly different from working on a novel in that you have to cut away all the writing, really discard it, retaining only a few key words, because it's the visuals that take over, and that's in the hands of the director and the actors. I wasn't comfortable doing that. For a long time I just clung to the novel and tried to stay as close to it as I possibly could. It had to be really torn out of my hands. The director suggested changes—*insisted* on changes—that I wasn't entirely happy with. I also realized that the actors take over. They're by no means puppets who just follow instructions, which I thought they would be. They're very actively involved, and they can't act unless they take over that role, take over the character. So again I had to relinquish a lot and leave it to them. It wasn't for me to insist on their remaining true to the book. The film turned out to be very different from my book. In the most obvious way, I thought of it as rather a dark book, black-and-white and shadowy. But the film was made in Technicolor and looks very gorgeous. No, I didn't enjoy it. Perhaps it would be more enjoyable to write an original screenplay, to be able to visualize it entirely from scratch as a film, but I haven't done that.

BG: Since the late eighties you've been in the U.S. for at least part of the year. What's made you stay?

AD: I first came here to take up a teaching job. My son was studying here at the time and my daughter later studied in the States as well. Actually I was quite certain I would go back to India, but since they both stayed on over here, I felt they very much needed a home here too, so I stayed on to make that for them. And I just have stayed on and on. I go back all the time on visits, but it's become harder for me to live there now. Having gained a sense of an independent life, it's very hard to go back and become a dependent again, which one does in India. One immediately becomes a dependent of one's family and circle of friends. It's painfully obvious. Over here you're expected to have your own opinions and to voice them, and when you go back to India, you find yourself continuing with that and then noticing that everyone's staring at you, wondering, What's got into her? [laughs] You learn all over again to be quiet and keep things to yourself. Similarly, you have to do things the other way round when you come here. People ask your opinion and think it's a bit odd if you don't have one.

BG: I was fascinated by your admission that American literature didn't really prepare you for American culture in the same way English literature did for English culture. Do you think there's more of a disconnect between American art and American life than exists in other cultures?

AD: Certainly the British literature that I had read prepared me for what I encountered when I first went to England in my twenties. England was exactly the way I had read of it and imagined it. I could recognize scenes, characters, objects, because I had encountered them already in a previous incarnation. The reading I had done about the States comprised the classics: I had read Faulkner and Steinbeck and Hemingway and Tennessee Williams. When I came to the States, it was New England, it was Massachusetts. I couldn't recognize anything. This was *not* the world that I had been reading about. I can't quite explain that. Perhaps you could help me understand it. Were these imaginative worlds of the writers which didn't really exist?

BG: I guess they were worlds that existed at the time the writers wrote about them. I suppose America would have changed as much between that time and the time you arrived as you've described India as having changed. Then, too, there often seem to be pronounced cultural differences in America by region, as there might be in India as well—I don't know. But New England is certainly distinct from each of the places those writers were writing about.

AD: Yes, New England is a different world again. Somehow those American books had not created for me the world that I found when I came here, which made me feel a foreigner as I had never felt before. I felt totally foreign. There was just *nothing* in my world in India which was similar or could connect. After all, there were many things British in India with which I could make connections. I wasn't totally at sea in England. In that sense, nothing American had ever really figured in my life. But I must say that when I reread *Huckleberry Finn*, which I think is the first book I went back to read on coming to Massachusetts, it all came vividly, gloriously to life. I understood the book as I never had before. I realized that all these were experiences I hadn't really had in reading before. Somehow the book and the experience had to come together. I had read Nabokov in India, one of the writers I had hugely admired. Always. But the books had not meant so much to me till I came to America and saw the scene he was describing.

Then there were other writers I discovered only on coming here who became very important to me. Don DeLillo. Reading *White Noise* and *Mao II* were wonderful experiences. I suddenly felt as though a window had been opened. Or Flannery O'Connor, whom I had not known before. I enjoyed her work so much. All these writers suddenly began to matter so much more once I was here.

BG: What's been the hardest part of living in America?

AD: As I say, I'd never felt a foreigner before. *Baumgartner's Bombay* turned out to be prophetic in that sense. [laughs] I had had to imagine what it's like to be a foreigner to write that book—my mother had never given me a sense of being a foreigner. I have found myself being rather like Baumgartner, walking along streets where he obviously doesn't belong and trying to make sense of the lives of the people around him, mostly failing.

I was also very frightened that I had lost the material out of which all my work grew. I felt that I wouldn't be able to write about India again because the American experience was so powerful, it was so preoccupying. Even further, I was teaching myself to be a teacher, which I hadn't been before. I didn't know how to teach; I had to learn it, and learn it from the students, which made me feel even more helpless and inadequate.

BG: You've said that since September 11, America is a frightening place for outsiders. I wonder if you might expand a bit on this American paranoia that you've mentioned elsewhere.

AD: I came here in order to teach, and having lived on university campuses, I had always found them such welcoming places. And I encountered so many other foreigners, especially at MIT, where at least half the students come from elsewhere. It had seemed to be a place where everyone could find a foothold and make something of their lives. And then after September 11, I gradually realized that the scene was changing, that people here were beginning to think, Whom have we let into our midst? That there was a great deal more suspicion around. Everyone didn't change at once. After all, I was still among friends, among students. But I became aware that people would become more careful of whom they let into their midst, of what kind of ideas you were bringing in. You learned to be more careful about expressing your opinions or thoughts. For one thing, I didn't quite understand how people felt, wasn't able to guess, was sometimes taken by surprise, even among those of my colleagues who I thought were friends. For instance, I felt that they didn't quite understand where these attacks were coming from and that perhaps being from the East myself, I had some glimmer of what kind of simmering anger, rage, resentment would bring about such attacks. And later I was far more angry than I think my colleagues were about the death and destruction in Iraq. I wasn't able to tell them how very angry I felt, because they felt angry too, but about different things. I felt that the attacks of September 11 weren't carried out by a country, by a government: they were carried out by certain individuals. So I couldn't see why one had to attack a government or a country for this reason. I couldn't see what these people had done to deserve so much destruction of their own lives.

BG: Both Afghanistan and Iraq?

AD: Yes, except that Afghanistan is a much older story and much more complicated. It's not the same story as Iraq. That's why I felt that people weren't taking the trouble to learn anything about the situation—just accepting whatever was told to them, much too easily, much too lightly. Iraq isn't Al Qaeda.

BG: *Clear Light of Day*, your seventh novel overall and second to be published in the U.S., was your first of three to be nominated for the Booker Prize. How did the acclaim affect you? Do you think it's good that it didn't happen until you were already a well-established author?

AD: Those early books of mine were not what one would call a success at all. I was just so delighted—over the moon—to get them into print. But there was no success in the sense of huge advances or a great deal of publicity. That's all such a recent trend, to turn writers into celebrities or to have publication become a kind of public event. I never thought of my books as huge successes which would in any way change my life, and they didn't. I certainly never encountered the celebrity trend in my life. Even with the Booker nomination, you're one of six, seven, or eight writers who get nominated. You don't stand out by yourself.

Certainly you're happy for the recognition. It's very gratifying to have that kind of recognition. But on the whole it's such an unpleasant experience. Prizes in general are an unpleasant experience, not necessarily one I'd like to repeat. For every one writer who wins, ten or twenty lose. I really dislike all these Pulitzer Prize and national award lists. It's an awful thing to put a writer through. I still feel that if your book is published, it has readers, it gets read. I don't even follow the sales figures ever. I have no clue how many copies I've sold of any one book.

BG: Is there any difference, that you know of, in the way Indians read your books and the way that, say, the English or Americans read them?

AD: Definitely. Indian readers read them with much more intimate knowledge and are therefore much more critical and quick to jump on you if you get the slightest detail wrong. These different reader-ships have different expectations of your books. If you get a reputa-tion for writing a certain kind of book, they want you to keep repeat-ing that kind of book and not write another kind of book. My pub-lishers were a bit worried about *The Zigzag Way*. They thought, Well, you're an Indian writer, you've always written about India. Why are you coming up with this new subject? You're not a Mexican writer. And this attitude is very limiting. One doesn't want to repeat what one's already done. Each book should be a kind of challenge, a new territory for you to explore. Otherwise there's no excitement to it at all.

BG: Do you think trying to analyze and dissect the creative process robs it of any of its magic?

AD: I think writers are always happy to talk about the *craft* of writing or how they employ it. Some writers are happier to talk about their books than others, or better at it. And there are always certain things that you haven't even articulated to yourself, because so much has to do with the subconscious in writing. You can only explain so much. It's important in literature to leave spaces into which the reader can enter and engage with the text. For every reader it will be a different engagement, a different relationship. It's good to leave those spaces.

A CONVERSATION WITH
RODDY DOYLE

Tom Grimes

Roddy Doyle is as productive as a writer can be. He's written in every literary genre there is. Among his works are seven novels, a memoir about his parents, several screenplays, plays, a teleplay, three children's books, and a cycle of stories for a monthly multicultural paper. His novel *The Van* was a finalist for the Booker Prize in 1991 and two years later his novel *Paddy Clarke Ha Ha Ha* won the prize. The three novels that compose his famous *Barrytown Trilogy*—*The Commitments, The Snapper,* and *The Van*—were made into films. He's two-thirds of the way through a second trilogy, called *The Last Roundup,* and so far *A Star Called Henry* and *Oh, Play That Thing!* have made their way from his Dublin study into the world. We met a few years ago when he came to visit the Katherine Anne Porter Literary Center and the MFA Program in Creative Writing at Texas State University. We exchanged e-mail addresses and stayed in touch. Recently we discussed his views on music, keeping current with slang, and the changing fortunes of Ireland and America.

Tom Grimes: In *Oh, Play That Thing!*, Henry Smart escapes from Ireland and lands, as did most immigrants from Europe in the early twentieth century, in New York, on Ellis Island. From there he wanders into American culture and myth, first as Louis Armstrong's manager, and at the end as an actor in a John Ford film. Why is America attractive to you as subject matter?

Roddy Doyle: I come from, and live in, a very small country; America is a vast country. Ireland, until very recently, exported most of its people; America imported most of these people. I grew up looking at American TV and movies, listening to American music. I felt I knew America, or several versions of the place, before I ever visited. It was so big, so full of possibilities. I have tried to make Henry Smart somewhat larger than "normal" life; America is the logical place for him to run to. Note: we both refer to "America," not the "United States of America." Even that tells us quite a lot about America, and why I wanted to send one of my characters there.

TG: You once described America to me as "your great, tragic country." Why does America strike you as tragic at the moment?

RD: I've spent quite a lot of time in the USA in recent years, and it reminds me of Britain when Margaret Thatcher was prime minister. Many Americans are beginning to despise their own country; they're embarrassed, and feel powerless. I often encountered this in London and Liverpool and Manchester and, most especially, Glasgow, in the late eighties and into the nineties. But Thatcher eventually went, and so will Bush the Lesser. That's the great thing about liberal democracy: tragedy can be temporary—it doesn't have to be Shakespearean. In actual fact, America's greatest tragedy is Christian fiction. It frightens me more than any flu pandemic or "Jeb for Pres" campaign ever could.

TG: I know you're no fan of hypocrites or Christian claptrap, which you couldn't get away from fast enough in your youth.

RD: The Christianity of it all worries me. Bush's use of the word *crusade* was truly frightening. It's a battle of two fundamentalisms that feed off each other, and need each other to thrive. We kill one of yours, now you kill two of ours. Why don't these people watch *The Battle of Algiers*, or read up on what happened in Northern Ireland immediately after Bloody Sunday, in 1972? Drop a bomb, shoot an innocent victim, and you will have a line of volunteers, and more bombs, and more victims, and more volunteers, and on and on, until Iraq is virtually everywhere. I saw Laurie Anderson perform in New York last year, and she said—I'm paraphrasing—"This war isn't going to end. It's going to move." And maybe that's their plan, an endless, shifting war that will stifle opposition, debate, basic human rights, and do great things for cement-company profits. But, calming down a bit, I actually think that all religion is ridiculous. I went to a Christian Brothers school, so my scars are Catholic ones. But I'm glad I didn't go to a Muslim Brothers school; I don't think it would have been a happy alternative. All religion is nonsense. Christianity, all the branches, Judaism, Islam, all the branches, Taoism, Hinduism, and I throw in yoga and vegetarianism—they're all silly.

TG: Do you think the U.S. really can remain a liberal democracy, as you might still find in the EU, or do you see us becoming a pop culture theocracy?

RD: Yes, I think the USA will remain a liberal democracy. You'll always be allowed to vote for your own idiots. But this, again, is where I'm reminded of Thatcher's Britain. There was an air of defeatism—"there's nothing we can do"—for years, and no real alternative offered to her and her ideology. There was no point in opposing her. That went on for years. It's easy to sneer at Blair now, but he did break that Tory hold on Britain. He made doable what people had been longing to do for years. There's a not-dissimilar problem in Ireland. There's a coalition in power that few people actively like, but an opposition that doesn't seem to believe that it can win the next election. So we'll probably get more of the same. My big objection to American politics is the two-party system. It seems fundamentally undemocratic.

TG: What's your impression of Harold Pinter's denunciation of the U.S. in his Nobel Prize speech? According to the *New York Times*, Pinter said it was the duty of the writer to hold an image up to scrutiny, and the duty of citizens "to define the real truth of our lives and our societies . . . . If such a determination is not embodied in our political vision, we have no hope of restoring what is so nearly lost to us—the dignity of man."

RD: I agree, and disagree, with him. I don't think writing, or the duty of the writer, should be too tightly defined. The duty of the writer is to write—as simple as that. If more comes out of the writing—an image that demands scrutiny, a story that provokes guilt, joy, rage, impatience—good. I've been lucky. I've written words that have caused controversy here in Ireland, and have provoked people to examine the way we live. But if this is to be the only purpose of writing, we'll be left with a lot of very worthy, but dull, work. Writers can never anticipate the reaction of a reader. That's the magic, and danger, of the experience. I wrote something to anger an audience, and I got yawns. I wrote something else, to bring people to real life on a TV screen, and I received death threats. But Pinter is right. We're living in very ugly, damaging times. When is torture not torture? Has that question been asked before? Language has always been abused but the practice seems to have become routine. Deny, deny, deny; only the stupid tell the truth. Here's where I contradict myself, and perhaps agree with Pinter. The duty of the writer is to be stupid—and tell the truth. It's *how* we tell the truth, *how* we tell the story—that's where the writing, the hard work, comes in.

TG: You taught in New York a couple of years ago. You said you couldn't believe how incredibly cold the place is. Winter feels like a character in "Home to Harlem," a story you published recently in

McSweeney's, and at the same time the city streets seem vibrantly new. The place obviously affected you, and very quickly turned up in your work.

RD: When I referred to New York as cold I meant only the weather. I found it shockingly cold. It's early December here in Dublin, and colder than usual. There was light snow last week and I don't recall seeing snow in late November before. Yet it's mild. "Will I wear a jacket?" is a question I ask throughout the Dublin winter when I go to the front door. That's why New York was a shock. I'd experienced cold before. I'd even been in Lapland in the middle of winter, but this was different. The wind coming off the Hudson; Jesus—it shaved me every morning. But I loved it. I loved walking in it. I loved getting out of it. I loved the taste of espresso when my hands were still cold. It was a novelty. It made me think. When writing about Ireland, I rarely mention the weather. It goes without saying. If it isn't raining, it soon will be. But having an Irish character walking the streets of Manhattan, as I did in "Home to Harlem," I had to describe what he felt—what I'd felt when I arrived in early January 2004. I loved the blueness of the sky over New York. Cold, blue days are very rare in Dublin. In New York, they are normal. I loved trying to capture that on paper. The cold, the noises, the accents, the subway—I was looking and listening like a kid.

TG: I've just read Joan Didion's *The Year of Magical Thinking* on your recommendation. She continually returns to the fact that the sky was blue on 9/11, and that everyone mentions this when recounting the events, as if the planes couldn't possibly have hit the buildings on a sunny day. Do you think the images of the towers bursting into flames and then collapsing like cigarette ash would have been as powerful if they had happened on a gray, rainy day? What do you look for when you're creating images in your work—the battle scenes in *A Star Called Henry*, jazz clubs in *Oh, Play That Thing!*, a pint in a pub, the streets of Manhattan?

RD: I think those images would have been powerful, and terrible, regardless of the weather. But I suppose there is something even more obscene about the fact that it was a glorious day, and the knowledge in the backs of people's minds that it might be the last such day before the onset of fall and winter. We don't expect people to die on their holidays. We don't expect footballers to have heart attacks while playing. We don't expect to hear bad news on a sunny day. We don't expect to see it. Isn't the sun glaring in the Kennedy/Dallas images?

When I'm writing and researching, trying to re-create a place that's gone or a place that won't be familiar to most readers, I try to find images that are very visual and promise meaning beyond the visual. For example, I read that in 1916, the glass in the dome of the General Post Office in Dublin started to melt because of the heat during the bombardment. That would never have dawned on me. It's two miles from my home. I'll be walking past the building in a few hours. I went in many times while I was writing *A Star Called Henry*. I stood there, and looked around—and up. But it never, ever occurred to me that the glass above me would, or could, melt. Discovering that, and deciding to include it in my overall description, seemed to bring the thing alive for me. I wasn't just listing off events or images. This one image brought heat and sweat, and something terrifying—the British are outside but look what's falling from the roof. With jazz clubs, again, it's heat—and lyrics. Pictures are less important. They're important, but the sweat and the words really capture it—I hope. It's what I immediately thought of when I was deciding how to re-create a 1920s jazz club—heat and sweat. Like any music club. The streets of Manhattan in winter? Shadows and sun, and cold, and layers of clothes. They're images that allow readers to imagine themselves there.

TG: In "Home to Harlem," a black student from Dublin named Declan comes to New York to write a thesis on the Harlem Renaissance's influence on Joyce and Beckett, which is a poignantly absurd premise, and an incredibly funny one. Declan's Irish but no one really believes it. All the other characters think of him simply as black. So he's looking for an identity, but he can't seem to locate one.

RD: A lot of my work seems to be about identity. We take a word like *Irish* for granted; we know what it means. But I don't think we ever do. *A Star Called Henry* is narrated by an Irishman, but he's present at the creation of what came to be known as Ireland. My father's uncle joined what was called the army in 1914, and went off to war. He survived and came home in 1918. But now he was in something called the British Army, and home wasn't the same place. Something happened in those four years. A few years ago we could have said, reasonably, that Ireland's was a rural population. That's no longer the case. Things change; conditions change—definitions have to be constantly reexamined. Hence the black Irish kid wandering the streets of New York in "Home to Harlem." When I was a kid, and in a Christian Brothers school—I shake as I write; those men were unbelievable—the Irish ideal of what we were supposed to be was rural, Gaelic speaking, and Catholic. The color went without saying; I'd never seen a black man or woman. Those days are gone, and the Christian Brothers are dead or in jail. Ireland has become an economic magnet. People from Africa, Asia, and, most recently, Eastern Europe, the states that joined the EU at the start of 2005, are arriving and staying. The old definitions of Irishness are becoming out of date; they might be dangerous. Am I more Irish than the kid beside me on the bus whose parents are Nigerian? Am I a traitor because I think *Riverdance* is shite? America is full of hyphenated people. I like the hyphens. Polish-Irish, Nigerian-Irish, Estonian-Irish, and, my own self-definition, Dublin-Irish. We live in exciting times.

TG: But Declan's not above using the stereotype of being "Irish" to pick up a girl. "Give her lots of 'grands,'" he thinks. "They love that."

RD: And fair enough. He's no eejit.

TG: You've been writing stories about immigrants in Ireland, too. These have appeared in a monthly paper. Immigration is a major concern in Ireland right now. During the economic boom of the nineties, immigrants flooded the country. Now there seems to be a reaction against this situation. Why do you feel that stories have something important to contribute to the argument? And what audience are you trying to reach by publishing the work in city newspapers?

RD: Labor strikes have been rare in Ireland in recent years but there's currently a big dispute in a company called Irish Ferries. The company management wants to make its Irish employees redundant and replace them with Eastern European workers, who will work for less. We have a minimum wage here but, apparently, it doesn't apply in this case, and the company is planning on re-registering in Cyprus. It's worrying, as it could result in a lot of hostility towards immigrants; the old "they're taking our jobs" argument. And, naturally, management isn't replacing itself with a cheaper Eastern European version. So it is working people being thrown against each other. And this, I think, is where stories come in. The paper I write the stories for is called *Metro Éireann*, a multicultural free paper, founded by two Nigerian journalists living in Dublin. (*Éireann* is one of the Gaelic names for Ireland.) I divide the stories into eight-hundred-word chapters, and I've been writing them for more than five years. I'm on the seventh story now. I'll collect them into one volume soon. The idea is to bring characters together, some born in Ireland, some recent arrivals, to see what happens—to make stories. New stories. The whole idea is to bring the "old" Irish and the "new" Irish together, to see what happens. To make it seem natural, and exciting, and fun, and frightening, and thought-provoking. In 2006 I'm going to be writing with a Nigerian writer/actor called Bisi Adigun; we'll be working on a new version of Synge's *The Playboy of the Western World*, but this time the playboy, Christy Mahon, will be African. It should be fun, but only if Bisi does exactly what I tell him to!

TG: How has it been, working with a fixed word limit for each installment?

RD: The eight-hundred-word quota is fun. I'm writing a story at the moment. I finished the first draft of the sixth chapter yesterday, and it's about one hundred fifty words too long. I can't simply carry those extra words into the seventh chapter, because each chapter has to be a little story in itself. I have to get rid of the extra words, and that's often fascinating—how the deletion of a couple words can have a huge impact on the shape and power of a sentence. It's not something I'd want to do all the time, or even much of the time. But I really enjoy it. And I don't plan ahead. I'm finished with chapter six, but I've no solid idea about what's going to happen in chapter seven, and I don't have to worry about it until a month from now. Then it'll be a fresh little terror.

TG: You also like to get out of the writer's study and into the world. You've worked with others on a series of forty-minute plays that are done in high school classrooms. What are some of the plays about, and why stage them in classrooms rather than theaters?

RD: I love my office. I've a cup of good coffee beside me now, and I'm playing the soundtrack of Martin Scorsese's Dylan documentary, *No Direction Home*, and there's no one telling me to hurry up. So life is good. But, yes, I like to get out. I'd hate to catch myself writing about a version of Dublin that's twenty years out-of-date, and think that it's contemporary. I like to keep my eye on things outside the door. I like to listen.

The school plays were an Amnesty International project called Voice Our Concern, which I helped develop. In Irish high schools there is what is called Transition Year, when the students are fifteen—a gap, a nonexam year, between the Junior Cert and the final two senior years. They do work experience; they form minicompanies; they go on field trips; they do drama, et cetera—it's a great life. Anyway, the idea was that ten writers would visit ten schools on the tenth of December—International Human Rights Day. We'd talk to the students, about their ideas, their concerns, about what sort of a play they'd like to see or act in. I went to a school, a convent, in a town called Dundalk, about forty miles from my home. I ended up writing a short play about racism—a big topic among the students, some of whom are originally from Africa, or have one or two African parents. They were all working on their minicompany projects, so I made that the setting—a school room; a group of students; the tension—they are working to a deadline; the "casual" remark; the arguments; the resolution. I got ideas from the students, and some of the local geography and slang. Then I went home. I actually wrote the play in New York, in the winter of '04. I later saw some of the same students perform the play, which, by the way, is called *The Chocolate Colin Farrells*. It was a great experience; I loved the whole thing. The ten plays, which are now in book form, are short, so they can be "done" in school, in a school room, in the conventional forty-minute class period. There are plays by, amongst others, Maeve Binchy, Peter Sheridan, Dermot Healy, Conor McPherson, and Hugo Hamilton. They're for school use only, the "property" of Irish high school students.

TG: You've returned to certain characters in your books. You traced, for instance, the Rabbitte family in *The Barrytown Trilogy*. And Henry Smart is scheduled to appear in book three of this new trilogy. Now you're revisiting Paula Spencer, the character in *The Woman Who Walked into Doors*. You've even resurrected Jimmy Rabbitte in a new story. Why does catching up with your characters at different points in their lives appeal to you?

RD: In the case of Paula Spencer, having spent quite awhile working on two novels set in the past, I wanted to write a novel set in contemporary Dublin. Which is why I wrote *Paula Spencer*. I thought that Paula would be a good guide, someone who'd be close to the changes that have been occurring to the city and country. For example, she's an office cleaner. In *The Woman Who Walked into Doors*, she worked, and went to work, with other working-class women, like herself. Now, in 2005, she works with Romanian men and African men and women. She's the only white Irish-born woman. How does that make her feel? I was also curious about her, generally. How was life treating her? Was she still drinking? How were her children? Were they all alive? Was she a grandmother? But the real appeal, the reason I wrote another book about her, was her qualities as a guide—an interesting person to observe, and an interesting, wise observer. In general, it often seems like a good idea to revisit characters, if they're older, if their surroundings and circumstances have changed—to avoid sequel hell, The Further Adventures . . .

In the case of Jimmy Rabbitte, from *The Commitments*, I went back to him because with the recent immigration it seemed that the people on all his best-loved record covers were arriving in Dublin. There's a line in *The Commitments* that has become quite famous: "The Irish are the niggers of Europe." That was written in 1986. Ireland is now one of the wealthiest countries in Europe. I thought that the line, and what was behind the line, and the man who says it, Jimmy Rabbitte, were worth revisiting. So, again, it's the changing city and country that suggests going back to a previous character. He's much older; he has kids and a bit of a beer gut. Other characters, I've absolutely no interest in after I've finished with them. Paddy Clarke, for example, from *Paddy Clarke Ha Ha Ha*—I don't think I'll ever go back to him. It's never seemed like a vaguely good idea, not even a vaguely bad idea. I don't think there's anything creatively exciting and rewarding in going back to Paddy. I might, on the other hand, go back to Jimmy Rabbitte Sr. some time. In my third novel, *The Van*, he's an unemployed plasterer; it's set in 1990. Now, fifteen years later, there's no such thing as an unemployed plasterer in Dublin. Men who were out of work fifteen years ago are now buying holiday homes in Spain and Turkey. Also, he'd be in his sixties now. It's an interesting age— not old, no longer anything like young. There'd be plenty there to write about. But it's not a plan. I've also revisited characters in the books I've written for children, because children grow so quickly; their vocabulary, the rhythm of their lives change. Also, in the case of Rover, the talking dog from my children's books, writing about a character like that is just too much fun to resist.

TG: Music is an essential part of your life. Does music affect your work not only in terms of content but also in terms of structuring your narratives and writing sentences?

RD: Yes, music seems to be essential. Cleaning the kitchen is fine if you're listening to Wilco. I'm a great admirer of Radiohead. I loved *OK Computer*, and what they did after it—*Kid A* and *Amnesiac*—"difficult" music, when they could have gone for something more world conquering. And *Hail to the Thief* is a masterpiece. It's a bit like *Highway 61 Revisited*, a different experience every time I hear it. There's nothing quite as exciting as finding new music.

I listen as I work. But I rarely "listen," if that makes sense. I don't listen to lyrics; I don't sit back and admire. I just play it as I work. At first, I played music because I had a long day to fill and I thought music might help fill it. This was after I gave up teaching and starting writing full-time. My first four novels, including *The Commitments*, were written music-free. Then I began to play classical music as I worked. My ignorance of classical was almost total but even so, virtually everything I played seemed already familiar. This piece had been used for a bread commercial; that piece was the theme music for some television show or other. Some of it fairly captivated me—Pergolesi's *Stabat Mater* and Mozart's *Requiem*, for example—but a lot of it I found dull. So I began to root around in the "contemporary" section. And Philip Glass and Steve Reich and Michael Nyman and Gavan Bryars and many others started filling my day and, actually, they began to do much more than that. For big chunks of the day, I'm concentrating on the words in front of me—choosing the next one, deciding on the final shape of a sentence. I might be playing music but often the music has stopped and I haven't noticed. But perhaps equally as often I need music to get me going. When I was writing *A Star Called Henry* I played two pieces of music almost incessantly in the last six months or so of writing. They were *After Extra Time*, by Michael Nyman, and *Music with Changing Parts*, by Philip Glass. Those pieces were like my petrol; their rhythm is somehow in the book. Their energy was what I was after. That was the case too with Steve Reich's

Different Trains. But I also loved the way he uses the voices—the pieces of sentences, the fragments of sense—in a loop over the almost overwhelming music. I thought it was astonishing. I know: music is music and prose is prose, but I wanted to attempt something a little bit similar in *Oh, Play That Thing!* The rhythm would drive the story forward, but repeated words and phrases would bring it back and, sometimes, forward—would remind the reader of previous events, would somehow hint at future events, would knit them together. So music, in those two instances, has become more than a way of filling a long day or of masking outside noises.

I have to emphasize, though, that essentially it's me and the page and the words on the page. But even there, on paper, music is useful. In *The Woman Who Walked into Doors*, Paula Spencer recalls music as she recalls events from her life. Frankie Valli was singing "My Eyes Adored You" when she first talked to her future husband. As she remembers a childhood event, "Take a Giant Step" by the Monkees comes into her head. Her life has a great soundtrack, except for the 1980s, when she was being beaten by her husband, or recovering from beatings. The absence of music is important. She hears something from the eighties, and it means nothing to her. Which is why, in *Paula Spencer*, when Paula gets a stereo for her kitchen, the first CD she buys is by U2. They're from her city, and her part of the city; they're only a few years younger than she is. But she missed them. As they were off conquering the world, she was on the kitchen floor, trying to get up. So, she buys *How to Dismantle an Atomic Bomb*. And she loves it.

TG: Louis Armstrong and his music fascinate Henry Smart. How did you make the switch from soul and R&B to jazz? Was it tougher to write about it?

RD: The switch from soul to jazz was, finally, easy. Because in both cases I was listening to, and trying to capture on paper, three-minute songs. I saw no difference. I was listening to the Armstrong recordings of the late twenties and early thirties, deciding which songs I'd use in *Oh, Play That Thing!* and, as with choosing the soul songs to

include in *The Commitments*, I homed in on the lyrics. The way to capture the rhythm of the songs on paper was by using the words of the
songs. Luckily, Armstrong sang. It's one of the reasons I chose him
as a character. He'd been persuaded to sing as a way of resting his
lips from horn playing, and that meant he stepped forward and sang
into a microphone, and I could try to "invent" his performance by
breaking down the lyrics and weaving them with the narration, their
rhythm infecting the prose and somehow—I hoped—suggesting live
performance. When I was doing this I was strongly reminded of
writing *The Commitments* twenty years ago. So, no, it wasn't hard. The
hard work came in researching, coming to grips with the era, and trying to imagine my narrator listening to the music then and there.

TG: You've mentioned the rhythm of the dialogue and "deciding on
the final shape of a sentence." How do you locate the particular
rhythm and tempo of a piece? When do you know you've reached
the final shape of a sentence, that it can't exist any other way?

RD: These are hard questions to answer, because I never ask them.
I just discover the rhythm as I write, and write in deeper. I decide:
that's it. I don't ask: why? It just seems right; it seems to fit. When I
was writing violent passages and the narrator's reaction to the violence in *The Woman Who Walked into Doors*, then broken, unfinished sentences seemed right. When she tried to be calmer, short, unadorned
sentences fit. The notion that "it can't exist any other way" doesn't
arise. It's more a case of, "This is exactly the way I want. It knits well
with the last sentence, and the next. It's sharp. It brings the story forward. Time for coffee."

TG: You've also talked about the current slang being different than
what it was in the late eighties, when you wrote the Barrytown trilogy. Have you given up on writing sonorous phrases like "ya fuckin'
eejit," "ah Jaysis," and the universal "fuck off"?

RD: I haven't abandoned slang, for fuck's sake. It's just, it's tricky.
Words hop up, and disappear; they go in and out of fashion. "Fuck

off," happily, is fashion resistant. I'll be taking it with me to the grave. "Eejit" and "fuckin' eejit" are also holding their own. "Gobshite" tends to be a word middle-aged people use. I recently wrote a story about three young lads who go to Liverpool for the weekend and they use "eejit" occasionally. But they also call each other "muppet" as an alternative to "eejit." This is interesting, because its use is quite recent, despite the fact that the lads weren't born when *The Muppet Show* was first broadcast. "Man" has became quite common, but not in the hippie sense. Pronouncing it on paper—if that makes sense—I'd write it "m'n." "How's it goin', m'n?" Adding the "m'n" to the end of pieces of dialogue affects the overall rhythm of the passage. I have to make sure I hear how people speak today, and not fall back on what my ears took in twenty years ago.

TG: How has it been, moving from novels and plays to short stories, which I believe you're writing for the first time? Has it changed the rhythms of your prose, or the way you conceive of characters?

RD: I've always divided my working day, which is eight or nine hours long, into different projects. I wouldn't want to write a novel all day, and I couldn't write two novels at once. So I work on different pieces, as long as they're very different. I've been writing scripts for nearly twenty years, almost as long as I've been writing novels. It's a very different exercise, much more mechanical—never literary, although they do have the dialogue in common. But even there, it's different. There's more elbow room in a novel; there's far less space in a script—there's not the room for the meandering conversations I love. For some reason, in the last few years I've been having ideas that lend themselves to the short story form. I never wrote short stories when I started writing, despite Irish writing's reputation for them—or maybe because of the reputation. But, for example, I want to write a story about a funeral. It can't be part of a novel, or a scene, or scenes, from a script. It's the funeral—that's all. The characters are there, fully formed—no development, none of what the movie people call "back story," what the rest of us call "a life." It's a short story, or it will be. I don't think it changes the rhythm of the writing, sentence by sentence. But it does have a big impact on how I approach the character. It's like a photograph instead of a film. In a few cases I haven't named the character. It seems to make sense. We only get a glimpse, albeit a significant one, of the character, so the name doesn't seem important, or even honest.

TG: You've turned several of your novels into screenplays. Do you have any sense of how it will feel to adapt someone else's piece, as you're doing with Synge's *A Playboy of the Western World*, assuming that Bisi does everything you tell him to?

RD: I've written scripts from four of my novels, three of which actually became films. I was always happy enough to hack away at the novel, and I liked the opportunity to retell parts of the story, to create new dialogue, bring in new characters, et cetera. But it was my own work I was mangling, so I never felt anyone at my shoulder with a machete. I also adapted Liam O'Flaherty's novel *Famine* for the screen. It's a great, sprawling book, set during the Great Irish Famine, which started in 1845. I loved the novel, absolutely loved it. And I was very precious with it at first, very reluctant to chop at it; I was overrespectful. The first draft was too long; it was actually more like a synopsis of the novel. Then I copped on, and put the novel aside and wrote a draft of the script without consulting the novel. I went back to it later, for the dialogue. But putting the book aside was liberating. It freed me to tell the story in script form. I also realized that I wasn't harming the book by adapting it. It would still be a magnificent novel, even if I made a balls of the script, or if Ben Affleck ended up playing one of the starving peasants.

I haven't started work with Bisi yet, but I suspect we'll probably leave the original play aside a lot of the time. It's already a play, so we're not adapting it for any other form. We're writing a version set today, instead of 1907, when it was first produced. I don't think it'll be too nerve-wracking. Synge is long dead, and I don't know if there was a Widow Synge or any little Synges, or if they were violent little lads, but they'll be long gone too. The plot is incredibly tight, and the lines, back and forth, are so sharp—that's when we'll be looking at the original, I'd guess. Not at the lines, as such, but the pace and the momentum of the plot.

TG: Does switching forms keep things fresh for you? No plans to bear down on a seventeen-year project like *Finnegans Wake*? Nothing Homeric in the offing? No *Ulysses*-like seven-hundred-page pub crawl for Jimmy Rabbitte Sr.?

RD: Hopping from one project to the next does keep things fresh, I think. An important part of the writing is anticipating the writing. If I'm working on a novel, I often think about what I've just written and what I'm going to write, and try to figure out how a character will behave or act. Instead of walking the hillsides or pacing the garret, I work on another project. It might be, say, a book for kids. I can concentrate on it and have the novel on the back burner, so to speak. If something occurs to me, I'll jot it down, and go back to the novel later, or the day after. I can also keep the excitement and concentration levels reasonably high throughout the day. It's a bit like teaching. The class is beginning to wind down—we're all beginning to get bored. But the bell will soon go, and a whole new gang will walk into the room, demanding knowledge and entertainment. Moving from one project to another is a bit like the class bell. Did Joyce know it was going to be a seventeen-year project? The decision to write a novel is, always, quite a flippant one. It's easy. "I think I'll write a book about a kid in 1968." That's it. I've never known how long it'll take. The duration only becomes distressing in the third, fourth, or fifth year. Five years has been my limit, so far. I'd love to write a novel set in one day, but seven hundred pages? That's nearly thirty pages an hour. I can recapture most of my hours in a few lines.

TG: It seems like you've taken Beckett's advice: "I'll go on." In the end, what pulls you back to the desk and the blank page every morning? Faith, fun, neither, or both?

RD: I love writing. I love the words. I love building the story. I've been very, very lucky. I've watched children laugh at lines I've written. I've seen scripts I've written become films I'm proud of. I've seen great actors make my lines their own. I've been told by women that they are Paula Spencer, the woman who walked into doors, that the book captured their lives. I wrote a television series, called *Family*, which changed the way domestic violence was viewed and treated in Ireland. It was an extraordinary experience. I have copies of my books in Hebrew, Korean, Icelandic, Slovenian. I do exactly what I want, and I believe in it. I love what I'm doing. And now and again, I play hooky.

A CONVERSATION WITH
RIKKI DUCORNET

Rachel Resnick

Like the lick of a whip, Rikki Ducornet's bold, bawdy fiction leaves its mark. Ducornet rigorously explores the darkest terrain of the human condition, and her sensuous and surreal novel *The Fan-Maker's Inquisition*, which was published shortly after we met, is as daring and satisfying a work as we've come to expect from her.

The Fan-Maker's Inquisition is a dark, erotic tale of a fan-maker on trial during the French Revolution for her friendship with the Marquis de Sade, and for conspiring with Sade to draft a manuscript revealing the crimes of Bishop Landa, the man responsible for the destruction of the Mayan culture. Like an intricate fan, the book unfolds and creases, revealing stories within stories, meanings upon meanings. Ducornet layers in Sade's explosive voice from prison and evokes the conquest of the New World, while in the background heads never stop rolling. By turns playful and horrific, the book also asserts the sovereignty of imagination, celebrates books themselves, and explores the risks of passionate living and thinking.

Ducornet is the author of seven novels (*Gazelle*, *The Fan-Maker's Inquisition*, *The Stain*, *Entering Fire*, *The Fountains of Neptune*, *The Jade Cabinet*, *Phosphor in Dreamland*), two collections of short fiction (*The Complete Butcher's Tales*, *The Word "Desire"*), five books of poetry, and a book of essays (*The Monstrous and the Marvelous*). In 1993, Ducornet was a finalist for the National Book Critics Circle Award for *The Jade Cabinet*; that same year she was awarded a Lannan fellowship. Before embarking on writing, Ducornet was an accomplished and internationally exhibited painter. She has also illustrated numerous books, including Jorge Luis Borges's *Tlon, Uqbar, Orbis Tertius* and Robert Coover's *Spanking the Maid*.

When I called to request an interview, Ducornet graciously invited me to stay at her South Denver home, which she shares with Jonathan Cohen, a psychoanalyst. When I arrived at midnight, my flight two hours late, she was outside weeding the garden.

Inside, we shared rosemary tea. Small, graceful, and full of sensual and earthy charm, Ducornet seemed decades younger than her fifty-six years. Her bewitching eyes were heavily lined with kohl, lending an exotic accent to her beauty. I was surprised by her breathy, little-girl voice. It is only recently, she said, that people have stopped asking for her mother when she answers the phone.

The next day was unusually hot and humid. We retreated inside the house, which was late sixties in design, with high wood-beamed ceilings—sparsely decorated but for some Javanese puppets, tribal masks, and Mexican carved-wood snakes that seemed eager to slither from the walls. The dining room was filled with light, and the large picture window revealed a sea of tiger lilies just outside. We sat down to talk at the table over juicy, white-fleshed halves of casaba and diced mango nestled amid mint leaves from Ducornet's garden and garnished with freshly decapitated tiger-lily blooms. Fresh ciabatta bread, four-pepper goat cheese, and copious amounts of Turkish coffee completed the feast. Ducornet was wearing a gauzy red

Moroccan dress splashed with wild colors and thick silver hoop earrings. A portrait of a wax albino Renaissance man stared down limpidly on us as we talked.

Afterward we walked to a local restaurant for dinner. On the way back, a carload of boys hassled us. While I kept walking, my suspicious urban instincts instantly activated, Ducornet responded warmly and openly to the boys' slurred queries about directions. Only when they asked if she wanted to go to a bar with them did she finally walk away. Ducornet assured me this was an odd occurrence in her upper-middle-class neighborhood. The next morning, we learned that shortly after our encounter with the boys, a woman was knifed to death only one block from Ducornet's residence. The boys were prime suspects. I flashed on Ducornet's thematic obsession with evil, her insistence that evil is inevitable, banal, and must be confronted in ourselves.

Rachel Resnick: How did *The Fan-Maker's Inquisition* come about? Was it born in a postcoital fever dream? Did it start as a forbidden glimpse of a woman's thigh?

Rikki Ducornet: Yes, the fan like the thighs of a woman opening and closing! I think Murasaki Shikibu's *The Tale of Genji* and the fascination of the fan and the hidden face, the hidden body, the revealed body, and the incredible eroticism of that book were percolating in my mind. The fan-maker character simply surged forth. Her voice was clear and strong and engaging. I quite fell in love with her! I'd wanted to write about the Marquis de Sade. Then when I wrote the first few pages of *The Fan-Maker*, I realized I was in the French Revolution and this woman was being questioned by the Comité de Surveillance. Sade was just around the corner. When I began research and reread Restif de la Bretonne, I found his voice still interesting, but also self-serving and pompous. I imagined he could have been jealous of Sade. Restif saw himself as a libertine and a pornographer, but he lacked Sade's unbridled imagination. In fact, it was Restif who portrayed Sade as a monster. When Sade made Spanish-fly candies for his whores and got them sick because he'd ignorantly used too much, Restif claimed Sade poisoned the women with arsenic. Suddenly I had one of the major villains in the book.

RR: Another villain is Bishop Landa. In the book, you draw a parallel between Landa and Sade. Yet there seems to be a vacillation about whether Sade is a monster or not.

RD: The book confronts the true monster and the false monster. The one who wrote about monstrosity was Sade, but he never committed murder. History has marked him as the perfect monster. Whereas Bishop Landa, the man responsible both for the genocide of the Maya people in the Yucatán and the destruction of their books, is not generally known. Landa was like a good Nazi. He was interested in the Mayan language and culture, and requested their books. Then, once he thought he understood, he had everything burned, because he believed the Maya were devil worshipers. So the main confrontation in the book is between the one who writes the dangerous books and the one who burns the dangerous books. And I am posing the question, who's the real monster here? Another connection between the worlds of the Maya conquest and the French Revolution is sodomy. One prime reason Sade got in so much trouble was that he was a sodomite. And one reason Landa and his Spaniards despised the Maya was because supposedly they were sodomites. Apparently sodomy was part of some sacred Mayan rituals.

RR: You've said that to see a writer's work as biography is unsophisticated, and yet one could say all your characters are on some level explorations of various aspects of your psyche. If you buy this, are you Sade? In what way? How about the fan-maker? The inquisitor? Or is that my role!

RD: A writer, like an actor, takes on an infinite set of possible (and impossible!) selves. It seems to me that so much of being human is our capacity for empathy, our far-reaching imaginations. Writing *The Fan-Maker*, I was inhabited, turn by turn, by the fan-maker, by Sade, by Restif de la Bretonne, by Landa, by Olympe de Gouges. I was seized by "their" voices. In other words, at some point the dream becomes tangible, palpable. At this point the characters have bodies, they have voices. The book becomes their book.

RR: Were you thinking about theater when you wrote *Fan-Maker*? Because the opening reads like a play. The fan-maker on trial. The spectators functioning like a chorus.

RD: Sade's imagination functioned in set pieces; he was a spectator above all—even in his own fantasies. For example, many of the imagined scenes in *The 120 Days of Sodom* take place behind a peephole. Perhaps it is this distance that makes it possible for Sade to come to pleasure. In prison, cut off from the world, his own fantasies are twice removed. Perhaps this distance explains the violence of the dream. Sade liked to say that had there been a whore in prison with him, he would not have become a writer. Prison set the stage; his reverie functions as a stage; the fixed tableau, obsessive and static, defines the structure and mood of his phantasms.

RR: Did theatrical concerns inform the book in a larger way? Mentions of theater crop up repeatedly. Were you forging a link between theater's sacred space and the sacredness of text?

RD: The novel is structured like a play—the opening literally takes place on a stage and unfolds as a courtroom drama. Language is magic; it evokes worlds of the mind and, for a time at least, manages to keep the fan-maker alive. But because of its subversive power, her clarity enrages those who hear her. In the end language "damns her" and yet . . . the word will not be silenced. Sade will not leave us alone!

RR: Have you done any acting yourself?

RD: When I was a kid, I was cast in the lead role of *The Bad Seed*. I was worried they saw something in me I didn't see. Ultimately I didn't pursue acting because I wanted more privacy.

RR: Charlotte Innes has called your work "narrative painting." I was struck by your work's cinematic quality—the bleeding of images, the quick-cut associations like a kind of linguistic montage, the graphic freeze-frames. Do films feed your work?

RD: Just as a painter of the nineteenth century could not help but be influenced by photography, a writer cannot help but be influenced by cinema. Cocteau's *The Blood of a Poet*, Satyajit Ray's *The Music Room*, the Brothers Quay's *The Epic of Gilgamesh*, these have all had a profound impact on my imagination, as profound as the paintings of Bosch and Vermeer, or the cities, the faces, the landscapes that have touched me deeply.

RR: I loved your essay "The Death Cunt of Deep Dell," from *The Monstrous and the Marvelous*. That's a gnostic concept, right? Woman as seduction and downfall; cunt as trap, snare, coffin. I know buttocks are the order of the day, but is there a Death Cunt in this book?

RD: The Death Cunt appears once, I think, selling sweet rolls in the shadow of the guillotine.

RR: Why do the female characters die? I kept thinking of *Thelma and Louise*. Women break free, show each other the pink, then have to die. Maybe it's because the chameleonlike Death Cunt wasn't around enough to demagnetize the hostility of men toward women?

RD: If the women die it is only because so many women died—especially the strong ones—during the Revolution. The Revolution hated feminists!

RR: Again, why Sade, why now? Is the Devil's Arsehole our new mascot?

RD: I wanted to come to terms with Sade myself. Writing a novel is such a great excuse to see how you think about something. Writing the book was a way of thinking rigorously about Sade. I can't say I was influenced by Sade as a writer at all. What I'm grateful for was that somebody dared to push boundaries perhaps as far as they can go. And I think Sade raises important questions. For example, when he says, "Why can't someone kill his daughter if kings can kill the children of their enemies by the tens of thousands?" he's doing just what Swift did with A Modest Proposal: "Well, why don't the Irish just eat their children?"

RR: Are you drawing a parallel with Sade and something in the current climate?

RD: Well, I see a link to the gnostic vision, which intrigues me. It's a vision of the material world as a hopelessly dark place where the body is a prison, the world a cage, and so on. I think Swift's vision fits because of his terror of the body. Sade's fits too because despite his obsession with the body, he's also frightened of it. And he's convinced the world of Nature is an evil place where anything is possible.

RR: The world's a stage, the world's a cage. Hmm. How does the fanmaker fit into that?

RD: She is a very moral being but she's also a free spirit. While she recognizes that Sade's vision is a horrific one, she also comes to believe it's absolutely essential. I, too, turned away from Sade for a long time. I thought him beneath contempt, narcissistic. But I think it's more complex. Sade had tremendous difficulty ejaculating, which I think explains in part his unbridled imagination. He was alone, he was desperately unhappy—all he had was his cock for company. He was totally engaged in masturbatory fantasies, yet he realized and played with the moral implications. What's important about Sade is that there are no bad thoughts, no bad words, only bad acts. And I think we should be grateful to him for putting the worst evil on the page, ready to be examined with all its terrifying implications. Because it's true that the Sadean world leads right to the Holocaust.

RR: What about when Sade trips on the power of his own fantasies, when he thinks his jack-off scribblings have given birth to the guillotine outside his window?

RD: It's a paranoid's worst nightmare, that one's own dark dreams are realized out there in the world. It's also what readers of Sade have said. What I think is, maybe if we had really read Sade, if our species was capable of dealing with the shit within ourselves, then maybe we could overcome this need to maim and torture others. So in that sense, we have to read Sade, but we have to read him responsibly.

RR: Do you personally subscribe to the gnostic vision?

RD: No. Simply: the moral dilemma gnosticism proposes is interesting; if the world is corrupt and the body filthy, if the entire cosmos is a gigantic mistake, then why bother with concepts such as freedom and responsibility? Why not, in the words of Cesar Vallejo, just blow everything and that's it! Sade, you've noticed, is asking the same question. If matter is intrinsically evil, well then, why not blow everything, who cares!

RR: In *Fan-Maker*, you also present Sade as full of longing, tenderness even. Was that invented?

RD: It's true. He had tender friendships. He actually had a very tender relationship with his wife and, at the end of his life, with a much younger woman. One has to make the distinction between life and books. Which is why I went to the letters. The way I see it, the letters are the voice of the man. The books are the voice of the writer.

RR: Would that apply to you as well? Your books are the voice of the writer, and distinct from you as the woman?

RD: The woman/writer writes the books; the books belong to her characters.

RR: I know Gaston Bachelard was a big influence on you. Bachelard talks about letter writing being necessarily an act of love. And also an act of reverie. Did that come into play?

RD: It's interesting you mention Bachelard. I often do have people writing letters to each other in my books. Because indeed the letter is a space where one dreams the Other. The letter is the living reverie of the Other. Which is why letters are so important.

RR: But when Landa dreams the Other, it's nightmarish, and dangerous.

RD: That's right. Because he can only imagine the Other as enemy. Whereas Sade is imagining his friend.

RR: If the fan doubles for a book, and also suggests a cunt, as you have said in *Fan-Maker*, would you say you want the reader to fuck the book as he or she reads?

RD: Perhaps rather than fucking the book, the reader is seduced by the book, by the voice of the fan-maker and Sade's dark humor.

RR: Are you trying to implicate the reader in the book? To induce reverie?

RD: Of course I am trying to implicate the reader. A book is all about thinking; thinking and dreaming. I think a good book always induces both. An acute reverie. Questions.

RR: In martial arts, there exist war fans, weapons which when opened are studded with razors on one edge and designed to kill. Did you consciously decide to focus on the erotic possibilities of the fan and leave death to the guillotine?

RD: Yes. The fan is seduction, aesthetic delight, the infinite theater of erotic arousal.

RR: What research did you do for *Fan-Maker*?

RD: I read what Sade read in prison—Rabelais, Laclos. I read his letters, which are very unlike the books; Sade's voice is bawdy in the letters, in the manner of Rabelais, and, in the manner of Laclos, very elegant. Sometimes he ties himself into knots with frustration, or he succumbs to crazed schemes. But for the most part the letters are engaging, sometimes very funny, even touching. I researched the French Revolution, of course, and the conquest of the Yucatán;

I reread Diderot and Restif, and all of Olympe de Gouges—which was painful. I researched fans and spoke with a Parisian dealer. She attempted to sell me an eighteenth-century fan from China that was, in fact, ugly. I studied maps of Paris during the Revolution and dress styles and menus. I read countless letters and journals from the time and so on . . . But the book was a wild horse from the first moment, and I had to struggle to keep up with it. I was certain Sade would give me a hard time, but he showed up, panting and obese, yet somehow impressive and even elegant, every morning like clockwork.

RR: On the cover, the book says "a novel of the Marquis de Sade." Do you consider this book to be a novel?

RD: Well, it certainly is a small novel. I write small novels. I don't write sprawling nineteenth-century novels, much as I love those books. I'm really into concision. I think of Calvino as somebody who also writes concise, down-to-the-bone novels. I think *The Fan-Maker* is very much a novel, because of its scope. I seem to write very small books that engage big issues and sprawl intellectually.

RR: Is your ethnic heritage important to you as a writer?

RD: My mother's background was Jewish, my father's Cuban and Catholic. I could not help but be influenced by politics and the collision of cultures. We ate picadillo and we ate pastrami, and if my father introduced me to *Justine*, he also introduced me to Cuban music and a species of old-world dandyism.

RR: What do you think of women writers, or do you think the category "woman writer" should not be made?

RD: I think the category "woman writer" is absurd.

RR: And yet your work is celebratory of female sensuality. How does that fit with your feeling that the work is not gender-specific?

RD: Any work worth its salt will cause the reader to empathize with the characters, to engage with them fully. The reader and the writer both shed their skins. They become permeable, elastic, haunted. In this way every novel is transsexual, fluid, a kind of fabula/chimera. And the reader is, too.

RR: Since dreams, reverie, and memory are so crucial to your work, I wonder what your earliest memory is.

RD: My earliest memory goes back to about eighteen months. I was happily sucking on lobster legs in a restaurant with my parents. There was a big window, light was pouring in, and I was sucking on tiny legs. Bright red and beautiful and very tasty.

RR: What's the most perverse eating experience you've ever had?

RD: Eating snails I had fed thyme and parsley to for a couple of weeks.

RR: Do you think imagination is a precursor to action?

RD: Well, that's the interesting dilemma. We're creatures of infinite imagination. The problem is not to contain the imagination, but to make the distinction between fantasy and behavior. To make those moral choices. It seems to me that in a racist culture, and ours is profoundly racist, people need to be attentive. Because if that attitude's not examined, you are engaging in evil. The banality of evil is an everyday occurrence.

RR: Are you a drug addict? A junkie? Pill popper? Do you drink cough syrup at bedtime?

RD: I do not take drugs, I'm not interested in the drug experience at all. But somebody gave me psilocybin mushrooms a couple of months ago and I had a wonderful experience. I was totally myself, totally rational. But there was a slight shift in my perception. I was in my house, the entire space in which I live was glamorized. A tantric experience! The material world was imbued with light. Even the bathroom tile was pulsating. "Light as knowledge!" And I wondered, what if our species had evolved with this slight shift in perception, where would we be?

RR: Are you now an advocate for consciousness-expanding drugs? Is this a new phase?

RD: I can't even drink coffee, and I get high drinking tea. Perhaps we should all give these mushrooms a try. The problem is they wear off! And yet, one has to have an experience like that. It's like a profound amorous experience. One says to oneself, "Remember this is possible." It reminded me to live fully in the moment.

RR: The word *glamour* appears a few times in this book. Coming from Los Angeles, the self-proclaimed glam-slam center of the world, I was curious what you meant by it.

RD: "Glamours" are those phantasms created by witchcraft. To be "glamorized" is to be bewitched. It's a wonderful term dating from the Inquisitions. Hollywood is the modern place where we are glamorized. That experience with mushrooms was glamorizing. I'm surrounded by things of potency: Javanese puppets and Mexican masks. They're things of power because they're involved in symbolic theaters, with potent places in people's cultures. Under the influence of the psilocybin mushrooms, they took on their primary attributes. They were animated as they are on the stage. They were moving slightly, their bodies turning. I was bewitched.

RR: The intricate designs the fan-maker painted on the fan's mounts seem like self-contained reveries, miniature tableaux, homages to imagination, eroticism, and beauty. Were beauty and aesthetics concerns in this book too?

RD: How lovely. Yes. The Revolution made a terrible mistake, as did Castro, of thinking that beautiful buildings were not for the people. This idea that beauty is only for the precious few is a mistake that both elitists and anti-elitists make. It's fascist ideology to reduce everything to the lowest common denominator. What I'm calling for is the contrary: we should surpass ourselves. We should have the wildest imaginings, experience the greatest beauty. Places of beauty are also places of mystery, places that set us dreaming—like Old

Havana. And at our very best, to use Bachelard's term, we're imagining beings.

RR: Now I'm going to ask a series of technical questions, if I may. Do you have a writing regime?

RD: I usually write every day. But it isn't really interesting, is it? I get up, make a big pot of tea, dance for an invisible audience for about an hour, and then I write for about four or five hours.

RR: You're lying!

RD: I lost patience with yoga and everything else. But if I can wake in the morning and put on some Cuban music or some Ravi Shankar, I actually dance for an hour. So that's what I do every day. Leap around the house. Get my blood going. Then I write so I'm still close to a dream state, before the aggravations of the day set in.

RR: Do you write by hand?

RD: Ink on paper, by God.

RR: What kind of pen?

RD: A fountain pen. I'm a great fan of very light fountain pens. So I can write without cramping.

RR: Since you have this background as an illustrator and painter, do you ever sketch out ideas for fiction?

RD: Yes. Sometimes I find it useful to sort of plot where people might be in a room. Or just when I'm kind of fooling around and dreaming, doodling.

RR: Do you do a lot of drafts?

RD: Yes. Things begin to fall into place after maybe five, six drafts. My early books went through ten or twelve drafts. This one didn't. It fell into place the way I wanted it to. It had that quality Calvino talks about when he says, "light as a bird." I didn't want to overwork it.

RR: How do you name your characters?

RD: They usually appear with names. With the fan-maker, I didn't know what her name was. She was the fan-maker until Sade wrote to her and then I realized her name was Gabrielle because he named her.

RR: What was the significance of withholding her name until Sade named her?

RD: I write very organically and it just happened that way. I liked it, so I kept it.

RR: Do you keep a notebook?

RD: I try. I have various notebooks, none of them finished. They're absolute chaos. And I always lose them. For *Fan-Maker* I had a notebook from Mexico, then I lost it. But my memory of the notebook gave me ideas. What I've learned is, I get excited, take notes, and lose them. But if the notes are supposed to be in the book, they'll reappear on their own. I never find the notebooks until I'm done with the books. That's when I realize I'd had the ideas earlier.

RR: Do you procrastinate?

RD: That's where cooking comes in. It's very nice to be a writer who loves to cook and garden because I do procrastinate but I don't feel guilty. How can you feel guilty baking bread?

RR: You have been called a "writer's writer." Do you agree?

RD: Well, I consider myself a writer's writer insofar as I consider myself a reader's writer. And writers are very good readers. But no. I think there are all kinds of readers out there who can read me, and they're not necessarily writers.

RR: You've traveled extensively and moved often. Was there some sense of always looking for the perfect place?

RD: Recently I found myself thinking, maybe it's Finland with all those trees. Or the Yucatán. And I love the Val de Loire. Though I felt lonely there. I don't know if I'll stay in Denver. It's hard to imagine staying because it's not mysterious enough. But I've come to realize that if landscape is essential to me, people are more essential. But of course I have exceptional friends scattered all over the globe. That's frustrating.

RR: While you're writing, do you also read other writers' works?

RD: I find when I'm writing, and I'm writing all the time, I have to pull myself out of that space in order to read things that don't have anything to do with the book. I did this recently to read Donald Antrim and Rick Moody.

RR: Do you like the act of reviewing?

RD: Yes. I wish I had more time to do it because I like it and think it's important, but it takes up a lot of time. It's demanding.

RR: One review that I tripped across said there was the "whiff of the schoolmarm" about you and your writing. How would you respond to that?

RD: Bullshit!

RR: You've talked frequently about believing in a sexual soul and feeling you have one. Can you elaborate on that and how it was manifested in this latest book?

RD: I think the sexual soul has to do with sexuality informing one's entire being. I always think of sexuality as the heart of who one is. I think the sexual soul means one delights in the natural world and isn't frightened of other bodies or new experiences. A sexual soul is intrigued by other cultures, delighted by new music, by the sensuous experience of language.

RR: Now you talk a lot about delight and pleasure. Does pain figure into your vision of the sexual soul?

RD: It does if you consider the pain of living. When we give ourselves over to someone, perhaps part of the exhilaration is knowing one's entering a risky space, that one can be hurt. I think the sexual soul is one that is profoundly open to the Other. I can't imagine a life that's not informed by pain. It's part of being human. I worry about our culture, which feels pain is unnatural. A culture in which people are popping pills so they can detour around pain. Then I think the entire culture enters into another, greater pain, a limbo of nonbeing—the most painful space of all.

RR: So, do you like to whip or be whipped?

RD: [laughs] I like pleasure too much . . .

RR: You have said that our society is obscene. What do you mean by this?

RD: Pornography is about objectifying the Other. It's a way of diminishing the Other, of making the Other safe. If you're frightened of the body, what better way to negate its reality than to render it pornographic? This is what torturers do all the time, jabbing at cunts and anuses with broken handles. Often torture is sexual. I think it's a way of denying the Other's intrinsic reality and beauty and capacity for transcendence. It's like saying, "You're just a piece of meat, and nothing more. Here's the proof."

RR: Do you ever consider when you're writing that there's a sadistic impulse?

RD: No. I write about difficult things at times, and it's often painful to do that, but it seems necessary. I'm not doing it to be sadistic or masochistic. I'm not trying to hurt myself or the reader. I am trying to move the reader, bring the reader to a place of understanding, a place that might lead to anger, or even action. But mostly I'm trying to lead the reader to knowledge. Then it's up to the reader to act or not.

RR: Have you read *The Body in Pain* by Elaine Scarry?

RD: Yes. I love that book, especially how she links war and torture, and says the tortured body is a microcosm of the destruction of the country. There's no way out; your body becomes the whole world. That's what pain does. There's no way of remembering or imagining anything else because you're swept away by the intolerable reality of pain.

RR: I'm still curious about the connection between pain and pleasure, since this is very much a territory of your book—separate from the realm of torture. Do you think ecstasy is only possible if there is a nexus of danger and pleasure?

RD: For me what's involved with ecstasy is awareness. Ecstasy is by nature fleeting. So it's not so much danger as it is the sense of impermanence. If one loves deeply, whether it be a beautiful painting or a beautiful face or a beautiful soul, there's always sadness springing from an awareness that this cannot last. I know there are personalities for whom danger is essential to that experience, but that's not my way. Thought I do feel as a writer and artist there's some territory that's risky because it edges toward madness. Ecstasy is not far from madness.

RR: The risk for the artist then is madness?

RD: The risk is not knowing when to pull back.

RR: Does the exploration of boundaries between pain and pleasure interest you in human relationships?

RD: When people go there, it seems to be a lack of faith in the health of the relationship. I think it's self-destructive.

RR: There are also conceivably experiential boundaries. Like how sensation feels when it's pain versus pleasure.

RD: True.

RR: Is accessibility to readership important to you?

RD: I think that's dangerous. Calvino talks about writing books that are smarter than oneself, about upping the ante, and I really go along with that. I want to write the books that I want to read. That's my primary concern.

RR: What are you working on now?

RD: In my book *The Word "Desire,"* there is a story called "The Chess Set of Ivory." This story—one of the few "autobiographical" pieces I have ever written—has become the first chapter of a novel. I lived in Egypt for a year as a child, and, after all this time, am ready to write a book informed by the memory of that place and time.

RR: Why do you end *Fan-Maker* with an incomplete reverie, and the word *sadness*?

RD: The final reverie Gabrielle tells is also obviously about the book itself at this point. And it's a sad book. I mean, it's about the failure of a great promise of the Revolution. And the failure of love. And a life imprisoned. The risks involved in writing real books.

A CONVERSATION WITH
DEBORAH EISENBERG

Anna Keesey

After thirty years on West Seventeenth Street in Chelsea, Deborah Eisenberg is moving house. The closets have "disgorged" their contents, books tip sideways on their shelves, boxes lie here and there. Eisenberg and her beloved comrade, the playwright and actor Wallace Shawn, will be moving to a sixth-floor walk-up a few blocks away, a small "palace" of elegant moldings, terraces, a willow tree. Shawn says, in his wry, bemused way, "We think it will make our declining years more . . . acceptable." And the exercise they'll get apparently makes their doctor "ecstatic." It's no accident that some people in sixth-floor walk-ups are ninety years old and going strong.

But even for the casual visitor, such a move seems laden with loss. This apartment, with its air of industrial romance, clarity, and ghostly chic, seems right for Eisenberg's literary aesthetic: radiant, complex, dense, fierce, and comic. In a closet-sized study here, she has composed some of the most ambitious and memorable works of fiction in the contemporary literary landscape. Like her peers Alice Munro and Mavis Gallant, she has predominantly written short stories, and what short stories they are: "Flotsam," "A Lesson in Traveling Light," "Under the 82nd Airborne," "In the Station," "Someone to Talk To," "The Custodian," "Mermaids," "Revenge of the Dinosaurs." For them, Eisenberg has received numerous awards: Best American Short Story and O. Henry prizes, a Whiting award, a Guggenheim Fellowship, and the prestigious Rea Award for Short Story, made to writers who have contributed substantially to the short story form. Her prose is fresh and lyrical and pungent; by any accounting she's one of the country's most distinctive stylists, and her capacity to describe fleeting states of mind and heart is unmatched. All her work shows a species of stubborn courage in dissecting the mind, with particular attention to the space where consciousness and conscience overlap. She resists the blandishments of conventional wisdom, particularly those of her own cultured kind; like a diplomat on an eerie planet, she has beautiful manners but takes no creature's self-presentation as the truth.

Her characters—generally some variation on that class that used to be known as "middle"—are struggling to stay on their moral feet in an America—or an American satellite—that is slippery with hypocrisy, pain, deception, and exploitation. To their confusion and chagrin, the characters often find that they themselves are implicated in the production of the grease beneath their feet. Eisenberg says, "I've always been interested in power relations," which is, perhaps, not unusual for a writer, but the fictional permutations of that interest are so diverse and subtle that their main commonalities may be the sensations they provoke in the reader: venous dilation, prickling, unease, and ferocious enjoyment. In "Windows," a woman leaves a man who has beaten her, taking with her his child; it's a decision that's not really a decision, but a deep, unconscious impulse, and it dooms woman and child to permanent flight and pursuit. In "Tlaloc's Paradise," the arrival on her Mexican doorstep of an inquisitive young tourist causes an expatriate American woman to recall with pain the Communist hunting that sent her south decades before. In "Some Other, Better Otto," a curmudgeonly New Yorker is nearly crippled by grief for his schizophrenic sister. In "Twilight of the Superheroes," upwardly mobile millennial youths, contemplating the pleasures of their future from the terrace of a fabulous Manhattan sublet, are presented, one beautiful morning, with the sight of dark figures sprinkling from the destroyed World Trade Center.

Power relations, indeed, but not paraded in front of us with academic righteousness; the subject of interpersonal, intersocial relations is subsumed in Eisenberg's characteristic and inimitable rendering of thinking, feeling, and perceiving. Her sinuous use of point of view displays—without shrinking—the layered, elusive nature of thoughts and the illusory quality of what we may believe are convictions.

Eisenberg, now sixty-one, is strikingly beautiful in a way that probably didn't go over big in fifties Winnetka; large-eyed, slight, and leggy in tall boots, she resembles a black swan, a Jazz-Age divorcée, or a European ballet mistress with a haunted past. When we had our conversation in the quiet of the disassembled apartment, she shared my terror of the recording device, and it took a couple of minutes to arrange ourselves in a sufficiently oblique relationship to it.

Anna Keesey: It's one of my missions in life to get more people to read your stories. They're amazing.

Deborah Eisenberg: Thank you. But it could be an uphill battle.

AK: I mean, a lot of people do read them, but they tend to be the smartest and most well-read people I know. I wonder why the next tier of smart and well-read people don't read them?

DE: I gather that there is something kind of intimidating to some people, or, not intimidating, but inhospitable about the stories. I mean, I don't see it, but I know sometimes they're greeted with impatience: "Why does this have to be so complicated, why can't you just say it immediately, why do I have to find my way around in the scene?" Well, I never think of myself as presenting obstacles—it's not a game, in my view. I'm not making a game of some sort.

AK: You're not purposefully withholding information, to get an advantage . . .

DE: Never. I don't withhold information to achieve an effect. In fact, I don't withhold information at all. I don't hide information that the characters know. I'm trying to be faithful to experience, or sensation. But I think there are readers who are confused by having information come to them in the way it does in my stories—it's not parceled out in tidy, discrete bits.

I remember asking my friend Craig Lucas, the playwright, to read a story. I don't remember which one it was, but I do remember that I considered it finished, and it was pretty much what I'd wanted it to be, but I was sending it around and it was being greeted with what I'd call complete incomprehension. Naturally, I wanted to figure out what the problem was, so I enlisted a few people, including Craig, who I consider to be very good readers, without really telling them why. Anyhow, Craig didn't seem to have any trouble with the story at all, and I asked him why he thought other people might find it so baffling, and he said, "Well, you have to be awake when you read it . . ."

It wouldn't seem to be much to ask of a reader, but actually, it turns out that a lot of people like—and expect to be able—to read fiction while they're half-asleep. And it's just not possible to do that with my stories. You might not consciously realize what something is doing in one of the stories, but there isn't anything in them—in my opinion, of course—that isn't doing something; I don't just chuck in idle stuff for the fun of it. And if you miss detail, it will be at a cost to your understanding or enjoyment of a story. Things are placed at angles, and unless you're receptive to the way a given story is coming toward you, to the way you're moving through the story, you're going to miss a lot, and then you'll be confused, frustrated, and angry.

I think that some people have to slow down quite a lot to read the stories. I'm such a slow reader that it's a natural pace for me to have to move slowly through a piece of fiction.

AK: Well, the fact is you're writing short stories, but they are the longest, most complex short stories that anybody is writing. I imagine that even Alice Munro is sitting in her kitchen in Ontario, drinking Nescafé or something, thinking, Wow, this is so fucking complex! I just don't know if I can follow it! You have these webs of characters, who have all sorts of different, and sometimes obscure, relationships to one another, and each brings in an overt agenda, and a covert agenda, and an unconscious agenda; then, often, they are getting drunk, or getting high, so their perceptions are changing dynamically over the course of the story, and beyond that, we have another level, which is that they're not just talking about their boyfriends, they're talking about American privilege, or race, or McCarthyism. Well, they're sort of talking about those things, and sort of talking about what's right in front of them. You can see that if the reader's brain is not firing on all cylinders, he's not going to get it.

DE: Absolutely. And then the whole story just seems like static, or papier-mâché or something.

AK: Where does that come from? You talk about being a slow reader, or a literal reader, someone who as a child had trouble learning in a conventional way, and I wonder if this deep level of detail—this capacity to stay in a given moment that doesn't resolve immediately or easily—is an aspect of the way you think? Is it a neurological personality, or is it an aesthetic commitment: this is the way the world needs to be represented, and other ways are fake?

DE: I'm guessing it's an aesthetic commitment based on a neurological fingerprint. Condition, actually, is the word I think of, but in its broadest sense, not as pathology. It's very much the way I experience the world—not very streamlined—and therefore it does feel appropriate and necessary—natural—for me to represent it that way.

AK: People are so used to seeing experience predigested for them, and they expect to see those markers, and when they don't see any of those—what they're seeing is an original story—they throw up their reader hands.

DE: Yes, and I'm always perplexed when a reader is perplexed, when a reader says of one of my stories, "What was that?" I think, Well, it's what I said it was. It's the thing I said.

AK: One of the things I notice is that the point-of-view characters seem always to have information, perceptual data, flooding over them. They aren't armored. Their capacity to predigest information, to strong-arm the data away from them, to filter or ignore it, is—

DE: Is compromised.

AK: But they are often the characters who can then pay attention to what people . . .

DE: Actually say and do.

AK: Yes. So when you're writing a story, and you are rendering that experience—when light and sound are behaving in strange ways, when the character is overwhelmed by sensory perception—are you recalling it, or are you inventing it?

DE: It doesn't feel like recalling. But it can't be inventing—I mean, what would you invent a sensory perception out of? So it kind of has to be some sort of mental act related to recall. There's the vaguely odd paradox in my life that I can't actually pay attention to anything, or I don't seem to be able to pay direct attention, but things do apparently slide in somehow and live vividly in some area that's usually unavailable to me . . . There's a news broadcast, *Amy Goodman's Democracy Now*, that I love to listen to in the morning, it's indispensable, but usually after it's over I have to ask Wally what the news was!

But if Wally's not around, I still seem to end up—often much later, and very mysteriously—with a lot of the information, somehow, even though my brain seems to have been just an impermeable obstacle while I was listening. I miss stuff—I'm really like Mr. Magoo, of all the senses. The elephants are walking by, and I don't notice.

AK: But you're noticing that the light looks like apple cider.

DE: I don't notice the elephants, but I do register, say, out of the corner of my mind, some toenails and trunks and fuzz on great big ears. I think something like, Huh, yeah, toenails, trunk, ear fuzz. What seems to be going on in my brain is nothing. Absolutely nothing. And I have no memory at all, which can be kind of alarming. That is, the years have stacked up—I must have had some sort of experience at some point in all that time! But when I'm trying to picture what the light was like in a room at a certain time of day, well, I sort of *can* picture it—so I'd assume that something of the sort was taken in by my brain at some point, because something like that, a sensory experience, is, I would suppose, uninventable.

Fiction is making stuff up, but I would suppose that it's making stuff up by analogy. If you've never been beaten up but you need to describe what it's like to be beaten up, you probably won't have more than the routine difficulties involved in describing something that you have experienced directly. Because you're almost sure to have some experience in your sensory repertoire, some feeling of being physically violated and shamed—maybe it was tripping over your ice skates when you were a kid—but the knowledge of the experience common to both getting beaten up and tripping over your skates is somewhere in your body.

AK: It also strikes me that you can tell when you move from something that is an authentic analogy into something that is phony or invented or a cliché or somehow received or self-serving—a lot of writers who are good don't catch themselves there, they aren't as vigilant. Do you just never go to phony places?

DE: I always go to phony places. For a long time when I'm working on something, I can't look at what my hand has produced the day or week or month before, because it's just hideously phony. You'd think that phoniness would be something that's achieved with work—that the natural would precede the artificial—but it's actually the opposite for most writers, I think. There are famous exceptions, of course. But generally, unphoniness is what you achieve with work. The first impulse is always a cliché, or something that's inaccurate. It's a kind of inaccuracy that is the most powerful siren song, because although it's very difficult even to approximate something, it is actually possible. And you're so proud of yourself for having approximated it, you think, Well, that's pretty good—

AK: That'll pass.

DE: That'll pass. I've so often had the experience with a gifted student, when I say, "You know, that doesn't ring true," and the student says, "I know, I knew it, I knew it." And they didn't quite let themselves face it, because it's so hard. It's a bit of a habit, a discipline, which I acquired under the tutelage of the wonderful man I live with, who would just never let anything pass—and I feel that the reason it's hard to acquire is that you're terrified that you're never going to be able to get it, really; you're going to be able to get pretty close, but not close enough—it's just not going to be adequate no matter how hard you work, and so you allow yourself to think, This will do.

But if you can build up the confidence or patience—simply patience—or steady nerves, you think, Well, I didn't do it today, and I'm probably not going to be able to do it tomorrow either, but I will be able to do it sooner or later, then you can just relax. I think one of the reasons I'm so slow is because I'm so mortified by all the horrible writing that I do, and instead of just thinking, Okay, I'll let it be for now and go crashing forward and I'll get it to work eventually, I lose heart, because I don't really have the confidence that I will be able to get it to work. You see people who write swiftly and also extremely well. It's pretty thrilling—you can just tell that they've got that kind of nerve.

AK: So you can't go crashing forward, but you return eventually to the scene of the crime; you linger and start figuring it out again.

DE: Well, unfortunately, I don't know what something is until I've already figured it out! So maybe I'll always have to work backward like that. I do think that the caliber of a piece of fiction is pretty much proportional to the fiction's urgency and seriousness of purpose—even if it's something funny, of course, or apparently light as a feather—and I usually can't locate the purpose of what I'm doing until I've already spent a very long time on it. People say to writers, "How do you find the right word? You're good at finding the right word, how do you do that?" Well, that is really not the problem. The problem is to think of the thing—what it is that the word needs to represent—and then the word will eventually be there.

AK: So you must believe, then, that eventually all things you experience can be described in words.

DE: I do. I don't necessarily have all that much evidence in support of this belief, but I do believe it. Although, I would say that over the course of the effort the returns can be substantial in their diminishment. I fervently wish I were a composer or painter or something so that I would be able to render a lot more expeditiously the incredibly ephemeral effects I yearn to render. Writing really feels like you're down in the quarries with your axe. I grew up with H. T. Lowe-Porter's translation of "Death in Venice," which is no doubt wildly inaccurate and wildly flawed, but at the end of the story there's a description of Aschenbach thinking about writing that's translated as, if I'm remembering it correctly, "to liberate from the marble mass of language the slender forms of his art." Well, I don't know how much of that is really Mann and how much is Porter—or, at this point, come to think of it, how much is me—but it's just so accurate! You think of the duomo in Siena, those thin, ethereal marble forms. The thing that wants to be written really does seem to be hidden in the marble mass, and you think—

AK: You think, How is that done? How do you do it without breaking it? How do you know it's in there?

DE: Yes. And you think, Argh—if I were a composer, or a painter, I could do this in twenty seconds!

AK: And what do the composers and painters of your acquaintance think of that?

DE: Well, I haven't actually run the theory by them.

AK: Back to the idea of choosing the right word, which we agree is not really the problem, it seems to me that one of the great pleasures of your stories is the outrageous richness of the diction. In "Rafe's Coat," for example, there's a line in which "Cookie ratified her little witticism with raucous baying." I think, Ratify? Raucous? Bay?

DE: I was pleased with that. It seems correct and efficient to me.

AK: There's a lot of the language of unpleasant physical qualities: things are "gummy," "bulbous," "oozing." And then we have all those Latinate words: witticism, lambent, ratify. So there's a rich range of diction. And I thought, Well, when did she gather those words? Did she get that from being attached to Wallace Shawn by a string for years?

DE: Well, I was a big reader as a child. As a child, up until about when I was fifteen. And I was a very big talker, when I finally did learn to talk. I was a very late talker. But when I did finally start, evidently I talked in whole paragraphs and plenty of them. I remember being shushed a lot. But apparently I wasn't about to talk until I could use relative clauses.

AK: You have an older brother. He might have colonized the language thing.

DE: He was much older. Now he's not, but he was then—six and a half years. And always very articulate. And my mother, I believe, was very exact as well. I myself talked in volume but not necessarily well. I still feel pretty helpless when I try to express the simplest thought without a piece of paper in front of me and a lot of time. But I loved language-y things when I was little. I loved "Pogo," for example, long before I was old enough to understand it. I mean I *loved* "Pogo." It's always a source of fascination for both me and Wally—on what basis are children enjoying these things they can't possibly understand?

AK: There's something about the physical profile of the words on the page that is intriguing. It seems to me that there are some people who have a kind of mind for whom the word, the signifier, doesn't turn immediately into the signified. They don't drop instantly through the hieroglyphic into the imagined thing, but rest on the surface of the word for a while. A lot of those people turn out to be poets, of course.

DE: That's so interesting. That sort of abstraction, which you think has nothing to do with the content, with no value of its own, actually does represent content in some way. So [gesturing to teapot on table] you think TEEEAAAAPPOTTT. Hmm, what are we saying?

AK: Certain things hit you at a certain age, when you're developing certain skills cognitively . . .

DE: We both should have been brain scientists. It's a shame.

AK: So you were a huge reader, and you were gathering these language trinkets that you were not yet deploying. But you were not very compatible with school, not able to remember what you were taught . . . what was that like?

DE: Well, I don't know. It's still the same, though. Now, this is an unpleasant story and I can't remember it very well, but we were having dinner with some people the other evening, some of whom we didn't know, and there was one guy of whom I kept thinking, Boy, is this guy dumb, he doesn't understand a single word anybody is saying, it's unusual to run into somebody this dumb, isn't it remarkable. And then about ten minutes later I realized that *I* had no idea what people were saying.

AK: It was you! You were the dumb one!

DE: Well, I think it was both of us, maybe. It was really shocking. I was sitting there and nodding, but I couldn't understand a single word. Everyone might as well have been saying, "Arf, arf, woof, woof." It happens to me a lot, I'm sorry to say.

AK: I remember you saying once that you started writing because you had to figure out something to do.

DE: Yes—well, at some point during the years when I was just managing to entrench myself in writing, I heard a young woman, much younger than I was, talking about going to a writing program. She said, "Oh, yeah, I thought maybe I'd try that." Well, I almost went through the ceiling, because to me writing wasn't something you'd casually *try*. It was as if someone had said, "Yeah, stigmata? I think I'll give that a whirl."

I wasn't thinking of suffering, but I was thinking of exaltation. Writing fiction does seem to me like going on a vision quest, and not something to be taken up lightly in any way. And for me, starting to try, or trying to start to start to try, was a court of last resort. I mean, my life—you see that brick wall [pointing out the window]? Well, that brick wall was here [hand in front of face.] It was upon me. It was kind of a desperate situation. Those are the circumstances in which I started to write.

And of course I couldn't do it at all. And if I hadn't been living with a writer, I would have thought, Oh, that's because I can't write. I'm not a writer. I have friends of course who are writers who were just born being able to do it, or were able to learn rapidly when the time came. But because I started so late and was so inept, my embryological struggles with writing are still very present in my mind, so I have a lot of sympathy for young writers, particularly those with an acute sense of the difficulty of it. And had I not been living with a writer I would have thought, Well, this is ridiculous, of course I can't do it. But he was able to inform me that the fact that I was bad at it, that I couldn't just sit down and toss off a reasonable sentence, let alone a trilogy, bore no relation to whether I was suited to it. And that is precious, precious information. A lot of people don't—well, how would they know unless they found out from other writers?

AK: So, did you start writing with the play *Pastorale?*

DE: No, I started with the story in my first collection called "Days," which concerns someone quitting a heavy, long-term smoking habit. It's the only autobiographical thing I've ever written, and it is auto-biographical because I didn't think I was writing fiction. I thought I was keeping a journal about going to this wonderful, kind of scruffy gym in a neighborhood YMCA. This was long, long before people considered it, as so many now do, de rigueur to go to a gym—it was pretty novel, in fact. And it was all I could do at that particular point in my life to get out of bed once every month or two and go to the Y with my friend Kathy, so I thought, Here's this wonderful institution which is going to save my life, and if in fact I am going to try to write some tiny thing, I'll write about what it's like to go there.

And I was completely unequal to the task. Wally was encouraging me, but my threshold for frustration was low, very low—I kept tearing up what I'd written. After a very long time—I'm guessing about a year and a half, I gave what I'd done to Wally, and I was very excited about having filled up some pages, but very uncertain about what I'd filled them up with. And Wally said, "Well, you haven't written a factual piece about the Y, you're writing fiction, so now turn it into fiction." So I was in a state of intense frustration and anguish, and I spent another year or so turning it into fiction. And I gave it to him, and he said, "Great, you've turned it into fiction, but it's lost its life. Do it again." And I thought, Well, which of us am I going to kill? But I wrote it again, and he said, "Wonderful—you've written a story!" It took about three years, altogether.

AK: I have a question about that story. The character comes to understand, and says, that the point of life is to have a good time, to find out what one wants to do, and start doing it. In the context of the story we understand how it's a revelation to her, because she has told us that previously, whenever she had a feeling, or something to say, she stuck a cigarette in her mouth and inhaled smoke instead of speaking. So it seems as if she has, actually, no self. Did that experience characterize you? Was it an exaggeration of something you experienced?

DE: Far from being an exaggeration, it was an understatement—to the most remarkable degree, you would hardly believe it. There was this little prisoner waiting inside a shroud of smoke, inside the personality that had been able to survive with the aid of that smoke—a very angry, starved little creature—so when the façade crumbled because I stopped smoking, the creature stepped forth, without a shell, without skin, totally unformulated, and was just this volcanic, lavalike, terrifying, inchoate, dangerous, endangered thing.

AK: How old were you?

DE: I was thirty. I'd been smoking since I was fifteen. By that time I was a very heavy smoker, and I loved it, I loved every cigarette I ever had in my life. I can practically remember their names. Stopping was like a death. I knew I wouldn't be able to stop by exercising my willpower, so I made it non-negotiable.

AK: How did you do that?

DE: I decided that I would never, ever, do it again. Never, ever. No, worse—there was no "never again" to contemplate; the future was closed as far as smoking and I were concerned. Because I knew that if I had to rely on willpower to stop smoking, I would lose. I went to a hypnotist, who taught me how to hypnotize myself, but there was something about the physical sensation that I couldn't stand. I just couldn't bear it, so instead of using that technique or using my nonexistent willpower, I just put smoking behind me.

AK: So all you had to do was suffer, not decide.

DE: Yes. It was horrible. I was in mourning—not only for the fantastic consolation of nicotine but also I suppose for the person, the smoker, I had just killed, as well as the person inside the smoker whom I had allowed to be stillborn long before. And here was this new person, entirely unequipped. Probably if someone who had known me in kindergarten saw me now, he'd say, "You're exactly the same." And in many fundamental ways I'm sure I am. But in some critical ways I'm very different. Or maybe I'm substantially the same as I was in kindergarten, but very different from the way I was at sixteen.

AK: It was a challenge to know yourself, to act on your own behalf, that sort of thing?

DE: I'd say maybe acting on my own behalf. Authenticity of experience was never the problem. Autonomy was. It was an incredible problem. A lot of my experiences were fairly bitter, because I was so reduced, so reduced and rather damaged. Have you ever seen or read the play *Kaspar* by Peter Handke? Well, I don't remember it much, so I'm talking about something I don't really remember, but the only character is Kaspar Hauser, who was a feral child. It's very beautiful. Handke has a lot of views that I consider pretty loopy, or anyhow, I don't agree with them, but what a writer! I mean, that guy is *fabulous*. So, there's a phrase that might be reiterated for half an hour, or maybe it just occurs a few times, but Kaspar says, in the translation I encountered, anyhow, "I want to be someone like somebody else was once." Or maybe it's "I want to be a person like somebody else was once." I never really felt like a human being. But just now I'm embarked on this huge apartment move, and the other day I was calling Con-Ed to change the account, and calling the movers, and I thought, Wait a minute, I *am* someone like somebody else was once. When did that happen? Because I sure wasn't always someone like somebody else was once.

AK: You turned into a person who could make phone calls. I've probably told you this story before, about when we were all at Iowa and Denis Johnson was there briefly. At the Mill one night he talked about how grateful he was to have married his wife, and we said, "Why is she great?" and he said, "She can talk to those people." We said, "What people?" and he said, "Those people who call on the phone about the mortgage. I can just say to them, 'You're not human,' and hand the phone to her."

DE: I think he's the funniest person alive. I'm sure I've told you that I used to follow him around at Iowa?

AK: Just to hear what he said?

DE: Just to—that luster, to travel in its wake or something. I'd see him at the grocery store and say, "Denis, Denis, hey, hi, Denis, can I carry your beer, Denis?" Well, I'm sure it wasn't beer because he wasn't drinking, but potatoes or whatever. And you know he didn't have a clue who I was, I think, that he and I were teaching in the same program—I was just some weirdo following him around the grocery store.

AK: Let's see. You wrote "Days," and then what came next?

DE: What happened next was that my friend who appears in that story as Kathy—her name is Kathy, and she's a writer and director, Kathleen Tolan—said she wanted to direct a reading of that story at the Public Theatre. And I said, "No, no, it belongs on the page, blah blah," and she said, "Well, what kind of a friend are you?" So I said okay, and she got a wonderful actress, Karen Ludwig, to do the reading. So a little later Joe Papp, who had initiated the Public and ran it, called me up and said, "I'd like you to write a play." And I said, "Well, Joe, I can't write a play." And he said, "Well, I'll pay you." I said, "Oh, that changes things considerably."

But I had a very good waitressing job at the time—I mean, good in that nobody had bothered to fire me, and believe me, no one else would have hired me, so I was very reluctant to give it up. And Joe said, "Drop a couple of nights a week, and I'll pay you, and you'll write." I was totally panicked. He said, "You'll come in and show me what you're writing." And I said, "Oh sure, of course," but I never show anybody what I'm writing and I wasn't about to then, and of course, actually, for a long time there was nothing. Wally basically moved out so I could just be a lunatic, doing it.

AK: He's the best man in the world.

DE: He's the best man in the world. So after five months, *bonk*, there was this play.

AK: But it can't be true that *bonk*, there was this play. Was there . . . fragmentary chaos that suddenly resolved into a play? All those funny characters, who are turning coffee cups upside down over dead mice and dropping acid accidentally—

DE: There's an autobiographical component to that one, too. Actually, I sort of tried to write something as a story that then became that play and partly a different story—very different—later. And, really, it was remarkably *bonk*. I've never written anything so fast. Except for "Revenge of the Dinosaurs," which I wrote very, very quickly, for me, that is, over a few months. But with that story I had real clarity of purpose from the outset.

So I gave this play to Wally and he said, "Gosh! Gee! Great, a play—but I don't get it." And I said, "Believe me, this is really good." I don't know why I had such confidence in it, but I did—complete, serene confidence. I said, "Don't worry, you're in good hands, it works, it's good." So then I brought it to Joe, and Joe said, "I hate this play." And I said, "But, Joe, it's really good!"

And Joe loved to be the guy dishing out favors, so he was infuriated at having to be the bad guy. It drove him sort of wild, so with every second that passed while I sat in his office with him, he became more and more vehement about how much he hated that play. But I didn't mind at all. I just found it hilarious, for some reason. So Wally said, "Why don't you invite the people you work with at the bar to read it." We got a bunch of food and everyone came over, and afterward Wall said, "I see. I see."

AK: He got it.

DE: Yes, because it did work, after all. And by the time I'd written the play, I'd begun to think, This is great. This is really fun. That feeling you can't get from anything but making art. And I'm very grateful to

Joe, because if he hadn't encouraged me—of course as it turned out, he was trying to *dis*courage me, but it was too late by then—I very much doubt I would have kept on.

AK: Making the thing that no one else has written before, because no one else could, because only you can.

DE: Yes. And that's every writer's birthright.

AK: I suddenly had a vision of a writer taking her hand off and putting it on the street for everyone to look at. It's that disturbing, that real, and that much ours.

DE: Yes, that's absolutely right.

AK: But after having the pleasure of that reading of the play, you went back to writing stories. You were living with a playwright, and you were around actors and directors and playwrights a lot, and you'd had that communal experience, and yet you went back to the more solitary world of writing stories.

DE: Yes. You might well wonder why, because of course theater is so much more fun, a million times more fun. But for one thing, I don't have the nerve for plays. It really takes steady nerve. You can't imagine the terror of production—all the things that can go wrong with people that just won't go wrong with a pencil and eraser; your pencil won't get sick, for example, or be cast in a movie during rehearsals. It's exhilarating, but you have to be strong. Also, I don't think that the form is that compatible with the way I tend to look at things. What I do is a little fragile for theater. And I like to control things much more than you can control a play.

AK: I would say that in a play you can't render consciousness, the elusive quality of consciousness, in the same way.

DE: That's it, that's exactly right. You really can't do that so well in theater, though of course there are many things you can do that you can't do in fiction.

AK: Was it produced fairly soon after?

DE: No, it sort of floated around. I sort of forgot about it. As far as I was concerned, I'd had the fun, though it turned out there was so much more fun to be had. Carole Rothman, who I knew a little bit, called me up and said, "I'd like to direct your play," and I said, "Great! Just don't change anything." And she said, "Well, er—don't be ridiculous, plays are always changed." I said, "Not mine." But I did end up changing it a little bit.

AK: What was it like to see it?

DE: Rehearsals were the most fun I ever had in my life. In fact Christine Estabrook, who played Rachel, said, "You've just got to stop laughing! You're disrupting rehearsals!"

AK: "We can't have a maniac in the house."

DE: Yes. I mean I couldn't believe what they were doing. I couldn't *believe* what they were doing. They were so funny. I was screaming. Because the writer can't imagine anything as concretely as the person who is going to get up on stage—it's going to be their voice, their body, their rhythms of speech, of breathing, of moving—the particular quality of their concentration.

It was amazing. But I don't enjoy sitting in the audience. I really hate it. Just having other people experience your work. Just to be sitting there noting how other people are responding—you don't have to watch people reading your book!

AK: And you're so close to other people, when you're in a theater. So, I'm interested in what order the stories were written in. I think it might be of interest to posterity—

DE: I'm glad you put it that way.

AK: —and so what came after "Days"?

DE: "What It Was Like, Seeing Chris" was the second. That's a story I'm pleased with. Now I see lots of things that are clumsy about it, but I'm still pleased with it.

AK: Is that common? When you look back, are the stories meaningful? Do you remember their composition?

DE: These days I almost never look back. I did at first, but not now. And I remember very, very little about making each story, though I do remember certain things about certain stories.

But early on, there was no pressure on me at all—I had all the time in the world. "A Lesson in Traveling Light" was my third story. The fourth one, which I don't like, was "Rafe's Coat." But it was the one that got my first book published. I was Laurie Colwin's waitress, and she kept asking me what I did, and I kept telling her I was a waitress, which was absolutely true, but then there was a review of my play in the *Times*, which, incidentally, compared my writing to hers. So Laurie, who was a wonderfully generous and lively person, demanded to see something I'd written, and I had just finished "Rafe's Coat," so I gave it to her, and she passed it on to her editor, Alice Quinn, who liked it, and offered to publish a collection when the time came. But in fact, I had no interest in making a collection then. I was amazed that I could even produce a piece of paper with a mark on it.

AK: But "Rafe's Coat" does have some of the funniest things in the world in it. Doesn't Heather, the soap opera actress, describe something or someone as being like "a stack of fish on a plate" or "fish on a plate"? And it does have Cookie ratifying things with raucous baying. What don't you like about it?

DE: First of all, that quality of consciousness that you mentioned. The story's more superficial. I mean, it doesn't attempt not to be superficial, it is the way it was supposed to be—

AK: It's about manners, and so on—

DE: It's sort of brittle. The narrator is obviously a very self-deceptive person, and that was the fun of it, keeping up that big edifice, while also making it transparent. It was fun. Well, it wasn't that much fun to write, but it was interesting. I think I needed to write it, to teach myself some technical skills.

AK: And then?

DE: Then "Transactions in a Foreign Currency," then "Broken Glass."

AK: There are certain sorts of women in some of the stories—perhaps they attract each other, or create each other—a confident, rapacious woman and a nervous, naïve, inchoate sort of woman. I'm thinking of Cinder and Charlotte in "Flotsam," Amanda and Jill in "The Robbery," Marcia and Patty in "A Cautionary Tale," and Melanie and Rachel from *Pastorale*.

DE: Well, I suppose they come from . . . me. I mean, thankfully things change when one gets older, but I remember being extremely attentive to, dazzled by, that sort of competence, that sort of confidence.

AK: How did your political consciousness grow?

DE: I'm not sure that it really has grown. I'd say that maybe what you're calling a political consciousness is just an amalgamation of a few attitudes I've had from very early on that have been sort of forcibly refreshed from time to time.

For one thing, I was always rather acutely aware of inequities of various sorts, imbalances of power. I think many children are—after all, they don't have much power, and most children aren't in very benign situations, in my view. But that feeling never abated for me— the painful awareness of inequity—perhaps it was an element that my family was Jewish in a Midwestern suburb that was not Jewish—and I think it's a simple jump from noting the fact of inequities to noting that different circumstances are bound to create different attitudes toward the same things.

That sounds moronic, but actually it's something that has to be learned over and over again, at least in my case, because it's really easy to lose sight of. It's very difficult to remember that not only are other people experiencing things that are quite different from what you're experiencing but also that the difference is important and it doesn't go away when you yourself stop thinking about it. And the more privileged you are, the more comfortable you are, the more obtuse you're likely to be about the experience that other people are having, the fact that the experience of other people is different from yours and every bit as real.

I've always—always—been marked by my class. I mean, there are things I will never know about the world that any factory worker knows. Even when I've done menial or degrading or unpleasant work, even when I've felt that my financial prospects are disastrous, I've always had a big cushion of a middle-class background and middle-class expectations.

As a child, I had a rather tortured relationship with the people who were known as "the help." My mother did not, possibly because she had grown up poor, or relatively so. She was untroubled, I suppose, because she was just hiring people to help her do the work she couldn't get done by herself. But I felt awful about it. I suppose I had some awareness that I'd been born inalterably on the winning side of certain relationships.

Then when I was seventeen, I had the great good fortune to be sort of accidentally involved in an amazing civil rights thing. It had to do with the Highlander Folk School, a really wonderful institution, founded by Myles Horton, who had initially been very active in labor issues with the Cumberland miners. His son Thorstein, named for Thorstein Veblen, I believe, went to the same boarding school that I did, and he invited me to come down to Tennessee in the summer and join in on a project. The school had been burned down some time before, and we were in the Smokies, building a campsite, and the local police came up in the middle of the night and arrested us and took us to jail.

But the fact is, they wanted to kill us. I was charged with "assimilated intercourse," which meant interracial sex shows or something. Well, I was seventeen, and it was about two in the morning, and we were all asleep after a hard day of work, and I wasn't having any kind of intercourse. They took us down the mountain into town, and into jail, and in a couple of weeks there was an actual trial. And when the cops realized I was a minor, they transferred the charge to the one other white girl, who was eighteen.

As I remember, "assimilated intercourse" was a hanging charge, or anyhow someone said it was, but fortunately it was completely obvious that the cops weren't even trying to make any of the charges, which were plentiful, look legitimate. And somehow we were all let off with fines. They had refrained from killing us, apparently, in the first place, to make an example of us, but looking back at it from this vantage, that trial feels like a triumph of the justice system. I mean, when one thinks of the privatization of prisons and immigrants in detention camps and the undermining of habeas corpus, to say nothing of Guantanamo and "extraordinary renditions" and so on, that courtroom seems to have represented a tiny, fleeting golden age of American justice.

AK: What did they look like, the people who arrested you?

DE: I don't remember. That is, in my memory they were wearing Klan sheets with their badges pinned on them, but I simply can't believe my memory is accurate. I'm pretty sure my memory of the sheriff's daughter is reasonably accurate, though. She was about to go to teacher's college or something. It was the early sixties, you know, but it could have been the forties. She had blond ringlets and a blue gingham dress. And she sat demurely in the courtroom and took notes.

AK: That's amazing. What happened? Did your parents come down?

DE: No, actually. Things were terrible then with my mother, and had been for a long time—everything she did drove me absolutely crazy, everything I did drove her absolutely crazy. It happened, also, to be the summer my brother was getting married, and everyone was very anxious that the wedding go smoothly. Which it did, actually—it was lovely. But anyhow, I was allotted my one phone call, and I called my mother and said,"Hi, Ma, guess I can't get home yet—I'm in jail!" and she said, "You're coming home right now." And I said, "Er, well, I can't—" and she said, "No excuses."

AK: She didn't understand.

DE: She didn't. Neither did I, really. I thought, I'm from Winnetka, nothing can happen to me! It was the next summer that the three boys [Schwerner, Goodman, and Chaney] were murdered in Mississippi.

But the especially valuable lessons from that experience were reserved for my return home. Because when I got back, lots of people expressed interest or curiosity about what things were like where I had been, and when I told them, they flatly didn't believe it. I had been there and they hadn't, but they didn't believe me. Of course there were certainly those who knew that real courage was required of black people in the South—and the North, for that matter—but for the most part it was clear that this fact only retained its reality for a moment at a time, and the rest of the time it was like a movie that was over. That was true for me, too. There were moments when I had some insight that the life of another person went on coherently from one moment to the next, but for the most part, the lives of people I'd just met would be vividly real to me one moment, and the next moment it was as if no experience but my own was legitimate, as if there was in fact no experience but my own. Mine was the only experience that was wholly real to me for more than a minute or so, but at least I'd learned that. I mean, at least I'd learned how much I wasn't taking in.

AK: Then later you went to Central America with Wall, which shows up in both of your work, in stories like "Broken Glass" and "Holy Week" and in Wall's play *The Fever*. Did you go in the eighties?

DE: In the late eighties and early nineties.

AK: I always notice that your most caustic characterizations are of Americans abroad, people whose only interest in another land is where to get a good steak and how to relieve the locals of their indigenous textiles.

DE: Yes. And I include myself in that characterization. I mean, I'm one of them.

AK: What happened there? And what did you come back with, besides textiles? What did you come home knowing that you hadn't known?

DE: Nothing. Well, except for a great deal of specific information about where, exactly, I was situated in the workings of the planet, and what, exactly, was being done to certain people on my behalf. But in essence I'd merely been horrifyingly reminded of how parochial I am, of how difficult it is to learn, if you're in a comfortable position, what went into the construction of that position, and how extremely important it is to make an effort to learn what that was—where you fit in.

It's always a shock. It can never be assimilated, at least if you're even reasonably privileged, reasonably comfortable, you can never fully understand or accept it, that your particular experience is neither inevitable nor dominant in the world. People vary of course in their capacity to comprehend the reality of someone else, to comprehend the humanity of somebody else. Did you see the photograph of the Rutgers women's basketball team in the *Times* a few days ago?

AK: They were so beautiful!

DE: They were so beautiful. And the expressions on their faces—of such serious, painful, judicious reflection! And it was so fascinating to hear Don Imus, in contrast, trying to "explain" himself. He couldn't really understand what the fuss was about. He seemed genuinely confused that anyone would censure him, because in his mind he had just been making jokes about things that weren't real: women.

I don't know, I have no way of evaluating, but I do suspect that our particular culture has made itself unusually expert in dehumanizing other people and instructing people how to estrange from themselves the experience of people not themselves. Or the experience of people who *are* themselves, actually. For example, what about this prevalent, hair-raisingly weird attitude a lot of people seem to have that they themselves aren't real unless they're on TV! That their lives must be reflected in order to be actual—a complete inversion between internal and external. Television has been a very powerful instrument, in many ways, in colluding in this thing, a sort of derangement of humanness, that does have rather immense political consequences. And, yes, when we returned from Central America and were asked what was going on, we were received with a chorus of, "No. No. That's not happening. You didn't see that, you didn't hear that. You didn't understand the context, you were naïve."

AK: That willful ignorance shows up in a number of stories: "Broken Glass," "Under the 82nd Airborne," "Holy Week," all terrifying stories that take up the problem of not knowing what one should know. And the people who do know, who are able to hear, are driven almost crazy by what they know. They fall apart, their speech falls apart, they decompensate. Like Beale, in "Someone to Talk To," and Susan in "The Robbery."

DE: We live in a bubble. Everybody outside it, outside this tiny milieu, knows exactly what's going on. Yet unless we happen to meet or know someone who lives outside it, or we have a special motivation to find out, we'll be ignorant, no matter how "well educated" we are or if we read the *Times* every day front to back. Well, that will only embroider your ignorance, really. You really have to ferret out the information. When we went to Central America, I realized that a six-year-old child in El Salvador, a six-year-old, knew exactly who I was, and what I represented. I didn't know. I was there trying to figure it out. But the child knew.

AK: What did you represent?

DE: The very day we arrived in San Salvador, in fact, a huge graffito appeared on the U.S. Embassy. Like a lot of U.S. embassies I've seen, it was up on a hill, like a fortress, surrounded by a high wall and barbed wire, and so on, but someone had managed to get up there and paint, in Spanish, of course, "In this building is planned the torture and murder of the Salvadoran people." The next time we saw the embassy it was gone. I imagine the person who'd gotten the words up there didn't last so long, either.

If one is American one has to be very resourceful, very motivated, to find out what's going on, because you won't find out from TV, and rarely will you read something in the mainstream media that conflicts with the views useful to the corporations that own the mainstream media. There are lots of people very motivated not to tell you what's happening. Well, look at the war. Billions of dollars going "to the war," but what can that possibly mean? "The war" is an abstraction. Where, actually, does all that money go? It's not going to the soldiers. They're not adequately armed, they're not protected, they're poorly paid, they're poorly cared for, they're underinsured, when they come home wounded or disabled or traumatized, the treatment they receive is very inadequate, or they're actually disqualified for treatment. All that money is not going to the soldiers, so where is it going? It's going to buy airplanes, tanks, bombers—all sorts of instruments of annihilation that are manufactured by U.S. corporations. It's going to private military contractors like Blackwater, mercenary outfits, in short, which are run by private corporations from the U.S. A large amount of it is going to "reconstruction." That is, to huge corporations like Halliburton, and Bechtel, to reconstruct—or, it seems, to not reconstruct—at great profit, what has been destroyed by the airplanes and the tanks and so on that similar corporations manufacture.

AK: So there's no motivation not to destroy, when they profit from the reconstruction.

DE: Exactly. And now of course the big joke is that Halliburton is going to Dubai, where they won't have to pay U.S. taxes. So, in short, it's you and I, with *our* U.S. tax payments, who are funding profit-making corporations to knock things down and get people killed.

Because also, when you think about it, who are these "insurgents"? What does that word mean in this context? It means people who want the U.S. to get out of their country and stop destroying it.

AK: That truth, and the fact that we don't hear about it, or listen for it, fuels "Revenge of the Dinosaurs." Everyone is quarreling about her own little agenda, and no one is noticing that Nana is dying, and people are getting beaten up on the street, and the TV news is showing explosions. Nana, who once wrote a book on economics, on currency, is no longer compos mentis. And she's the only one who would have been able to look at the violence on television and say, "That is about money. That is money, there."

DE: Yes.

AK: Is it possible to be an American and live an ethical life?

DE: Well, that's the question. For the middle class—there used to be a huge middle class, but of course there hardly is one any longer—if you vote, and pay taxes, you're contributing to all kinds of destruction. Our money enriches big corporations and kills poor people at home and elsewhere. As we sit here, people are being killed, with our money. But what is there to do? On, in fact, Amy Goodman's show, I heard an interview with a woman who led a group of tax resisters, all of whom withhold portions of their taxes on moral grounds. As it happened, I was just on my way uptown to see my tax accountant, and make out my tax checks. Well, the woman was saying, "Nothing that can happen to a tax resister in the U.S. can possibly compare to the horror that we're inflicting on people in Iraq." And I thought, That's so true. I'm going to go tell my accountant that I'm going to withhold my taxes. Then Amy Goodman asked her what happens to tax resisters. And the woman said, "Well, some property has been confiscated—some of our members' homes." And after another moment she said, "And some of our members are in prison." And I thought, Plan B.

I know she's right, I passionately share her views, but not pas-sionately enough to emulate her courage. So, in regard to your ques-tion—I think that the overwhelming majority of people in this country would be considered perfectly nice, decent, upright people, if we happened to be living in other countries. But our private and local selves are overshadowed, now, by our public and global selves. I'm talking now about people like myself, who would be considered financially stable. It gets more complicated, obviously, when you think about the rapidly growing population of the impoverished. I can't do anything about my disproportionate power—none of us seem to be able to do anything about our disproportionate power unless it's something extreme almost to the point of self-immolation in one way or another. So the circumstances of our life, the historical circumstances, decree that we're villains, no matter what our convic-tions or character, unless we're willing to risk a lot more than I, at least, have thus far had the courage to risk.

AK: What I really don't understand, though, is how people like Dick Cheney can be so wrong, how they can not believe in the personhood of others. They don't understand the least thing about human feel-ings. I had a cab driver recently who knew more than Cheney—he said to me, "You come in my house, I throw roses on you?" meaning, of course, how ridiculous it was to invade another country and expect to be greeted as "liberators." But Cheney—he has children, he has daughters. How can he not know that other people are real?

DE: That would be the one to figure out. Because if you could under-stand Dick Cheney, you could understand everything. I mean, I think it's very likely that Dick Cheney had no expectation of being greeted as a liberator—though I think there were people in the adminis-tration, I'd guess including George Bush, who were sufficiently ill-informed to believe that they would be—but I don't imagine that Cheney cared in the least how he'd be greeted.

AK: We're skipping over a lot—the stories that use Europe as a setting and a force, stories that use addictions as settings and forces, extraordinary stories about children and young people like "The Custodian" and "Mermaids" and "The Girl Who Left Her Sock on the Floor," but I want to ask you about the most recent collection, *Twilight of the Superheroes.* I notice that in the title story you come back to the division of the story into pieces that you used way back when, in "Days." And the web of characters we're used to seeing gets even more broad. Did you—did those fragments have anything to do with the enormous intensity of the material [the immediate experience of 9/11]?

DE: I don't know. I don't think that was intentional. The broad range of characters is what I needed, I think, to represent a range of experiences. What I was focused on was representing what that huge event felt like in the moment before all the reactions inevitably set in. What was it like before we knew that this thing would come to be called "9/11"? I was in Virginia on that day, and as I remember, my class was ultimately cancelled, but not before a number of people had gathered. I think I said, "We just don't know what this is—if it's one horrible event that will be swallowed by history or whether it's the beginning of something." And one of the students said, "Yes, it might be the beginning of terrorist attacks all over the country." And that had never crossed my mind, strangely enough. I was thinking with apprehension of the retaliations and the political hay that could be made of it—and the things that I feared obviously came to pass.

AK: I'm curious about Kate, the protagonist of "Like It or Not" in the recent collection. Along with perhaps Lynnie in "The Custodian," she's one of the most conventionally middle-American characters you've explored. Who is she to you? And how and why did it occur to you to send her to Europe?

DE: I don't remember how—possibly I was just utilizing some stuff that was ready to hand, a fairly recent trip to Italy—and I don't know why. I suppose I just needed her to have an experience that might painfully reawaken a longing for a romance, and Europe is very good for that.

AK: I'd also like to hear you talk about "Some Other, Better Otto," in this recent collection. It strikes me as perhaps the most intimate of your stories, the most undiluted portrait of a person in persistent, insoluble emotional pain. How did that story start, and grow?

DE: I'm very happy with your characterization of that story. There have been lots of readers who feel that Otto is just an unpleasant person, which I certainly don't. All I remember about the genesis of that story is that it started very unfruitfully with a couple, or two couples—in some scrawlings they were heterosexual couples and in others they weren't. It went nowhere, and I put it aside. But then from its ashes another story arose later, and that one started with my feelings about the sister—with Otto's feelings about her.

AK: Do you feel your project or projects as a writer have substantially changed, in the years you've been writing?

DE: I don't know. I've never thought about it. I suppose my effort has been a consistent one—I just keep trying to make something out of words that you'd think couldn't be made out of words.

A CONVERSATION WITH
NURUDDIN FARAH

Anderson Tepper

Stepping into Nuruddin Farah's suburban home outside of Cape Town, South Africa, I am immediately put at ease by his warm, relaxed manner and the elegant, sunlit space itself. "You're looking at my lost book," he jokes, explaining how he spent almost three years consumed by the house's renovation. "That's why there is that extra gap between the novels *Secrets* and *Links*. This house is a novel in itself." Farah, of course, is a master craftsman, whether helping to construct a house, or building—book by book—his own elaborate, multitiered record of his native country, Somalia, and the intricate bonds of family, clan, and religion that have at times threatened to destroy it. Farah's writing is rich, vivid, even startling—a sensory overload of imagery and metaphors, psychological twists and turns, and folk wisdom. His books are completely modern, yet imbued, too, with the air of a timeless oral culture.

In his most recent novel, *Knots* (2007), the connections are as complex as ever: Cambara, a Toronto-based actress and makeup artist, returns to Mogadiscio and is plunged into a violent, alien world she hardly recognizes. The streets are overrun by *qaat*-chewing, gun-toting teenagers; a clan warlord has camped out at her family home; people seem to melt into the shadows of this war-ravaged ghost town. Cambara, haunted by her recent divorce and the death of her son, begins to disappear herself, cloaked in the anonymity of the *hijab*, the Islamic veil and headscarf. Tension is palpable on every page as Cambara navigates the mazelike city: How can she move around? How can she recover her house, reclaim her identity? How can Somalia itself survive?

The fate of Somalia, naturally, has been on Farah's mind for a long time. Born in the town of Baidoa, in Italian Somaliland in 1945, Farah has lived a somewhat nomadic existence—exiled in 1976, he's moved around Europe, the United States, and Africa, and only returned to visit Somalia for the first time again in 1996. In the meantime, he has said, he struggled to keep his country alive by writing about it. In 1998, he was awarded the Neustadt International Prize for Literature; in 2006 Penguin reissued his first novel, *From a Crooked Rib*; and Graywolf republished his Variations on the Theme of an African Dictatorship trilogy, *Sweet and Sour Milk*, *Sardines*, and *Close Sesame*.

When we met in Cape Town in December 2006, however, it wasn't only Farah's fiction that was drawing attention—the situation in Somalia was reaching a breaking point, with a tense standoff between the federal government in Baidoa (with Ethiopia's backing, as well as implicit U.S. support) and the Islamists in power in Mogadiscio. A brief war indeed erupted a few days after we spoke, and its repercussions continue to threaten to draw wider forces into the conflicts of the Horn of Africa.

Anderson Tepper: What is the latest news from Somalia? I know you were there recently yourself.

Nuruddin Farah: They're playing a cat-and-mouse game. It has less to do with politics than it does with power. And the reason is that there are several groups, including the Islamists, who are vying for power. Unfortunately for everyone, power, or the containment of the problems of Somalia, is equally shared between the Islamists and the federal government. The Islamists seem to have overrun the country, but they're not as organized as the government. What the Islamists have is the acceptance of ordinary people that Islam is everything—and that everything else has failed. Democracy has failed. Western education has failed. The American presence has been a failure.

So there's a lot of confusion. Because neither the Islamists nor the federal government can go on its own, there is some kind of stalemate. Now, with regards to the Ethiopians, the Ethiopians have never wanted a stable, centralized, functioning Somalia—because it's not in their interest. Ethiopia has actually complicated the situation more.

The Americans seem to be terribly worried about the Islamists. In my view, there is nothing to worry about. But the longer this thing goes on—the longer Americans continue alienating the Islamists, and the longer the Ethiopians remain on Somali soil—the more likely it is for more Islamists from abroad to come into Somalia. The internationals haven't come yet—or they hadn't when I was there this fall. I was there and I spoke to practically everyone. I was ferrying messages back and forth. I was a self-sent mediator.

AT: In *Knots* you actually foresee the decline of the warlords and the rise of the Islamists in Mogadiscio.

NF: Yes, well, this novel was actually written at the time when the Islamists had not yet gained the upper hand. There were enough intimations, though, that this might happen, because people were unhappy with the way the reconciliation had gone. By then, the government had already been set up. There was intimation that the Islamists were going to get the upper hand because Islam is the unifying factor in Somalia, in the same way that the clan is the great divisive factor.

Now even Islam is mediated through the clan. Even the courts are divided along clan lines. You see, there are families who in Somalia are known as "those for whom no one mourns or weeps," because they're weak. So if someone is killed, or whipped by the Islamic courts, people say they must be "those for whom no one weeps." And the reason is even the Islamists and the courts will not punish someone who comes from a major clan. Because then there will be war. In this particular pattern, where everything is continuously negotiated, the Americans have stayed out of it. *This* is the time to go in and say, "We are part of the talks." They should talk to their enemies, and get to know them—the way the E.U. has attempted to do. I saw for myself how, instead, they were just bringing in bags and bags of cash to pay off warlords again.

AT: As in your other books, Mogadiscio itself plays an important role in *Knots*, both as it is now and as it exists in Cambara's memories. There is a passage where she recalls "her young days in Mogadiscio, when Somalis were at peace with their identities, happy with the shape of their world as it was then."

NF: Well, sadly, that is no longer the case. The irony of it, however, is that there is the semblance of that peace returning to Mogadiscio thanks to the Islamists, who have now imposed their own order.

AT: Tell me about your own experience of returning to Mogadiscio. Did *Knots* grow out of your own effort to reclaim family property?

NF: No, it was a coincidence. I wrote an article for the *New Yorker* about returning to Somalia. It was going to go to press before some big Catholic Church–related scandal happened and there were two stories that week that were killed to make room for it, and one was mine. It was never published. My book editors knew I wrote that and just assumed that experience was behind this novel.

AT: And this book is part of your next trilogy, right? I'm also curious about how you first began your project of writing novels as trilogies.

NF: *Knots* is the second book in the next trilogy that started with *Links* (2004). You know, I started thinking in terms of a trilogy when I began writing my first novel, *From a Crooked Rib* (1970). It is connected thematically with my second novel, *A Naked Needle* (1976), but those books never became a complete trilogy.

From a Crooked Rib is a novel that is highly sympathetic to women. What I wanted to do as a young author was to write the second novel from a totally opposite point of view. And then when it was published something happened that I hadn't expected: It was greatly admired by many misogynists! That was not at all what I wanted to happen. So I took it out of print, and it has never been republished. When I wrote a letter to my publishers at the Heinemann Africa series, they said they had never heard of this happening—an author asking that his book be taken out of print. They were dumbfounded!

These two books weren't reviewed much at all, either, so they relied mostly on word of mouth. As for *From a Crooked Rib*, even when feminism became popular later in the seventies, many of the feminists were not interested in men writing about women. So it died a second death. It also died because I came from a non-English-speaking part of Somalia, so therefore nobody expected a novel, in English, from someone who comes from Italian-speaking Somalia. So that helped it to die a natural death as well.

And what's more: Here I am, age twenty-seven, country-less, in exile, with no, what you might call, home base. You see, Chinua Achebe, Wole Soyinka, Ngugi wa Thiong'o—they all had a home base and their books became textbooks in school, they were bought and sold in their countries, and, naturally, everyone was very proud of their own nation's writers.

So, a combination of things made sure that those early books died.

AT: And *A Naked Needle* was the book that prompted your exile from Somalia?

NF: Yes. My exile was a consequence of *A Naked Needle*, which is a very satirical novel. I was in England doing postgraduate work in theater at the time it was published, and I was told if I returned to Somalia I would be jailed. I was in Italy on my way back when my brother told me not to come. So I stayed on in Italy when I got his message. I then wrote a play that was part of that trilogy, but I couldn't produce it.

I asked myself, Why am I being forced into exile? The answer was, Because I've written a book. And, therefore, what I write must mean something, even if it was just a silly book. So I thought, From now on, I should try to write something that is worthy of my fate.

AT: That is when you began your first complete trilogy—*Sweet and Sour Milk* (1979), *Sardines* (1981), and *Close Sesame* (1983)?

NF: Yes, I decided I would continue writing about Somalia. That trilogy, Variations on the Theme of an African Dictatorship, is set around 1975 in the first book, and I took it into the early eighties. And then I began going back and forth in time.

The next trilogy—*Maps* (1986), *Gifts* (1993), *Secrets* (1998)—which I called Blood in the Sun, has a very interesting framework. Because of the precariousness of my situation, because I didn't know when I'd ever go back, I had to find a way in which the three novels of the trilogy would work together—not through character, not chronologically, not historically—but to link them to an idea, the idea of victory and defeat.

AT: But why not consider the books as separate, stand-alone novels?

NF: Well, because I'm a very long-winded person, and therefore like to look at things from different viewpoints. There are also repeating elements that I like to use within the three books. For example, in every trilogy there is a novel with a female central character and a novel with a male central character. And then there is a novel in which you can't quite tell whether it is the male or female who is central. In *Links*, which is very sympathetic to women, the main character is Jeebleh, a man. And then in *Knots*, you have Cambara, a woman, who carries the story.

AT: How do you see the framework of this trilogy that you're working on now? Some of the characters of *Links* return in *Knots*; will they also appear in the next book?

NF: Yes, they will return, but they won't be in the center. But, it's true, the characters are one thing that repeats. You also have the idea of someone leaving a life of comfort—in Toronto, in New York—and returning to Mogadiscio. In other words, now the Somalis are repatriating. And the idea of return—the idea of going back to something you thought you knew but didn't—is a very fraught framework for a novel.

AT: I wanted to ask you about your language, its almost Faulknerian excess. Was this something that you set out to do at the beginning or has it developed over the course of your books?

NF: Well, the language within the novels changes, and hopefully it changes with each subsequent novel. A lot of my imagery, you know, comes from other languages, and a lot of people, especially Americans, are frightened by it, worried by it. Faulkner did something similar, and he had difficulties for a long time. But some of the metaphors are also constructed, even if they do seem odd at first; and sometimes they do run away. I remember once there was a page where there were five or six long metaphors, and the editor said, "Can't we cut some?" And I said, "You know, there are people who are heavy in the upper part and not in the lower part. Why can't we allow one page to just be naturally metaphor-heavy?"

But, yes, there is a sense of Faulkner in some of the books, although when he had his greatest influence on me as a young writer it was when I was writing *A Crooked Rib*, which was the least Faulknerian. So probably these influences came later. The great models for my idea of writing at the time I was starting out, I would say, would have been some of the Irish writers, like Joyce and Beckett. And the reason is because the kind of writing that I like to do is the kind that makes one think there is a story behind the story, that there is a tale *beyond* the tale, that there is something that hasn't been said that needs to be said.

AT: It is intentionally overstuffed with possible interpretations?

NF: I wouldn't use the word "overstuffed." I would say this has the implicit in the explicit, and the explicit in the implicit. That there is another story behind the story, that you haven't been told everything.

Sometimes a novel writes itself in the sense that the characters write their own lines. And sometimes you write and there is no way to go but *that* way, the direction it's headed. The certainty of the novelist is to make you feel there is no other way to go but their way. Now I'm working on the third part of this trilogy, and it also has some similarities with the other books. For example, there is always an orphan, and this new book has one, too. The framework is more or less the same, deliberately the same. But each book is very different.

AT: You mentioned before the theme of Somalis returning home, and I was reminded that you also wrote a nonfiction book on the Somali diaspora, *Yesterday, Tomorrow* (2000).

NF: Yes, well, that was a break in my novel writing. It involved a lot of traveling, and took a long time. It was a consequence of an article I wrote called "A Country in Exile." The idea was, If I can't go back to Somalia, why don't I write about Somalis where they are?

AT: You've moved around quite a bit in exile. How does it feel now, living in Cape Town, to be an African writer based in Africa?

NF: Well, the irony of it is that while I was away in exile before, that generation of Achebe, Soyinka, and Ngugi were living in Africa. They were professors at universities in their own countries. Now, they are all professors in America. I happen to be the only so-called "major" African writer who lives on the continent. I'm also the only one who doesn't teach, though I do on occasion for a few months or so at a time. And, yes, Cape Town has been a very convenient writing base for me—it's close enough to both Nairobi and Mogadiscio.

AT: When did you return to Africa? And did that have an effect on your writing?

NF: Oh, yes, my return to Africa enriched my writing greatly. Let's see: I lived in Rome for a while when I first went into exile. Then I actually bummed around Los Angeles for a bit, writing scripts. After that, I returned to Africa, and taught in Nigeria from 1980 to '81, before moving to the Gambia. I was thrown out of the Gambia, and I went to the first country that would have me, which was Sudan. So I lived in Khartoum before moving to a place that had just come out of civil war—because I was training myself for Somalia, which I was convinced was headed for civil war—and I moved to Kampala. This was the early eighties and Kampala was just coming out of its own awful violence of the Idi Amin years.

From there, I was thrown out again, as I had been in the Gambia, because I got into a headlong confrontation with the heads of state. So I went to Ethiopia, which had also come out of a military dictatorship. After Ethiopia, I returned to Nigeria, and stayed there until 1999, when we moved here to Cape Town.

What's interesting is that in many of these places, like Uganda and Ethiopia, I was absorbing the experiences and using them to understand Somalia—either what had just happened there or what I thought was bound to happen soon. Like I said, these other countries were training me for Somalia, and they were helping me to write about it.

So that's the geography of my life, I guess. But all the time, even when I'm settled somewhere, I go away for several months a year to be alone and write.

AT: Do you read much of the new generation of African writers?

NF: Well, there is a new crop of younger writers in Nigeria and in South Africa that I'm aware of. There are a few that are very good, indeed, like Chimamanda Ngozi Adichie, Sefi Atta, Chris Abani. But, you know, there are two types of writers. There is what I'd call the marathon-type of writer—boring, old fogeys like me, writing long projects. And then there are writers who write fine novels but only the occasional one. Now, one doesn't know whether these young writers are marathon writers until they are further along.

The first novel is often, to my mind, an indication of what a writer might do, given the time. Now, if you compare a novel by Achebe with the first novels nowadays, you can actually see that the work produced by Achebe was not only full of depth but extremely mature. It seemed as if he was born walking as a writer. Look at the first novel by Faulkner, the first novel by Conrad—look at them all, and even if they might not even be adequate as novels, the germination of something more is already intimated.

As a young writer, I remember, what interested me was to write not about myself but about somebody as different from myself as possible. You know, I was born in a town and never spent one night in my entire life with nomadic farmers in Somalia, like in *A Crooked Rib*. But that was a testing of the waters. Take the Indian writer Amitav Ghosh, for example, who wrote about Egypt so masterfully in his book *In an Antique Land*. Well, these are the books you can compare to those of the navel watchers.

AT: You were joking earlier about how managing the work on your house cost you roughly a book, about how each book generally takes you the same amount of time. What is your system of writing?

NF: I write in longhand, and then after a couple of days I go back and cut it and rework it and then gradually begin to build it. Then, once the irritations have been removed and I've really thought it through and I know the story line, the first draft begins to take shape. And that is the bulk of the work right there. When I do have difficulties, it is usually because my plots are not sketched out. They are very elaborate, and sometimes things only occur after writing them.

But my greatest difficulty has always been in finding the time and the peace of mind to actually write. Much of *Knots* was actually done in a month in Piemonte, near Milan. I took myself off and locked myself away there and wrote. Every now and again, I vanish. I don't let people know where I am—I have my laptop and my mobile phone, so there's no need for them to know where I am. Right now, in fact, I'm trying to work on the third part of this trilogy, and I just might need to vanish again soon.

A CONVERSATION WITH
DENIS JOHNSON

Charles D'Ambrosio

The literary hagiography glosses over this, and the book jackets omit it, but Denis Johnson is a fine companion for a sing-along. An affinity for folk songs on a summer evening is not a trait one expects of a man whose debut novel, *Angels* (1983), announced him as a brilliant chronicler of the desperate and drug-ruined, a sympathetic but unwavering examiner of what the *New York Times* called "people who slip helplessly into their own worst nightmares."

After *Angels* and his third book of poetry, *The Incognito Lounge* (1982), put him on the map, Johnson has gone on to publish some of the seminal books of the last twenty-five years. His fiction includes *Fiskadoro, The Stars at Noon, Resuscitation of a Hanged Man, Jesus' Son: Stories* (which was made into a movie), *Already Dead: A California Gothic*, and the forthcoming *Tree of Smoke*, on which he has been working on and off for twenty years. His books of poetry include *The Man Among the Seals, Inner Weather, The Veil,* and *The Throne of the Third Heaven of the Nations Millennium General Assembly: Poems, Collected and New.* His plays include *Hellhound on my Trail, Shoppers Carried by Escalators into the Flames, Soul of a Whore, Psychos Never Dream,* and *Purvis.*

Johnson's work is distinguished by more than its fraught subject matter. His writing is muscular and fiercely concentrated, the fiction employing a poet's refusal to waste words. "Dark" is too pleasant a word for what occurs in a Denis Johnson book: disaster does not await; it's here. His work quite rightly earns descriptions like "gritty" and "melancholy," but those terms are only half the story. To see the grit alone—and you almost do expect a fine layer to adhere to the hands as you set down his books—is to miss the humor and empathy. Characters begin in dire straits and then make even more catastrophic choices—and yet the reader roots for them, nevertheless. Sometimes one hopes simply that these dysfunctional figures manage to stay alive.

It took some doing to coax Johnson from his home in northern Idaho to the Reed College campus in Portland, Oregon, for the Tin House Writers Workshop in July 2004. But once he arrived, the collective gaze of the crowd followed him as if a unicorn had appeared. An unexpected sing-along coalesced at a round outdoor table as dusk settled and continued for an hour or so, one sixties-era song easing into the next. Johnson relaxed in his chair, feet crossed at the ankles, and hit the lyrics like a pro. The feeling of ease lingered on through the reading from *Tree of Smoke,* and afterward, when Johnson sat down with Charles D'Ambrosio to discuss television, wars, and the immense utility of anecdotes.

Denis Johnson: I haven't read that excerpt before tonight, and it's a lot of prose, a lot of paragraphs. I appreciate your patience. It's always good to read those things, though, because suddenly phrases leap out at you just as you're about to read them and you think, Gyad, I wish I hadn't put that in there! Cross it out.

Charles D'Ambrosio: You could do what Chris Offutt does and bring a pen up there, and start scratching stuff out.

DJ: Well, Chris actually stole my pen.

CD: I was in a WaldenBooks once—you know, those kind of suburban bookstores, not particularly complete bookstores—and for some reason I was in the spiritual/inspirational section, just kind of wandering around—I don't know what kind of day I was having. Anyway, I was in that section, in a suburban WaldenBooks, and there were all those books like "Go to the Light" and "The Unicorn at the End of the Tunnel" and all of those books, and I was just kind of staring at them blankly. They have all those yellow and pink covers and stuff, and there was one little thin black spine in the middle of that and it was *Jesus' Son*. And I thought, being a good boy, Oh, I know where that belongs. It's that other section, the literature section. And then I thought, Well, I'll just leave it here.

I'm going to ask the sort of questions that the students want to talk about. In other words, how do you do it? Or, quoting one of my students, "How the fuck do you do it?" Those questions are very hard to answer and sometimes the most honest answer is, "I don't know." But the students didn't fly all the way to hear that, so I'm going to put you through this. Did you always read a lot? Since, to quote Chris, writing and reading are sort of twin activities.

DJ: Yeah, I did, particularly as a child. I'm of the first TV generation. I was born in 1949, and my family had a TV around 1954 when I was six years old, but they didn't let me stay up late. I went to first grade in the states, and when I went to school, everybody'd be talking about *The Life and Legend of Wyatt Earp* last night, *Gunsmoke*, some of these shows that I hadn't been allowed to stay up late enough to see. We moved right after first grade to Tokyo, where we didn't have a TV. I went for some years without one. I read a lot of books at the library, books that kids read, the Hardy Boys and books about baseball players, and elementary-level science fiction books and things like that.

I think I was about nine when I started reading more advanced books, *Huckleberry Finn* and *Tom Sawyer* and *Penrod*. And such like. I read a lot until—I don't know, there was a point in my fiction writing career, sometime in the last fifteen or twenty years maybe, when I didn't read that much fiction. I read Chekhov—the only fiction I read is stuff in translation. I like the sound of translated literature, I don't know why. I can't turn the critic off. I start wanting to correct the word order of the first sentence. It just gets in the way. So nowadays, I read a lot less than I watch TV. I think I'm one of those people who watches at least a couple hours of television a day. I watch sitcoms, the old sitcom reruns. They're like plays, like half-hour plays. The sets are usually very few and the characters are few and they depend on dialogue and characterization. And of course they're funny. So I spend a lot of time watching TV, and when I read, I read strange books, which I refer to as "research into nothing." It's hard to describe what they are—a lot of fourteenth-century, fifteenth-century German mystics—strange books, I would say.

So, overall, I think the answer is "maybe."

CD: Was there any reading along the way that made you turn a corner and suddenly see these books as writing rather than simply, say, an adventure story?

DJ: Yeah, when I was in high school I started to—well, even before that, with books like *Tom Sawyer*—I felt that here was something that expressed the dilemmas of being a human, a small American boy in any era. Same with *Penrod*. I gravitated toward books like that and I could see right away that made me feel less alone but confirmed my impressions about experience.

Later on there were books about adolescence. I think people still read *The Catcher in the Rye*. When my son was about fourteen, six or seven years ago, he picked it up and read it and was very moved by it. And I just felt that there was this thing that could happen. You could go to the library, you go to the shelf, some title catches your eye, you check it out, read it, and it makes you feel at home on the

earth. And I felt so grateful to these people. I was already claiming that I wanted to be a writer, because it was the only thing I could do at school that sort of mollified the authorities, or made me credible to them, anyway. So I thought, This is a worthy thing to do. I want to make a book on a library shelf that some kid will read and feel comforted by. That's not an uncommon experience, I think that there's a high percentage of us who get into writing because of that kind of experience.

CD: Are there certain writers who became literary influences or that you modeled yourself after?

DJ: Yes, thousands. I went through many phases. I'd say the first literary influence was Booth Tarkington, who wrote *Penrod*. That was the first one where I read it and thought, Somebody's got to write a book about me, and this guy is close, but it takes place in the early 1900s, so if somebody is going to write a book about me, it better be me. That was the first time I set out to write a novel, and I was nine or ten years old. I believed Penrod was writing a novel too. That's one of the things he was doing on his adventures. So I hid out and I wrote a novel, and it was very much like Penrod, only it was about me.

Actually, that pattern has continued ever since. One way or another, I'm imprinted by a lot of different authors. I think one of the books that really influenced me was *Fat City* by Leonard Gardner. He only wrote this one book. It's a novel about two boxers. The experiences and the circumstances of their lives are not at all like mine, but his attitudes toward these characters, the tender and matter-of-fact way he talked about them, made me want to write books. I felt that this is how I want to see the world, how I want to help others to see the world, and to see some of the more broken-up people in it. Man, I read that book a lot. My first published novel—it was called *Angels*—sounds to me like it was written by Leonard Gardner. It's not even an imitation; it's just a fact that his diction and impressions had imprinted themselves on me.

CD: *Fat City* is an amazing book, and I think I see it in *Angels* too. There's something in it—the people are so roughed up, but the prose is so—

DJ: Yeah, it tends to dignify them, by writing about their world as if it matters. It doesn't dismiss them. It's pretty generous toward them, without sentimentalizing them. But along the way, there have been many writers, and I also went through a Robert Stone period. There's a whole section of *Angels* that goes into Robert Stone country. Kind of late, like 1990, I discovered Cormac McCarthy, and I felt the next book I wrote I was trying to be like Cormac McCarthy.

Who else? I mean, there have been many. Isaac Babel is a big influence on me, and I think reading his short stories gave me permission to write the crazy sort of jumbled-up story you'll find in *Jesus' Son*. It's just lucky for me that I picked up a foreign writer to imitate, because I haven't been caught on that one. I hate to be busted on these things. In fact, sometimes people ask who is my favorite writer. When I am telling the truth, I say I am my favorite writer, because when I read something by me, I hear all these people, all my favorite writers, they're all in there, all in one thing.

CD: Just to extend that a little bit, what is the usefulness of influences for developing writers?

DJ: Well, I think it just gives you encouragement and grants you permission. That's the main thing it does. You go through a period when you begin to read technically, when you're at the end of the enjoyable part of your career as a reader. And then you're looking at how it's done. From our influences we get a deeper understanding of technique and ideas about tricks and strategies—simple prose strategies.

CD: Where does a work start for you? Is it something you hear? Do you have to hear the sound of the sentences?

DJ: It usually starts with the auditory. I do know where *Angels* started. I was on a Greyhound bus, and it was really late at night, and I heard a woman in the back abusing her child, and saying, "Move your foot. I'm tired now. Move your foot or I'm gonna have the bus driver stop the bus and we're going to put you off the bus in the dark and we're going to drive away."

I don't know—that just stuck with me for a long time. I kept thinking about that woman and eventually she became one of the main characters in a novel. I didn't really dislike her when I heard her talking—I could understand. It was late and, in fact, the kid was a nuisance to all of us! I wouldn't have minded a bit if she'd gone ahead and done it. I can vividly remember the very germ for *Angels*. You know, it took twelve years before the book was finished, and it went through many incarnations, but she was always there. It begins with a bus ride, with her saying that to her kid. That was always the beginning of the book. Other characters became prominent and began to take over in the book; I didn't know how to deal with them. It sort of went on for a long time. I also knew they would go to prison. There was quite a bit I was willing to do for research, but I wasn't willing to go to prison. But eventually a job opened up teaching in a prison and I practically held the interviewer committee hostage until they gave me the job so I could go see what prison life was like because I knew those guys were going to go there. That was when I was able to finish that book, actually.

CD: Twelve years?

DJ: Yeah, it took about twelve years. The first chapter was written when I was about twenty, and the last one was written when I was about thirty-three, so . . . thirty-three! That's like thirteen years!

CD: How in the world do you create structure in the midst of such amazing chaos?

DJ: Are you talking about a particular book?

CD: Well, I'm especially referring to *Jesus' Son*, but how does a story find its form?

DJ: During my early twenties I wrote quite a number of stories that weren't any good. I mean, I was operating in a fog. I did have a typewriter, a series of typewriters, and I did write, but nothing really ever held together. I didn't even save the stuff. And I wrote a novel, too, come to think of it. I didn't save that either, because it just wasn't working. When I began writing *Jesus' Son*, it was just anecdotes that I told people, things that happened to me when I should have been writing books, but I was just getting messed up instead. People would always say, "You should write that down, you should make that into a story!" And I'd always say, "Once you tell it, you can't make it into a story." I don't know who told me that. Maybe I told me that, and I believed it. But one day I went upstairs in my house in Massachusetts and I wrote four of these anecdotes down, or three and a half of them, say, and I really liked the voice. What I liked about it was the double voice. I was now thirty-five years old, but I was writing about stuff that happened when I was eighteen, nineteen, and so on. There was this kind of perspective of the older person getting caught up in the voice of the younger person.

I had written them very quickly, and there was no revision, and if I forgot something at the beginning, I would just say, "Well, what I forgot to say is . . ." I'd write it in and so on, something like that. But as to the form of the stories, I can actually answer you as a student of those stories. There was a period of some years when I gave readings and I had those stories to read, so I went through that book. And I would do four, five readings per year. I would just start at the beginning of the book and I would read a couple stories, and then at the next reading I'd read the next couple. I read that book out loud to audiences, several times, all the way through, and I began to see how they were operating. Most of these were anecdotes from my life, and then I began to borrow from other people's lives, and they were kind of interesting.

What was funny about the form of those stories was that to make it feel as if a statement had been made, or a story had been told, I would put a couple anecdotes together. So if you look at those tales, they often consist of two anecdotes put side by side, which created a suggestion that somehow they were related. There's a strange tension that's created by the fact they're really *not* related. It just gets strange.

I ran out of stuff from my own life pretty quickly and started borrowing from others, as I say. The story "Emergency" is based on the experience a friend of mine had at a hospital where we worked. I did not have this experience; I was not on the shift when this guy came in with a knife in his head. And I wrote that down, and it seemed fine. But that's all there was. There was no more to say. I moved to Idaho like three or four years after I'd written the first part of that story, and I had this cowboy friend and we went canoeing one day. And he was telling me all these stories, including one in which he and his friend were drinking and went driving around in their truck, and they ran over a rabbit. And the guy insisted that they open it up and eat it, and there were little bunnies inside. I went home and wrote that down, and the whole story came together from what this guy told me. Later, I showed him the story when it was in a magazine. I gave him the magazine. He was an avid reader—and he's never mentioned it to me. I said, "You should read this, it's your story." But he's never said anything about it one way or the other.

But that's just a case where something happened, and I waited, and another anecdote came along, and then they came together. And in fact, "anecdote" is a Greek term for unpublished piece. It's something that is not meant to be published. And I did not intend to publish these stories. I had seven of them before I showed them to anybody. At that point I was out of money and I gave them to my agent and he managed to sell them. I never thought anybody would ever see those; I thought they were too revealing. Eventually I just reached a point where I thought, Who cares what I reveal about me?

CD: Well, that brings me to a question that came from one of the workshops. When you draw on your experiences, how do you deal with friends and relatives that are part of that memory? The further part of that question is, what, if any, obligation do you feel toward them?

DJ: It's tricky—well, it's not tricky, you either do it or you don't—but the thinking about it can get complicated. Once you read a couple book reviews about your own work, and once you've seen one or two interviews in which the reporter is completely mistaken about what the hell you thought you said, you begin to see that there's no point caring about what is in print about you, particularly not when it's fictionalized. But people who haven't had this experience of seeing anything about themselves in print before will feel violated. They will feel that anything they see about themselves is an attempt to represent them, and that this attempt has been a callous failure, that there was no care taken in presenting their story properly as they remember it. I might be able to sit down with them and say, "Look, it's just a story, and it's not really about you, I just feel I happen to have a calling to write stories from all human experience, whether it's mine or not, and it's not really your experience, it's just filtered through my secondhand understanding of what it was" and so on, but they will feel violated. I have to respect that they feel violated, and at the same time I am aware that they are incorrect in believing that they have been violated—they really haven't. For myself, I just go ahead and do it. They have every right to say what they care to, and if they can persuade me that I shouldn't feel this way, then I'll retract everything I've ever written—I can't do anything else. But it is definitely an issue.

I will say that when it comes to revealing myself, I've stopped caring completely. In fact, now I'm way over on the other side. There's a Romanian sort of philosopher-aphorist named Emil Cioran, who wrote in French, and he says you should write only about those things that you would never confide in anyone. I think that's a great place to go. Another thing he says is, "A book is a postponed suicide." [laughter]

CD: Your new book, *Tree of Smoke*, is partially set in Vietnam during the Vietnam War. Were you in that war, or have you been to the country?

DJ: The book also takes place in the Philippines and Malaysia, places I've actually been. And in Honolulu and in Phoenix, Arizona, and a little bit in South Carolina. I was raised in the Philippines and Tokyo, and I've done a lot of traveling in Southeast Asia, but I've never been to Vietnam. I'll go there someday. I was not in the war. The only wars I've ever seen were in Africa and the Philippines and Afghanistan and places like that. But not Vietnam. I am a draft-dodging drug addict.

Vietnam was my era, and the war in Vietnam traumatized me in the way that it traumatized many of my generation who didn't go, but I wasn't there and I wasn't traumatized by the actual violence. The stuff I write about in this thing, most of the stuff in there, is like a lot of movies you see—they weren't filmed in Vietnam, they were filmed in the Philippines. And a lot of the book is based on my memories of other places in Southeast Asia. So that's a question too: To what extent am I appropriating the experience of other people who have been traumatized—veterans and so on? Yet I don't think it's that kind of book. It's not about what I did in the Vietnam War, but that issue has been of some concern. It has been troubling to me, to what extent I might be expropriating the very hard-won experiences of these people. To what extent do I have a right to do that? I'm not sure I have a right to do that. I just have a calling, as I've said. There's a difference.

CD: Are you doing additional research for *Tree of Smoke*?

DJ: Oh yeah, I have some books, stuff like that. I don't mean to seem cavalier about it. It's just that the things that will find their way into this novel are not going to be based on a broad understanding I develop for myself. They're going to be based on images that affect me from reading about that era and those places. I've been reading memoirs and oral histories of Vietcong guys and people who were in the war. The kind of research I'm interested in is what outfit would so-and-so be in if he were there. When did they leave, and why would he stay after they leave, and so on. It's very much a paper-thin illusion, the whole business. That means there's very little behind it in the way of actual—anything. It's words on paper.

CD: If you're a draft-dodging drug addict, why do you look so healthy?

DJ: I stopped everything in 1978, most everything. I had a little caffeine tonight.

CD: What are your vulnerabilities as a writer?

DJ: Vulnerability? What is my weakness, where do I wish I had more strength? I think I just don't have the breadth of experience that I wish I had in order to inform my work, and I don't have the vocabulary. I'm like the guy in Shakespeare's sonnet, desiring this man's gift and that man's scope. I haven't got the gift and I haven't got the scope. But I make do with what I have.

CD: You've been working on *Tree of Smoke* for something like twenty years. What's made it so slow a process?

DJ: It's not that I've been pondering over this thing for twenty-two years. I've written other books in between! But this is one that has not died. It's actually in some respects the sequel to *Angels*, because two of the brothers from *Angels* appear in this book. Some other characters from some other novels also appear in this book. So the world of the novel was kind of building, and I was just making notes, and I just kept getting interested in other projects. I generally have quite a few going at once. Every once in a while one takes off and I stick with it for a while. This was just one that didn't take off until about a year ago, and then I started really working on it.

CD: Are any of those other projects poetry?

DJ: I do write poetry in notebooks, in fragments. I haven't really finished anything. There are a couple fragments that kind of seem like poems. I think they are going to appear in—I can't remember the name of the magazine. A man is doing a critical piece on a few poets and he just asked me to give him something, so I am. But generally, no, I haven't been finishing any verse. I make these little notebooks with little fragments in them to give to friends, and I use a really nice pen—I have this MontBlanc pen that my wife, Sandy, gave me, and that's about it for my poetry. Although, I have written a verse play and I'm about three-quarters of the way through another verse play. The same kind of focus goes into it as any other verse I've written— the business of writing these plays is very much the same as writing a poem. It's not like writing prose. Playwriting is actually much more trancelike for me, except for the verse plays, which require a lot of attention to how the words are falling into place. The prose plays I've written—some of them—have come out really fast. When I wrote the second one, I had the flu, I had a fever, and I just kept hearing these voices and writing what they were saying. When I was done I had like one-third of it. I had other things that just came out like this too—I'd go to this one coffee shop in Austin and just make these notes. I kept hearing these people talk, and I wrote down the dialogue and I had another third of the play. Different characters. And there were some notes I had for something from a long time ago, and that became the final third of this thing. So I really had very little memory of writing it at all. It just kind of appeared one day.

There are three plays I've written, and the three of them together probably took me three weeks to write. And then I have these verse plays that took years. It varies.

CD: You spoke earlier about the books that imprinted you as a child. Do you want your work to do the same for other kids? Did your children read your books?

DJ: I want them to be over eighteen! My son read these books when he was about sixteen. I don't think my daughter has read any of them yet. She's saving herself. I've written one children's story for my goddaughter, and that was actually published in the *Paris Review*, and it

was called "Denis the Pirate." It's about my great-great-great grandfather, who, according to the story, was a pirate. Otherwise, I think
my stuff is for adults only. I hope kids don't go using the kind of language in my books around their parents.

CD: Earlier this evening you were participating in a little sing-along of
some Bob Dylan. Is he a big influence as well?

DJ: Well, it's mostly lines and fragments and things like that that stick
with me. The beginning of "Desolation Row": "They're selling post-
cards of the hanging / they're painting passports brown. / The beauty
parlor is filled with sailors, / the circus is in town." I love that opening. And that line—I think it's from "Stuck Inside of Mobile with
the Memphis Blues Again"—"Now the rainman gave me two cures,
/ then he said, 'Jump right in.' / The one was Texas medicine, / the
other was just railroad gin. / An' like a fool I mixed them, / an' it
strangled up my mind, / an' now people just get uglier / an' I have no
sense of time."

But there are so many, and he was really a great influence on me.
I think he is a great poet, but he's not exactly a versifier, you know.
His work I would call literature rather than poetry—it's very key, I
think.

CD: Can you tell us more about the novel and how it's progressed over
the course of twenty years? How about the title?

DJ: The book has changed. What I read from tonight is just one chapter; there are also chapters about two boys from Phoenix who are in
the military. One's in the navy and one's in the infantry. It's basically
about them drinking a lot and trying to have their first sexual experiences and pretty much the stuff that I've always written. For a while
the novel was called "The Years," for five or six years. Recently of
course it's been called *Tree of Smoke*. That comes partly from the Bible;
there's literally this pillar of smoke, this palm tree of smoke. Same
with "pillar of fire."

I met this religious painter by the name of Norbert Cox who has done, among other things, a fifty-three-foot painting of the Bible. He's one of these primitive guys. He was the one who told me about the phrase "tree of smoke," which is a very important phrase in the Bible. Then later on I heard this verse from the Bible in a song called "Angelina" by Bob Dylan. And it says, "Beat a path of resistance up those spiral staircases, / past the tree of smoke, past the angel with four faces, / crying out to God and praying in unholy places." Wait— "begging God for mercy and *weeping* in unholy places." These are all the sort of contexts in which this phrase occurs. It means something in the book, too, something entirely different.

A CONVERSATION WITH
KEN KESEY

Carla Perry

Ken Kesey, cultural and literary icon, was the author of the novels *One Flew over the Cuckoo's Nest* (1962) and *Sometimes a Great Notion* (1964), as well as children's books, screenplays, articles, and several other novels. Born September 17, 1935, he grew up in Springfield, Oregon. He graduated from the University of Oregon with a degree in speech and communications and received a Woodrow Wilson National Fellowship to enroll in the creative writing program at Stanford. During his college years, he volunteered at a Veterans Administration hospital in an experimental program involving mind-altering drugs.

Kesey's homegrown parties evolved into 1960s San Francisco Day-Glo "happenings" and "acid tests" with light shows, body painting, exotic costumes, strobe lights, Eastern mysticism, sexual mayhem, and, eventually, a hookup with Jerry Garcia's band the Grateful Dead. In the summer of 1964, Kesey purchased a 1939 school bus, painted it psychedelic colors, and took the Merry Prankster crew on a road trip to New York. Neal Cassady (made famous as Dean Moriarty in Jack Kerouac's *On the Road*) was the driver.

Later, Kesey wrote, directed, and performed plays, including *Where's Merlin?* (which toured England for the 1999 solar eclipse) and *Twister: A Ritual Reality in Three Quarters Plus Overtime if Necessary*. Kesey was awarded the C. E. S. Wood Distinguished Writer Award honoring his lifetime achievements at the Oregon Book Awards ceremony in November 1999.

In January 2000, I was in Pleasant Hill, Oregon, at Kesey's office. Kesey had agreed to do a "Thing" at the Nye Beach Writers' Series in Newport, on the Oregon coast. As coordinator of the series, I was given the enviable task of obtaining updated personal information.

I asked Kesey questions about his philosophy of benevolence, attention, and love. I asked him about writing as drama, novels as performance, books as money, and videos of the future.

Carla Perry: I noticed the concept of "benevolence" when others have written about you, such as Tom Wolfe in *The Electric Kool-Aid Acid Test*. You could have been the top of the power structure, the head of it all, the guru. Instead, when you initiated all that hoopla, created the psychedelic "happenings," the acid-test musical extravaganzas, the on-the-road escapades, you would step back to let others flow with the scene. You seemed to love the crowds, but you would inconspicuously cruise, keeping your eyes open, keeping things on track. When there was trouble, you were the peacemaker. You would step in and round up everyone else to pay attention to the trouble, which would solve the problem. When a person was having a bad moment on a drug trip, attention would be focused on that person. The attention would translate to love as it was received, and the person would eventually be all right.

Ken Kesey: There's a line in the *I Ching* that says, "The best way to fight evil is to make energetic progress in the good." I've pretty much lived by that. The idea was to go against something wrong by getting involved with it. We used to say we were Christ-driven, Jesus-driven, and would deliberately give someone all our attention and then just lie back and imagine what would Christ do in these kinds of circumstances. It's harder now to do than when we first started doing this thirty years ago because there are more things that it is easy to get angry at.

CP: Would you mind talking about the death penalty, since you brought that up in an earlier talk?

KK: Most of the people in favor of the death penalty consider themselves Christians. A lot of them go to church and that's where they get their religious energy. And the death penalty goes counter to their deepest beliefs. Anybody who has followed the death penalty, they know it doesn't help. It doesn't help in fighting crime. There are many things that could be done that would be a whole lot more beneficial. And everybody pretty much knows that. But when it comes down to a battle, the right wing is so ready to battle and the left wing is so ready to give in that you're stalemated there. There's always more solutions than people think.

When we were bombing Bosnia, it was as though there were only two choices: we either bombed them or we didn't. If you were creative, my idea is, you could have gone to one of those military camps with a fire-fighting airplane that carries liquid, fill it full of urine, and drop it on Belgrade. It would have just had a hell of an effect. It wouldn't hurt anybody, but it would put them down a set. Because we had pissed on them. That kind of creativity is hard to come up with in the heat of a battle. For us to be warriors now it takes a whole lot more creativity than it used to.

CP: Let's talk about the flip side. Let's talk about your idea of benevolence for a minute. How did you get this idea? Does it tie in with being ignored early in life, like the character of Chief Broom in *Cuckoo's Nest*? Were you born believing in the goodness of people?

KK: I got the idea of believing in the goodness of people because I come from a really good family. The whole group of us did. Strong, middle-class families. We had some very good teachers in high school and college. And after school, we had teachers like Neal Cassady and Kerouac, Ginsberg, Burroughs. So we were well schooled. As time goes by, I feel more and more gratitude to those people. I'm reading the Kerouac letters now, the second bunch, from 1957 through 1969. They get pretty depressing because he's a drunk and beginning to get a little bitter and feels put-upon by all these people and you kind of wish you could go back in time and put your arm around him and give him a big hug and say, "Hey, you were more beneficial than you'll ever know." That whole group of people was there to hand the fire on to us and we're handing it on to our kids and our grandkids as best we can.

Ginsberg was the best at doing this, at being benevolent. Always sweet. "Happy little Allen," Cassady used to call him.

Then there's another thing. We've had spiritual help. You look back at stuff and you think, Boy, that's a far-out coincidence. But it must have been right, because there it is. The first time I was over there at the Newport Aquarium, this woman came up and said, "Hi, do you remember me?" She was sixty-something. I said, "Kind of." She says, "Lois Learned. You know, Nurse Ratched." I said, "Oh my God!"

CP: The real woman?

KK: The real woman was there and she is a volunteer. She helps at the aquarium. I was absolutely dumbfounded. I was completely tongue-tied. She said, "Oh no, don't worry about it. You did the nursing profession a great service. Nobody wants to be like that." You talk about synchronicity. Going there to the Newport Aquarium and running into Big Nurse. You can't help but think, Oh boy, there's some little leprechauns in heaven working this out right now!

Coincidence is an element of mystery because it happens so many times. It's best if you just quit arguing with it. It's more than serendipity. It's more than coincidence. There's a sense of intelligence to it. This isn't just random magic; this is magic for our benefit. Things are arranged with a red line drawn under it saying, *Pay Attention To This*.

CP: I believe in magic, in elves, in spirits. I believe in the synchronicity of life. If we're doing things with a true heart and if we're on our right path, then the cogs fit in. I believe in your concept of the "creative warrior." And I'm interested in your concept of paying attention because it seems to me that if we don't pay attention we have a direct route to discord. It seems as though it's the children who fall apart when their parents don't pay attention. Children don't do well in school if teachers don't pay attention. We've stopped paying attention to children.

KK: Everybody is still paying attention. The kids are paying attention. But they're paying attention to the wrong thing. They're paying attention to the loudest noise. If you're a kid of three or four and your parents are paying attention to television all the time, and you get in front of the television just when there's a gun battle going on, the parents will say, "Get out of the way!" The kid is going to say, "Look, what do I have to do to get attention?" And what he does is he goes out and gets a gun, and that's the quickest way in the world to get people's attention. I think it's going to be a good long while before we get over television and the gun shows. The Wild West attitude. Let's kill all the buffalo because we're white. But we have to get over that attitude or we won't survive as a nation. We'll tear each other to pieces.

CP: You've been doing it on a very personal level, though, always.

KK: That's where your heart is.

CP: You've said you were more interested in helping warriors know more about their task than you were interested in trying to titillate with stories. And you said that you've got to write a novel every so often to make people pay attention to the other stuff you're doing. How do you see your role as writer?

KK: I think a writer owes the reader a new way of telling a story, using a technique that doesn't normally show up in a novel. What I'm interested in is mystery itself. Mystery in life, in literature. Not the solution. As soon as you get the solution, it's like, "Well, we've done that. What are we going to do next?" If each mystery leads you to another mystery, that becomes exciting and promotes magic in your mind.

CP: How does this concept of "mystery" relate to literary craft?

KK: I've never liked the mystery as a form—mystery novels or mystery movies—because the whole action goes toward trying to solve the mystery. I've always objected to them teaching *Cuckoo's Nest*, because it's an easy book. It doesn't need any teaching. *Sometimes a Great Notion* needs a whole lot more teaching. There's more stuff going on. The best part of that book was, as I was writing it, I knew I was dealing with a new form, like plowing new ground. When you break new ground with your plow, up from the ground wells this moist spontaneous feeling of Oh! This is new ground! That moment itself offers you energy, even if the writing is not any good. I'm a terrible plower, but I do like the smell of breaking new ground.

CP: The literature scene has changed from what it was back in the sixties because of computers, because of Web pages, because people are supposedly not reading as many books. What is your impression?

KK: I think people are reading a lot of books. These big places, like Borders, they say there's more people reading than ever before. *What* they're reading is another matter. Teachers may be teaching kids how to read, but they're not teaching them what to read. Not many kids get the guidance to read *Paradise Lost*, for instance. That book is out there and there's nothing else like it. And no kid is ever going to read it unless they're forced to. That's the job of the English teachers: to say, "Read this!"

CP: You've said it's important for writers to get out there on the road and read their stuff to an audience. How does performance fit into this?

KK: Performance is what I'm paying attention to right now. My work in the last five years or so has been centered around performance. I can do the kids' books now by heart; I don't have to hold the book and read. When we went to England we had this little play called *Where's Merlin?* It's a simple little thing. The main message is that you can take a bunch of people with no talent and put them all on the stage and kind of survive. Because the audience is then brought into it. The performances end up with the audience onstage, dancing and singing. That's the gear we want to promote.

Here's an example of performance and synchronicity. When we were in England, I learned what a "Thing" is. I'd been reading about it before we got over there, like in *Prince Valiant*, you talk about the All Thing. And the word Thing, apparently, is a Finnish word to start with. And it means the center of something. And while we were there in Cornwall, we went to visit one of these Things, which is a big circle of rocks with a big rock right in the middle.

While we were there, after going to this ceremony in which King Arthur presided and the archbishop of the Druids knighted us, we got back to the motel and a guy came out to look at the bus. A young guy, maybe twenty-five or twenty-eight. He asked about the bus and we talked to him a little bit and he said, "Oh, I love my circle!" We said, "What do you mean?" He said, "I'll show you," and he began to flick through the pictures in his little digital camera. And the pictures were of him and two of his friends getting a truck with a great big rock in it, a big stone, and dragging it out into a pasture and sitting it upright in the middle of this pasture during the total eclipse of the sun. The stone weighed ten tons.

As I looked at those pictures all I could think of was, Here's a very ancient thing going on. Cornishmen dragging a rock and sitting it somewhere. And we're seeing it through a digital camera. So, we're seeing the Thing now with one of the most recent of inventions and we're seeing probably the most ancient of rituals through it. And that's wonderful.

I see performance as a Thing. Performance is a form of publication. Performance is when you go public. And publication of literature is the point. When we go over on the coast to Newport in April to do a Thing in front of the public, that's publication. When we're doing e-mail on our Web site, that's publication.

CP: How does the Internet fit into this?

KK: A lot of writers think they have to be published by New York, just like a lot of people who make movies think they have to go to LA. But all of that is changing, very fast, with e-mail, with our ability to contact people outside the old New York literary establishment. Or the LA movie establishment. And they are a little afraid of it.

CP: They're afraid of what?

KK: They're afraid of us. The Internet is the new campfire we have to gather an audience around. To really get an audience, to keep the reader's attention on the Web site, you've got to have a different kind of prose. You can't meander around. In fact, when we go to the Web site, if it's more than one page, I usually delete it. This form is so new, and so exciting, that to not take literature onto the Internet is deliberately avoiding something. It's possible right now for me to write a novel and put little pieces up on the Internet day by day. So, it would be a page, maybe four pages. I would key it in. You'd get up in the morning and there it would be.

It means I just send the message electronically and the consumer does his own printing, on the equipment he has. We have that capability right now. Everywhere. What that means is I'm not having to move that paper back and forth across the United States. Paper is heavy. Anybody who works with books knows that books are heavy as hell.

We have the capability right here to contact anybody in the world. The Internet will make the business of books so much more competitive. What I'm speaking is blasphemy in New York. We've got the talent, we've got the energy, we just haven't quite figured out how to hook that together with money. Blasphemers, unfortunately, don't get any money.

CP: Haven't you made a fortune from your books?

KK: Quite the opposite. I've never had a best-seller. That's one of those things that's a mystery to me. We're as nonprofit as you can get. I would love to be a profit-making organization. It's not out of benevolence that we are poor. Gurdjieff said that enlightened people aren't meant to be poor. Our poorness is out of ineptitude. People ask us, "Why did you do it that way?" We always say, "We're cyber-hicks! We're inept!"

An old lawyer friend called up and said that he'd seen they were having a new opening for the play *Cuckoo's Nest* in Paris and that I should be prepared to have a lot of money coming in. But we don't get any money from that. I don't get a penny from that.

CP: How can that be? Who gets that money?

KK: When I was twenty-five or so, I signed this thing for twenty grand and it went to Kirk Douglas and this guy Dale Wasserman who get money from that. It's one of those things that if you dwelt on it, you'd have to bite your tongue.

CP: Okay. Then let's not go there.

KK: Right. Let's not go there.

CP: Why don't you just ask for money from unexpected sources? I found that worked for me.

KK: How did you do that?

CP: I wrote those words down on a piece of paper. I was already working as hard as I could; I didn't need more work, I needed more money. The usual sources weren't doing the trick. So I wrote down,

"I need money from unexpected sources. Substantial money. Enough money to make a difference."

KK: And money started coming in?

CP: Yes. After a lifetime of scraping by. It came right away. Within a month.

KK: Maybe we should put that up on the Web site . . .

CP: So, Ken, what are you writing now?

KK: I've been working for some time on what I call the Jail Journal. The full title is *Cut the Motherfuckers Loose* but "Motherfuckers" is with asterisks from M all the way to s so people understand it. *Cut the M***********s Loose.* The book is about my stay in jail for six months. I've got stuff from 1954 on—extensive journals—but I don't know what to do with them now. I think eventually I'll get them over to the University of Oregon. Next door to this office is where all the archives are. All the tapes, all the film. Piles and piles and piles of stuff; this detritus of rotting minds.

CP: Do you have a thought to leave us with?

KK: My dad told me a great thing: You never outgrow your need for compliments. And every writer needs to be stroked a little bit. It keeps us writing.

Ken Kesey died after cancer surgery on November 10, 2001, but his Web site lives on at www.intrepidtrips.com.

A CONVERSATION WITH
TRACY KIDDER

Win McCormack

Tracy Kidder was born in New York City and grew up in Oyster Bay, Long Island, the son of a New York City lawyer father and suburban schoolteacher mother. Following college at Harvard he served in the U.S. Army, including a year's stint in Vietnam as an intelligence officer, after which he returned home to attend the Iowa Writers' Workshop. Kidder's professional writing career began as an inhouse freelancer for the *Atlantic Monthly*, working under the tutelage of Richard Todd, who remains his editor to this day. An assignment from the *Atlantic* to cover the trial of Juan Corona, accused of murdering migrant farm workers in northern California, led to his first book, *The Road to Yuba City*, published in 1974.

In 1981 Kidder made his name with the publication of *The Soul of a New Machine*. The book narrates the frenzied creation of a super minicomputer by an obsessively driven team of engineers at Data

General in western Massachusetts in the late 1970s. It won the Pulitzer Prize and put Kidder and his family on a sound financial footing for the first time. There followed *House* (1985), an often painful tale of the construction of a couple's residence that is also a subtle examination of social class in America; *Among Schoolchildren* (1989), an exhaustive account of the workaday performance of a harried schoolteacher over the course of an entire academic year; *Old Friends* (1993), a warmhearted depiction of friendship between men nearing the end of their lives in a nursing home; and *Home Town* (1999), a narrative exploration of the town of Northampton, Massachusetts. *Mountains Beyond Mountains* (2003) focuses on Paul Farmer, an American physician who has almost single-handedly pioneered effective healthcare delivery to the poor in Haiti and throughout the world, and *My Detachment: A Memoir* (2005) recounts Kidder's posting in Vietnam.

Among his friends and colleagues, Kidder is legendary for his prodigious level of work on both the research and craftsmanship ends of nonfiction writing. "When I have put in a really hard day of work," he once memorably stated, "I feel my Puritan ancestors think well of me." One June, I made a two-and-a-half-hour drive north through New Hampshire and along a section of the sparkling Maine coast to my friend's summerhouse overlooking a saltwater cove. The following is the result of a conversation during a long evening, over more than one bottle of good red wine, in front of a fire kindled and stoked to warm the chill early summer Maine night.

Win McCormack: When did you first start thinking you wanted to be a writer?

Tracy Kidder: You know, when one is in college one tries to identify oneself as something and while I was at Harvard I took a creative writing course. Though I only took the course in the first place because I thought writing was going to be sort of a hobby. I was going to be a diplomat. Save the world from terrible things that one had read about in *The Ugly American*.

Some of the girls liked the stories I wrote, and it occurred to me that writing stories was a way to impress girls. Honestly. And actually, when I look back, I can't think of a much stronger motivation for becoming a writer. Also, at that time, it seemed like a very romantic thing to do. A writer. It was something to call myself.

WM: You studied with Robert Fitzgerald, the legendary Boylston Professor of Rhetoric and Oratory?

TK: Yes. He was a pretty good poet in his own right, and a really a wonderful translator of the classics. Also a wonderful teacher. He really paid attention to you. He cared enough to be mean, too. Well, not mean but stern. Demanding. It was a great compliment to a student. He made writing seem important. He would read stuff to us that friends of his had written, people like James Agee and Flannery O'Connor. The first time I took his course, I would stay up all night writing stories for him, then go to sleep about the time my other classes began. He made me think it was a high calling. I took his course three or four times. I performed best the first time. After that I got self-conscious. I started a novel at one point and I made all these notes and drawings in the margins, which were much more interesting and better written than anything in the actual novel. I left that stuff in, imagining my biographer's delight in finding them.

WM: You started out in the Government Department at Harvard and switched your field of concentration to English at almost the last possible minute, late in the spring term of sophomore year—because of Henry Kissinger.

TK: Yes.

WM: You and I have somewhat different recollections of how it happened. Mine is that we were both taking Kissinger's course in international relations—Government 180—that semester, the spring of 1965 . . .

TK: Right so far.

WM: And it was conducted in a lecture hall that had very bad acoustics. And Kissinger used to pace back and forth, projecting his voice.

TK: It was a little stage.

WM: Yes. He would pace back and forth on that stage, projecting his voice into the wings. On top of this, he had that extreme German accent. You often couldn't understand at all what he was saying. On this one particular day, as I remember it, we were sitting in the very back row. He was lecturing about some obscure diplomatic event from another century, perhaps the Schleswig-Holstein controversy, whatever that was. All of a sudden, you jumped up and said, "I've had enough of this! I'm switching to English!" And you went right to the English Department and changed your major.

TK: The way I remember it is that it had gotten to the point where I wasn't often going to that class, and my recollection is you had said, "You should come this time because Kissinger is going to defend the Vietnam War. He's going to have a debate about it with his teaching assistants. You should come because it is going to be an interesting argument." And it was in the middle of that argument when I decided to walk out. Actually, this is how I've written about it in the memoir about Vietnam. I didn't stay to hear the argument get finished. And I've written something like, "One should always stay at least that long."

WM: Norman Mailer has said that by the time he graduated from Harvard, because of the excellent writing courses he took there and the feedback he got, he already had the conviction that he could be a successful writer. Did you?

TK: No, I didn't know that. I wasn't that sure of myself, to tell you the truth. One of the things that happened to me was that I had gotten so self-conscious that not a lot of ideas and stories were coming to me. I felt desperate about it because I had been walking around telling myself, and everybody who would listen, that I was a writer, but I didn't know what I was going to write about.

WM: Then you went to Vietnam.

TK: Yes, but I wasn't in combat, so I came back without those stories to tell. I wrote a novel anyway, about the experiences that I didn't have in Vietnam, which I thought I had destroyed, but then a copy surfaced a few years ago and I have kept it carefully hidden since then. In fact, I've begun my memoir with it. For me, it's an interesting record of self-deceit.

WM: But Vietnam has remained a subject for you.

TK: I wrote a couple of short stories about Vietnam. One was called "The Death of Major Great," and the other was originally called "The Island of Flatdicks," but when the *Atlantic* agreed to publish it, they felt they had to change the title. I'm still surprised they published it. It was later called "In Quarantine." The story was based on one of those myths that apparently is common to almost every war: that if you contract an incurable venereal disease they'll send you to an island and you'll never get to go home. You know, these are stories that you half believe because you know that "they," the great amorphous "they," are capable of almost anything. I invented a venereal disease called "longitudinal herpes." It was characterized by a miniaturization and shortening of the reproductive organ in the male. Later I did a nonfiction story about Vietnam combat veterans in 1978, about ten years after I had gotten back. I went around and found people who'd had the experiences I had not had. It was published as a cover story in the *Atlantic*. It was just such a shame what had been done to these guys. This was a very small group of veterans. There was lots of money going to veterans, but these were the ones who needed it the most. They were by far the most screwed up and screwed over and they weren't getting what they deserved. Guys with missing limbs and paraplegics being put in rat-infested VA hospitals in the Bronx. Stuff like that. It was awful.

WM: You are now addressing Vietnam in a memoir?

TK: I'm writing this memoir, but I actually don't much like memoirs. There was a memoir craze and I suppose it's dying now a little bit. But you can see why it's so attractive to people—they don't really have to go and do any work. I thought for a while that people ought to have licenses, you know, to have to be issued licenses to write memoirs. And one of the preconditions for getting a license would be to have done something in your life besides having written this stupid memoir.

WM: How and why did you switch from writing fiction to journalism and what is sometimes called "creative nonfiction"?

TK: After Vietnam, I went to the Iowa Writers' Workshop to write fiction. Robert Fitzgerald got me in. I went there on the strength of that dreadful novel I wrote. And I got really intimidated. There were some really high-powered, wonderful writers there. They ranged from Stuart Dybek to Ron Hansen, Allan Gurganus, Michael Ryan, Thom Jones. Jane Smiley was there too.

WM: And Raymond Carver?

TK: Ray Carver was teaching there, as was John Cheever. I remember both of them pretty fondly. Carver was still in his wild-man phase. He had a blue Ford Falcon and it had an aneurysm in one of its tires. I remember great big Ray Carver and little John Cheever sitting outside the Iowa State liquor store in that car, each with his bottle in a brown paper bag, sitting in the front seat drinking away.

Anyway, the other students were high-powered and it was sort of intimidating. There was a man there named Seymour Krim who was an interesting man; he was sort of a beatnik, in the 1970s, a beatnik. He really knew and had lived through a whole period of wonderful jazz in New York City. He was proselytizing something that was then called the "New Journalism," which of course wasn't particularly new. But he was proselytizing that and I sort of thought, Well, this is something I ought to try my hand at.

WM: There is a lot of discussion these days about the overlap of fiction and nonfiction.

TK: If what you're really interested in is telling stories it doesn't much matter whether they're factually true or not. I mean, the techniques of storytelling don't belong exclusively to fiction any more than they do to nonfiction. There are different imperatives. Different rules. Mostly you lay them down for yourself. If I had to make a list of really interesting books I've read, Mailer's *The Executioner's Song* would be on it for sure. It's a mix of fiction and nonfiction. He carefully labels the parts that he invented. I don't mind that at all, if you ticket it, label it.

WM: At that time did you buy into Tom Wolfe's thesis that the New Journalism was going to supercede the novel as an art form?

TK: I couldn't buy into that. I love novels. Tom Wolfe is to me a very entertaining writer, sometimes really good, but like all the pronouncements of writers, that's just utterly stupid. Wolfe in his worst nonfiction believes that there's only one thing that motivates human beings and that's the quest for status. And anybody who's done any thinking about what drives people knows that there's never just one motivation.

WM: Well, that's the motivation that drives him. He's confusing himself with the rest of the world.

TK: That's a problem that writers have, I think. But I don't know why one has to talk about one form replacing another form. I think we ought to be glad we have them all.

WM: I have in front of me here a *New York Times* review of your second book, the book that made you famous, *The Soul of a New Machine*. The reviewer compares contemporary fiction very unfavorably to what you accomplished in that book. He says the contrast with the narcissism of most contemporary fiction is striking.

TK: Well, look, when people are saying things like that in order to praise you, of course it sounds much more intelligent than when they're criticizing you. There's a lot of really bad fiction, some of which gets praised. And there's some really bad nonfiction that gets praised. It all gets sorted out in the end. I do think that one of the problems for people who are writing fiction sometimes is a lack of experience in the world. I didn't have all that interesting a life, you know, compared to a writer like my dear friend Stuart Dybek who could mine his childhood endlessly because it was so bizarre. One of the most important things somebody ever said to me, I mean, in just directing my little life, putting it on a certain course, was a wonderful writer who isn't all that well known named Sam Toperoff, who, when I was young and just back from Vietnam, was really encouraging me and was extremely kind. He said in an offhand way, "You know the world, particularly this country right now, is so strange and interesting." He said, "If I was a young man, I'd go off and get a job at *Time* or *Newsweek*."

WM: To give him his due, that's exactly what Wolfe accused the contemporary novel of doing in the sixties, of abandoning the strangeness of America for abstract modernism. He said there's so much interesting stuff going on and the only people covering it creatively are us New Journalists.

TK: I think there's some truth in that. Although, there's no reason to dismiss all of the novels and stories from that period that have appeared. I don't think Raymond Carver, for instance, ever abandoned the strangeness of America. He got right into a whole piece of it and he provided extraordinary immediacy. Any person who aspires to be a good writer could learn an enormous amount from Raymond Carver. However, if you do choose to go down the road of narrative nonfiction, one of the cool things about it is you get to satisfy your idle curiosity about things. You get to go out and see and meet really strange and interesting people. If what you're interested in is story, then of course you're interested in people because, at least in my view, character is the engine of plot. I think there are people who automatically assume that if it's not fiction then it can't have anything artistic about. But the craft of writing narrative is not confined simply to fiction.

WM: That same reviewer called *The Soul of a New Machine* "a journalistic report that is also a work of the imagination." Are your books works of the imagination?

TK: Yeah, yeah. It's just that I don't invent dialogue, I don't invent the characters, I don't invent the settings. But yeah, they are. Of course, they have to be. Look, any kind of writer, anybody who has ever tried to write a story, a historian or anyone, who has tried to do it well with economy and to bring people to life on a page, making voices palpable, putting them in a scene, all those things, and has gone a little bit beyond the banal or at least has imagined his way beyond it, knows that of course all narrative writing is an act of imagination.

WM: You mentioned before that writers set themselves rules. Do you have rules you set for yourself?

TK: There are rules that I set for myself—I know I make mistakes and I'm sure I'm committing them all the time—but I try not to tell a story in which people say anything that they didn't in fact say. I try to catch that reflection of a real live human being on the page. I know that to the people I've written about it's often like looking in a funhouse mirror. If you're writing nonfiction you're always dealing with more information than you can present. For most of the projects I've done, I've filled more than a hundred notebooks, gathered tons and tons of stuff, and I've had to make some order out of that chaos. I try to make it the story that I think I saw. I try to. John McPhee has a good line. I can't quote it exactly. He says you shouldn't abridge the accuracy of what you're reporting, because that accuracy is what allows you to tell stories that would be banal in fiction. What you really don't ever want to do to your reader—and I'm afraid it's almost impossible to prevent this—you never want to break the deal you have with readers. That's when they stop believing you. That's where I stop reading, generally—when I don't believe it.

WM: Does that injunction hold true for fiction as well, to not let the reader down?

TK: That injunction of course extends to fiction and poetry, to Coleridge's famous line: "that willing suspension of disbelief for the moment which constitutes poetic faith." In fiction it has nothing to do with factuality, it has nothing even to do with plausibility, necessarily. But there's some kind of deal that one strikes with the reader. Dybek does this marvelously well in some of his more bizarre stories. He sets out the terms of the deal right at the start and he doesn't break them. He doesn't violate them along the way. I think an enormous amount of care goes into that. When Mary McCarthy said that everything Lillian Hellman wrote was a lie, even "and" and "the," I knew exactly what she meant. I rather like Lillian Hellman, but I know exactly what Mary McCarthy meant. Of course some books of narrative nonfiction attempt at least to be works of the imagination. Not in the same sense as a novel, but then I wonder how many really good novels have ever been invented out of whole cloth.

WM: How big an influence was McPhee on you?

TK: I was forbidden to read him for a long time by my editor, Richard Todd. I think he said it was time for me to stop trying to imitate him. So he was a big influence on me. When I first read him, a friend handed me *Encounters with the Archdruid*. I had never heard of McPhee. I stole it from my friend. I was really smitten with the prose.

WM: Richard Todd has been your editor for a long time. Almost since the inception of your career. If I recall correctly, he gave you the idea for *The Soul of a New Machine*.

TK: Yes. What happened is, I had written a really bad work of nonfiction called *The Road to Yuba City*. Really bad work. I've gotten the rights back and have kept it out of print. I'm not sorry I wrote it. It's not that. I did my best. It's naïve. It's stupid in many ways. I'm glad it's out of print. But Todd helped me after that. Todd really taught me how to write, to the extent that I know how to write. It's not that

I came to him without an ability to write a sentence, but I just glommed on to him. It's interesting, his wife once said of him that he's willing to work as hard as the writer is. And he is. It's amazing. I had so much to learn about writing magazine articles, which I did with the *Atlantic*. I didn't dare attempt another book after that one for about five years anyway. Five or six years. Then I had come to the end of another article. I think it was the article about Vietnam combat veterans. I was starting to feel like I knew what I was doing. I started to feel like I had a voice writing nonfiction. It wasn't the voice necessarily of the person I thought that I was, but the voice of a person I thought I wanted to be. So I felt much more confident. And I said to Todd, "What should I do next?" He said, "Why don't you look into computers?" This was 1978 and I just laughed. He said there were things called minicomputers. That made me really laugh. He knew this fellow Tom West, who became the main character in the book, and I went to see him. I trust Todd completely. He has a really good eye for cant. He's writing a book of his own now. I told him he should let me edit it, and he just stared at me.

WM: What makes him a good editor?

TK: One of the most important things is, particularly for constitutionally insecure people, he never makes you feel like you personally, deep down, are guilty of these crimes against the language. I think there's a kind of objectivity that he cultivates. You can sit and laugh about stuff that didn't work. He doesn't make you feel like you are necessarily a bad writer because you just wrote some really bad prose. Unfortunately, I've overused him. Poor guy. I've given him drafts of things and he'll always say, "It's fine, keep going." Then you get to the end and you wonder what it could have been that he thought was fine. He's very even, and part of it is simply trusting that he will know when the thing is finished. You could go on writing something or reporting something forever.

WM: How do you know when to stop researching? How do you know when to stop writing? Hemingway was accused of having made factual errors in *Death in the Afternoon*, his book about bullfighting. His response was something like, "I probably did but if I'd kept on researching till I knew every single thing there is to know about bullfighting I never would've gotten around to writing the book."

TK: I think that's true. Part of it is exhaustion. But I have leaned on Richard Todd for that. Saying, Does this matter? Does that matter? There is all kinds of research you can do on a person's life and that could also be endless.

WM: In many reviews, you're credited with being able to distill complex technical information in such a way that the reader can understand it. You can make a computer's workings or the intricacies of building a house comprehensible.

TK: But this isn't really a compliment to me. I had wonderful people helping me. That's also one of the reasons why this vein of writing is so much fun to do: With *House* I got to go and see architectural historians, people who are historians of the nail, for instance, and it was really fun. I really got into it. With *The Soul of a New Machine* I had very good instructors. I had these engineers who were willing, and I think actually eager, to explain their jobs to me. It wasn't all that hard. I was never any good at math and I avoided science in college, and I always felt that as a consequence a huge part of what makes up the modern world was simply closed to me. What a stupid way to be. So it was fun to be around people who did speak that language, the language of mathematics, and have them interpret it for me. I began to think, and this is no doubt a kind of special pleading, that the ones who could explain it to the likes of me were usually the ones who really understood it. And I'm glad to do that, to make those translations. I'm glad that people feel that I've done that well. It's nowhere near as hard as trying to find that mysterious combination of things that makes a human being seem alive on the pages of a book. One is just work. Just trying to find a way to explain something. It's complicated, but a human being is something else. I've been reading a lot of Graham Greene. One of the things that astonishes me about him is that he can depict people, sometimes, without describing them at all, and yet make them completely vivid. I don't know quite how he does it. It's alchemy, you know? I think that's an important thing. When I wrote *The Soul of a New Machine*, I really thought of that computer that they were making—which is, by the way, an infantile computer now, an outmoded sort of thing—I thought of that computer as the intellectual setting, the real setting of that book.

WM: If you look at the body of your work as a whole, what jumps out for me is that you've almost always chosen to write about work, about people in their jobs, which is a subject largely missing from modern fiction and even nonfiction.

TK: There was a guy at Harvard who taught a creative writing course, named Morrison, who kept telling undergraduate writers, "Try and write about a job you've had. Something you've done." I think that may have stuck with me. Work is where people spend so much of their lives.

WM: So did you do that consciously? Choose work as the subject of all or almost all your books?

TK: To some degree. When I began what became *House*, I wanted to write about carpenters. I had gotten really interested in carpentry personally. I had bought an old house and was trying to fix it up. I cut my thumb half off, literally. Took a few awful falls off ladders. I decided I really wanted to write about the craft of building houses. I wanted to write about craftsmanship. I thought that I was writing about craftsmanship when I wrote *The Soul of a New Machine*, what opportunities were left in an advanced industrial country like the United States for people to practice meaningful work, the kind of work that allows them to use their minds, in basically an industrial setting. That preoccupation carried over into the next book, *House*. Then in *Among Schoolchildren* I wrote about a schoolteacher, and then in *Old Friends* about a group of men going into a nursing home. Trying to make some kind of life in such a place, that's another kind of work, you know?

WM: That book would seem to be the departure from the pattern.

TK: No, not really. Because they weren't at their place of work, but they were at a place of wishing to work. Sometimes I think that the whole business of choosing what to write about has to do with that stupid joke about the bum who searches for the lost quarter not where he lost it but under the streetlight because that's where the light's better. I also think that a little bit of self-doubt, not the crippling doubt, but a little bit of self-doubt is extremely good for a writer or anybody who's trying to do anything. You should have some. Because not everything you write is really worth publishing.

WM: Do you ever reread your work?

TK: At a certain point the Modern Library decided to publish *The Soul of a New Machine* and they offered me the chance to change anything I wanted. I started through the book and I got about twenty pages in and there wasn't a single page that wasn't completely marked up. I talked to Todd about it and he said, "Well, it's kind of like taking down an entire brick wall to get at one brick." He advised me to leave it alone. It's a book I wrote when I was thirty-six years old. Fine. I hope that I've written better books since then.

Actually, I've liked every book I've written. I've liked them each at the time and I always thought when I finished them that each was the best thing I had done. Robert Fitzgerald used to talk about "the luck of the conception," mostly talking about poems and stories and novels. But it also works in nonfiction. He used to say that writers had to depend on the luck of the conception. Some stories are better than others, or better for an individual writer. He was right.

WM: How has this worked out in your case?

TK: With *House*, things just sort of fell into place. I thought I was going to write about a bunch of carpenters in the building season, and suddenly there was this couple who needed a house built and there was a six-foot-six-inch tall architect who needed to design a house, his first house—he's a pretty famous architect now. And there I was in the middle of it. Suddenly I had this ménage à trois, without sexual connotations. I've always found writing books difficult, particularly the first draft. In retrospect, that book seems like the easiest, the most fun both to research and to write. One of the things I like is you can write a book that appears to be about one thing and it's also about another thing and another thing. Basically, *House* is a book about social class. I didn't want to have to say that. I think the message or theme or whatever is stronger if it's implicit.

WM: Haiti has become a subject for you.

TK: I've been trying to write recently about American foreign policy toward Haiti, an evil tale, and it's the first time, I think, in thirty years I've had a piece turned down. It's been turned down by the *New Yorker*. I think I let myself try to hedge too much. Tried to make myself seem . . .

WM: Objective.

TK: Yes, objective. The point is, there's no need to be objective about this. This is a situation with people dying, starving. Dying of dirty water and things like that. Then we, the United States, are blocking assistance that would at least begin to try to remedy some of those problems. And there is an enormous history going behind all of this. Maybe I wasn't able to cultivate that state of mind that Wordsworth talks about: "emotion recollected in tranquility." But I'm going to keep writing that piece until someone publishes it.

WM: Can we talk about *Mountains Beyond Mountains?*

TK: The main character, Dr. Paul Farmer, is the most important person I've ever followed around. This guy is a very special kind of idealist, an idealist who demonstrates that what he says is true. That is, that what he says is possible really is possible. Or, as he once put it, he's an action kind of guy. He's a person who is, in the broadest sense, tremendously upset about the distribution of medical technology in the world—or, probably better to say, the distribution of public health in the world. The maldistribution is so acute. I hadn't realized that, really, until I started traveling with him. The disparity is just so enormous, it really almost takes the top of your head off. My God, I had no idea the world is in such bad shape. Farmer set to work as a young man, even before he was a medical student, trying to address some of the suffering he'd found in the worst part of Haiti. I don't know if he had calculated in this way, but he had chosen a very good spot to begin working, because it stands to reason that if you can do a good thing in the worst part of the poorest country in the western hemisphere, you can pretty much do it anywhere. If you can show that you can treat AIDS effectively in a place like that, if you can show that you can treat the whole range of human illnesses there, then you've wiped away the arguments that I think have been developed in the Western world in order to make people like you and me feel better. Arguments like, you really can't do AIDS treatments in Africa because people don't have wristwatches there. There are these enormous epidemics, terrifying epidemics, of AIDS and TB and malaria, and here's a person who has basically shown us that there is no excuse for not taking them on and trying to stop them. This really caught me in a way nothing else has. To see someone actually make such a profound difference in the world.

WM: It seems that the combination of your experiences in Haiti and what's going on now in the world with America's new foreign policy has reawakened some of your old political passion. How do you view the current American government and the way things are going at home and abroad?

TK: How many administrations have I lived through? Eisenhower's is the first I remember. And this one [George W. Bush's] is without any question the most radical that we've ever had in my lifetime. It's astonishing to me how far right this country has gone. If you look at Nixon, and you subtract the Vietnam War from his record, he looks like a liberal Democrat or even a left-wing Democrat now. These people I think want to take America back to a time before the New Deal—I'm not the only one to say that. In foreign policy, it's just been no-holds-barred. The notion that the United States can pretty much do whatever it chooses at enormous expense to other countries—and I'm not talking about some businessman in Paris not doing as well as he might have, I'm talking about people dying because of American policy. Dying of a kind of low-level warfare that doesn't have anything to do with soldiers or guns. And the level of hypocrisy—hypocrisy is part of government, after all, but the level of hypocrisy now is staggering in its proportions. To talk about democracy and trying to instill democracy . . . In Haiti they have a constitutionally elected government. A popular democracy, if there ever was one. Granted, it's all screwed up. Yet I think it's pretty clear we're systematically opposed to popular democracy throughout Latin America. What we really want is oligarchy, and I'm not entirely sure that that isn't what we have going on right here in the United States, with a few curbs on it. And those curbs are growing weaker. I'm speaking in sort of an alarmist mode. I'm living a very nice life now and I can say this to you clearly and not be worried that Ashcroft's people will come knocking at my door tomorrow . . . I guess.

WM: Not yet, anyway.

TK: Not yet. But I don't like it and I think these guys are really bad news. I think they have an agenda that's really unfamiliar to most Americans. I'm not a left-winger. I don't think of myself as particularly ideological. Still, I don't like what's happening to our country and I don't like what our country's doing in some of the places that I know about. These preposterous attacks on France, which may be one of the few civilized places left on this earth, that kind of thing really offends me. What function does a writer have if not to write about his times? I'm not happy about this stuff and I think I should try to learn more about what's really going on, especially in our foreign policy. The most powerful country on earth has a policy toward one of the least powerful countries on earth that is doing nothing to help that least powerful country and is in fact hurting it greatly.

I think that's a good story. I don't care what the various editors of magazines might think. I think that it's a tremendously important story. If nothing else, it's certainly emblematic of what is going on generally. I think it's important to write about these things, even if you don't have a great deal of faith that it will do any good or change much of anything. To lodge a protest on behalf of human beings.

WM: What about going back to fiction? Will you ever do that?

TK: I'd like to, but I don't want to do it until I really have some fiction that I want to write. I don't want to do it just because I want to write fiction. There should be some reason to want to write fiction. Some a priori reason. I have some stories in my mind but I have to let them percolate awhile and maybe some people have to die before I write those stories. Because I suppose any piece of fiction that I write will be thought of as a roman à clef—isn't that always the danger?—and it would be even worse in that case because you'd be making up things that people would imagine are true. The desire to write a novel is nowhere near as important as having a novel you really want to write. And I don't currently have one I really want to write.

WM: So might you address the political situation next?

TK: I'll write this little memoir and then I'll see what's cooking in the world. I think it's important to say that I've been very lucky. Anyone who makes a living in the United States by writing and doesn't admit to having been lucky is deluded. And we may be in the twilight of the written word, but there are always going to be people who will need to be told what to think and what to say. So there are always going to be writers.

WM: Personally, I'm not a big believer in the twilight of the written word.

TK: Neither am I. I agree with you. Sometimes it feels that way, that's all. Sometimes one confuses one's own impending twilight with the twilight of the written word.

A CONVERSATION WITH
FRANCINE PROSE

Elissa Schappell

Francine Prose sees the world with a laserlike clarity, which can make one feel—especially when asking personal questions—as though one is standing in front of her in a wet bathing suit. Nothing escapes her eye. One of America's most provocative and impolitic social critics, Prose seems to delight in fearlessly slaughtering society's sacred cows in writing that is compassionate, funny, and unsparing. Whether taking on the woeful reading lists of American high schools in "I Know Why the Caged Bird Can't Read" in *Harper's* or the way history becomes entertainment, with the Holocaust the ultimate tourist attraction, in *Guided Tours of Hell*—Prose makes enemies almost as quickly as she attracts new readers and fans. "If my fiction and non-fiction have anything in common," Prose says, "it's the desire to say the thing everybody knows, but no one is saying."

Elissa Schappell: In 1998 you wrote an essay in *Harper's* entitled "Scent of a Woman's Ink: Are Women Writers Really Inferior?" in which you presented alarming statistics pointing out how women writers are not taken as seriously as their male counterparts, though they sell more copies, and are woefully overlooked by critics and those groups that award prizes for literature. Do you think things have changed for women writers in the last four years?

Francine Prose: Do you?

ES: Do you think that if a woman had written *The Corrections*—a big domestic novel—she would have gotten the same kind of attention?

FP: Well, the interesting thing is when you look at the National Book Award nominees, Jonathan Franzen wrote the domestic novel that was taken seriously as the heavy-hitter novel, and Jenny Egan wrote the political novel [*Look at Me*] that was read as the domestic novel—interior, psychological, whatever . . .

ES: Is the domestic novel just more interesting in the hands of male writers?

FP: I don't know. The sad thing and the reason why I have so little hope for it changing is that it just seems chemical to me, like hormonal—the way certain guys of a certain age, their eyes glaze over when they think that there is some "female" subject about to be mentioned. That's not conscious, that's just their hormones, or whatever is left of them.

ES: Like Norman Mailer?

FP: Right.

ES: The title of your *Harper's* essay is from a Norman Mailer quote: "The sniffs I get from the ink of women are always fey, old-hat, Quaintsy Goysy, tiny, too dykily psychotic." Do you think he was serious?

FP: Of course . . . Do you know the follow-up quote? He was interviewed on some radio station in San Francisco and was asked about that and he said, "Blah blah, blah, Francine Prose . . ." and then he said, "Can you imagine what it is like to be married to someone like that?"

ES: One of the reasons you were the perfect person to write such a piece is that when discussion turns to women writers who don't "write" like women—others include Mary Gaitskill, Deborah Eisenberg, Helen Schulman—you are often mentioned. What does it mean to write like a woman?

FP: It means the same thing that those guys thought it meant in the fifties and sixties—sentimental, humorless, domestic, limited, narrow.

ES: How do you feel being referred to as being "like a male writer"?

FP: It sends me straight to the mirror. What are they seeing that I don't notice? It's just so annoying, and let me say that after that piece came out, *Harper's* sent it to a number of women writers, Cynthia Ozick was one of them, and she said, essentially—as if I had been arguing for affirmative action, that sort of thing—she said, "I don't want to be considered a woman writer." Well, that wasn't my suggestion, that wasn't my idea.

ES: Do you find it insulting to be called a woman writer?

FP: Yes. I'd rather be called a writer.

ES: I interviewed Toni Morrison once and she said she despised being labeled an African American writer. It made her really angry.

FP: She's right. You get called an African American writer and you end up in the African American section of the bookstore, where nobody ever goes.

ES: It seems a week doesn't go by without some white male writer being hailed as he who will write The Great American Novel. Why are we as a culture so obsessed with the idea of The Great American Novel?

FP: I don't know, maybe it's the satisfaction of being able to put *Great* and *American* in the same phrase. What do they think The Great American novel is going to do? Explain the entire society? Isn't that a little peculiar, as we are always celebrating our diversity? We expect one novel to sell the whole thing?

ES: When the topic turns to women who can go toe-to-toe with male novelists in terms of writing very seriously about ideas and writing big books, novels long and fat—read: The Great American Novel—the names that come up are Margaret Atwood, Doris Lessing, A. S. Byatt, even Zadie Smith—but not one of them is American. Ergo, not a one of them could write The Great American Novel.

FP: I think it's very hard for people to read anymore. They don't read that well, and it's hard for them, for some reason, to see what is actually in the book. It's easier to come up with these categories, hooks, the Woman's Novel, the Great American Novel, this is This Generation's Novel. And none of this makes any difference.

ES: Is that part of the appeal of the *Twenty Under Thirty* anthology, or the *New Yorker* issue in which they anoint the best young writers?

FP: Lists of writers under forty are just marketing techniques. Because by now there are very few people who could tell you who was older, Chekhov or Tolstoy, who belonged to which generation. Those categories are useless.

ES: Why do we need a great American novel? Do we have an inferiority complex?

FP: Well, no one talks about The Great Canadian Novel. Then you have non-American writers like Doris Lessing and Margaret Atwood writing these big books. I guess they are bigger, but even noticing . . . it's like being a size queen.

ES: Does size matter?

FP: Does size matter? No. *Madame Bovary* isn't that long. Chekhov's "Ward No. 6" is pretty short. Of course it doesn't matter.

ES: It seems it has become a rite of passage for American male writers—or those who want to be taken seriously to write these—

FP: Big motherfuckers.

ES: Maybe they're compensating for something else . . . Look at how big Philip Roth's books are. Look at *American Pastoral*—that *is* The Great American Novel.

FP: Right. Let's open it up and start saying, "*a* Great American novel." The Great American Novel implies hierarchy and competition and that there is only room for one. It seems like a sixties/seventies macho thing, like The Great American Diet Book.

ES: Do you think the fact that women writers aren't more critically acclaimed has caused them to lack ambition to even *try* to write these *big books?*

FP: For one thing it's completely specious to even imagine people can choose what they are going to write in that way. You don't choose what you are going to write. You don't sit down and say, I want it to be bigger and better, broader and more profound.

ES: You don't think when some of these guys sit down . . .

FP: [laughs] I don't know. I can't imagine what that would be like. I can't imagine even being able to say a work is going to be a novel or a short story. It is what it is. You find the form as you are doing it. Maybe some guys do that. I don't know. How do I know what guys do? But wait, I write like a guy, I should know . . .

ES: Is it possible that women writers are just less ambitious, or that they don't want to write big books?

FP: What? You think it's like, I just wrote a nice little book, and no one will notice me, and now I can go on and have my baby . . .

ES: Or is it because—like Raymond Carver, who said he wrote short stories because parenthood kept him "in a state of permanent distraction"—children are keeping women from writing bigger books?

FP: No, I don't believe that either. There is child care, kids go to school! Anyone who can't write a novel of any size during the school hours isn't worth their salt. I mean, what are they doing? I just don't think you get to choose!

ES: There has always existed an old boys' network. Do you think such a thing now exists for women? Do you think women are more or less likely to help each other out?

FP: I always assume women are going to be nice, and I am always shocked when they are not. I just think you can't make any generalizations; it's just as likely that a woman in power is going to screw you as a guy in power is going to screw you.

ES: It isn't shocking to discover a lot of men don't read women writers, and certainly don't want to be compared to women writers—but there are also women writers who hardly ever read other women writers, and don't want to be compared to them either.

FP: What do they do about Alice Munro?

ES: Well, she's a problem. Thank God she's Canadian.

FP: It's so nutty. I am just so grateful to be reading anything good. I am currently reading Patricia Highsmith, and this is what I mean about people not being able to read. I have been reading *The Tremor of Forgery*, and I got through it and thought, This is one of the best Vietnam novels I've ever read, although it's set in Tunisia and Vietnam is only going on in the background. The main character defines himself as being antiwar; he has nothing but contempt for his neighbor, who is this right-wing fascist nut, but by the end of the novel you realize that the supposed hero is exactly the kind of person who could have gone in and blown away an entire Vietnamese village because it was in the way, but she never says that. And where do you find this book? It's in the mystery section, just because of *Ripley*! She's incredibly instructive because she's the best of the modern writers at creating characters who are completely opaque to themselves. They have not a clue about who they are, especially their sexuality. Half her characters are gay and they don't know it! It's very hard to do, especially when you are writing from that character's point of view.

ES: Highsmith seems to be in vogue now, perhaps because of the Norton release of her collected works.

FP: Does she seem popular now? She wasn't when she was alive. She was the sort of angry, difficult, alcoholic lesbian who was not someone you would send out on book tour. Gertrude Stein would be a pain in the ass at a dinner party, while Truman Capote is like the perfect guest. But who ever thought that writers were supposed to do that? Be the perfect guest?! What do your social skills have to do with how good a writer you are?

ES: These days it seems all writers feel they have to go through an MFA program. What do you think about this?

FP: Look, I essentially think that if you *have* talent it doesn't make any difference what you do, and if you *don't* have talent it doesn't make any difference what you do.

ES: So you don't believe that "with-hard-work-and-a-little-luck-anybody-can-be-a-writer" theory?

FP: No. I used to think that. I no longer think that. I used to think that if you put fifty monkeys in a room with fifty typewriters—boy, that is a notion that teaching disabuses you of fairly soon.

ES: Your book *The Lives of the Muses* examines the relationships between nine women and the artists they inspired. What inspired you to write it?

FP: I got a fellowship at the New York Public Library and I wanted a research project. I found a book that had five hundred great letters of the past millennium, and there was a great letter from Samuel Johnson to Hester Thrale, and it was such an amazing letter it stopped me cold. That sort of started everything. The book said she was his muse. I thought: Muse—what does that mean, what's that all about?

ES: The most contemporary muse in your book is Yoko Ono. I tried to come up with present-day muses in the mold of Gala Dalí and Suzanne Farrell, but couldn't think of one, except for the Babe Paleys and Ann Basses of the world who inspire designers to cut new ball gowns. Why doesn't the muse-artist relationship exist today?

FP: I keep thinking it's some other step on the continuum. The step from the divine to the human, and then we've taken some other step—I think we worship ourselves and each other just to worship ourselves and each other and we don't even bother making art out of it.

ES: Why?

FP: Well, don't you think that the whole concept is fundamentally bogus anyway?

ES: No.

FP: What, you think, I'm going to sit down and say, "Oh, gee, I'm writing this book because I love my husband"?

ES: No.

FP: Listen, it must have been very flattering to think, Tolstoy wrote *War and Peace* because of me!

Also, you know . . . Look at Lewis Carroll, he met Alice when she was five. He took that photo of her—*The Beggar Child*, practically the most lubricious photo ever taken—when she was seven. Take these nine relationships and just look at how many of them were twisted in some way—practically every single one. And most weren't the kind of thing you'd want to talk about. Can you imagine some guy now saying, "Gee, I wrote this book because I was madly in love with a ten-year-old girl?" I don't think so. The fact is that you can't generalize about anything. Nobody in this book is like anybody else in this book, no work they created is like any other, and no relationship is like any other. The minute you start talking about art you are talking about something very individual and very personal and very particular.

ES: You never had a boy muse . . .

FP: Okay, let's just say this: back when I had boyfriends none of them was responsible for my work, forget it. I am sure it mostly works the same way for men now. We're too ironic for that. It seems too naïve, romantic. I think it also seems too much of a surrender to someone else. It's better to say, "I sat down and wrote this. I did this, no one else had anything to do with it." But then of course you get the hideous acknowledgement page, the thanking to the wife or girlfriend for the proofreading or the cooking.

ES: One constant in all the artist-muse relationships was that after the muse stepped down from her pedestal and into her artist's bed or, worse yet, married him, her shelf life was then like . . .

FP: Zero.

ES: Who was your favorite muse?

FP: I loved each as I was writing them, but I did Alice Liddell first and she was a hard act to follow, she and Lewis Carroll were a hard act to follow . . . *that golden afternoon*. Also, so much had to do with how I felt about the work that came out of the relationship. The artist's actual work . . .

I re-read *Alice's Adventures in Wonderland*, and I loved it. It's amazing; it's a work of genius—it's like the Marx brothers. And right after that I did Lizzie Siddal and Dante Gabriel Rossetti. Not so great. Their story is a heartbreaking tale, a cautionary tale, her opium addiction and his exhuming her after she died. But the work is so fundamentally crappy compared to *Alice in Wonderland,* so that kept getting into everything and influencing my feelings. The next one I wrote was Lou Salomé and Nietzsche—with all the God and overeating—there was something so fundamentally unpleasant about her. When I finished it I sort of couldn't face it, so I called up Richard Howard and said, "Richard, I just figured out why Lou Salomé was so difficult, such a monster," and he said, "Oh, my dear, she was the worst thing that ever happened until Livia Soprano!"

Yoko Ono was the easiest to research. There are books, videotapes. I had the most fun writing about Yoko.

ES: The Salvador and Gala Dalí section was deeply amusing.

FP: Well, Salvador Dalí wrote that part for me. I mean, *The Secret Life of Salvador Dalí* is the funniest book ever written, all I had to do was quote it. I had to stop myself from quoting it.

ES: I love him preparing to meet Gala for the first time and painting his armpits red, pulling out his hair, slashing himself with a razor . . .

FP: Smearing himself with goat shit. I was at the library and I kept pulling people into my office to read to them, I couldn't believe how great it was.

ES: How is work on the new book coming?

FP: You know, you have to be like a kid with your eyes closed. It's the only way you can write. The only way to write is to assume you are going to be perfectly understood, taken in precisely the way you mean it, but obviously that is the last thing that is going to happen.

ES: How do you work?

FP: It's different from day to day. Ideally, I am up in the country, and the phone doesn't ring, no one knows I am there, I start work around eight and write fiction until about two, then do other stuff.

ES: Do you find you have one brain for fiction and another for non-fiction?

FP: Completely. Because the nonfiction brain knows where it is going to get to by the end of wherever it's going to get. The nonfiction brain has an end in sight. The nonfiction brain has a structure as inchoate as it needs to be, nonetheless a structure in mind, sort of, even if it isn't tappable all the time. Whereas the fiction brain depends on scrambling every impulse, disorganizing all that, and saying, "Where is this going to go that I didn't think it was going to go, what is that unforeseen possibility?" Plus, doing voices, personalities, characters, seeing things from other people's points of view. When you are doing nonfiction, it's your own voice, whatever that is, or you are pretending to sound like yourself. In fiction it's so much more fun, you are out of yourself, and the more out of yourself you are the better it is. That is one way. The really thrilling thing is when I find myself doing something that is so unlike me, and so scary.

ES: What do you mean, not like you?

FP: Well, I am about to do a chapter from the point of view of this youngish guy who is this flat-out, unredeemed, unregenerate racist. It's a lot of fun, and it's scary. The title of the novel is *A Changed Man*, which by the middle of the book has become a marketing concept, so it's sort of about moral change. Part of it is set at a human rights foundation.

ES: You ought to have fun with that. I can already hear the mirthless thought police sharpening their pencils. You drew fire for attacking New Age feminism and goddess worship in *Hunters and Gatherers*, and in *Blue Angel* you rankled some feminists by asserting that not every young woman who gets involved with a professor is a victim, but may indeed be the aggressor. Do you generally start with a character, or an idea?

FP: The character. What I am beginning to realize is really the most unproductive aspect of my so-called method is that I think by writing. I can't sit there and think. I don't know what it means to think, I don't know what I think unless I am writing. It is completely Pavlovian, and so essentially I will write a whole first draft just to figure out sort of what the story is, and who the characters are, and the scenes I am writing are really just place markers showing me where the scenes are going to be. Other people sit down and make outlines, they have ideas and characters, and I have zip.

I remember once Stephen Dobyns calling me up after just writing a novel and saying he thought his novel was going to be 240 pages and it was 244 pages. He had come that close to his idea of what it should be. It was just the shape he imagined it would be when he set out to write the novel.

ES: In *Blue Angel* the main character, a writing professor at a small liberal arts college, is charged with sexual harassment when he gets involved with a student. Was the lawsuit that was brought against Stephen Dobyns (though, in my opinion, throwing a drink in the face of someone who insults you hardly constitutes sexual harassment) the inspiration for *Blue Angel*?

FP: When all that happened—Stephen's case—I was already halfway into the book. So, no, it wasn't. Life imitates art in the most hideous ways.

ES: One of my favorite bad sex scenes is in *Blue Angel*. Any time you can combine a hideous dental emergency with foreplay.

FP: It is so much fun to write about bad sex. It's so much easier. Sex is impossible to write about. It's one of those experiences, like drugs, that looks completely different from the inside than the outside. You can't re-create the experience. There's nothing quite like it, and also the whole thing about good sex is: Why is it good? It's good because your consciousness shuts up for a few minutes. So if the point is suspending consciousness than what are you writing about?

ES: Is there a lot of sex in the next book?

FP: No, but I do try to write about the aftermath of sexual rejection from the woman's point of view, which has rarely been written about—except, I guess, by Alice Munro, but again, she's not American—and that was sort of fun. Again, you don't sit down and say, "I want to do this because I don't see it in fiction," but when you are writing something and you think, Where can I look, you realize you haven't seen anything like it anywhere. We'll see. The other bad thing is I don't know until the very last line of the very last draft if it is going to work at all.

ES: In your fiction, and certainly now in *The Lives of the Muses*, you explore the evils and rewards of seduction. Why is that of such interest?

FP: It's inherently dramatic. Is the person going to give in or not? Are they going to be seduced or seduce or let themselves be seduced, and doesn't it get back to—again, let me just go on record right here and say, I don't have any ideas, have never had any ideas—doesn't it go back to the idea of the will and the self and power, and what you surrender to, and what you give in to, where you draw lines?

And try to think of ten novels, or ten novels that you like, that don't involve seduction. I guess *Mrs. Dalloway* doesn't.

ES: I think one thing that unsettles readers is the way that you are able to insinuate them into the minds of characters they find despicable.

FP: That's so close to what I am trying to do, or what I later decide I am trying to do. I find myself writing about people who are trying to do the right thing, but are fucked up in some way that is so fundamental that it is so hopeless for them. No one would automatically think this sort of character is a nice person, but I happen to think they're human, and they interest me because of a complexity that has nothing to do with goodness or niceness.

ES: For me, part of the writer's job is to take readers places they are afraid to go, or wouldn't want to go alone, to make them confront their own hypocrisy or the irony of their feelings . . .

FP: Nobody wants to do that! You would be amazed at how resistant people are.

ES: Right, they will say Francine Prose likes Nazis.

FP: And they'll say, "Why do you write about such unsympathetic characters?" And I don't think they're unsympathetic. I mean I got that a lot with *Guided Tours of Hell* and it just made me insane. I kept thinking: I must be the only person in the world acquainted with ego, pettiness, and vanity; apparently I am the only one who knows these things exist because everyone else thinks it's just so distasteful they can't even stand to imagine that anyone else is like that. Am I the only woman who went through a period in my life when I was young and passive and would let any guy tell me what reality was just because he was a guy? I must be the only person that that ever happened to! Because no one else is willing to acknowledge that they know anything about female characters like that.

ES: So is there any real difference between your fiction and your non-fiction, in terms of the spirit of the work?

FP: One of the things that is different is that I feel that writing for a certain kind of magazine is like ventriloquism, whereas writing fiction and certain nonfiction pieces, the *Harper's* pieces, it's like having Tourette's. You just can't stop that thing from coming out of your mouth, you have to say it. You just *have* to say it.

A CONVERSATION WITH
MARILYNNE ROBINSON

Regan Good

Marilynne Robinson says she did not intend to write a novel when she started trying her hand at extended metaphors. She began with an image of a grandfather finding a watch on a lakeshore; then came a grandmother hanging laundry on a line. There were people in these descriptions and the passages were firmly connected to place, namely the wild, deep woods and darkly vegetative lakeshores of rural Idaho. One of the earliest metaphors she worked on was the image of a passenger train sliding silently off the tracks of a trestle bridge and slipping into the lake below. It is this image that begins *Housekeeping*. The accident, from which there are no survivors, occurs decades before the action of the book takes place, but the train functions as an uncanny anchor throughout the novel. The children of Fingerbone swear they sometimes brush their feet against the train's windows while swimming in the lake. Winter skaters invariably think of the iron locomotive under their bladed feet as they etch circles on the ice. A reader can unpack the image in a seemingly endless proliferation of metaphysically profound ways, which is exactly what Robinson intended.

Marilynne Robinson was thirty-three years old when she published *Housekeeping* in 1980. The novel was an eccentric piece of work by any standard, a kind of nineteenth-century novel written in the twentieth. The prose was Old Testament-rich, composed of long sentences and dense metaphorical passages verging on Melvillian grandeur. The critic Anatole Broyard wrote in the *New York Times Book Review*: "It's as if, in writing it, she broke through the ordinary human condition with all its dissatisfactions, and achieved a kind of transfiguration." Take this passage, for example:

> Imagine a Carthage sown with salt, and all the sowers gone, and the seeds lain however long in the earth, till there rose finally in vegetable profusion leaves and trees of rime and brine. What flowering would there be in such a garden? Light would force each salt calyx to open in prisms, and to fruit heavily with bright globes of water—peaches and grapes are little more than that, and where the world was salt there would be greater need of slaking. For need can blossom into all the compensation it requires. To crave and to have are as alike as a thing and its shadow. For when does a berry break upon the tongue as sweetly as when one longs to taste it, and when is the taste refracted into so many hues and savors of ripeness and earth, and when do our senses know any thing so utterly as when we lack it? And here again is a foreshadowing—the world will be made whole.

The book follows Ruth—a solitary child who feels different from her striving sister and the starched and pleated citizenry of Fingerbone, Idaho—as she begins to determine who she is. When their

aunt Sylvie arrives to take care of the girls after their grandmother's death, Ruth cleaves to the woman, feeling inexplicable sympathy
with Sylvie's wordless reveries and mysterious disappearances. The
novel ends with Sylvie and Ruth burning down the family house and
forming a rootless, hobo society of their own invention.

Flap copy for the original hardcover indicated Robinson was at
work on another novel, but then she seemed to vanish. What some
readers missed is that Robinson did publish two more books after
Housekeeping, both works of nonfiction: *Mother Country: Britain, the Wel-
fare State and Nuclear Pollution* in 1989, and then *The Death of Adam: Essays
on Modern Thought* in 1998.

Mother Country was a decidedly strange follow-up to such a *literary*
literary debut as *Housekeeping*, and it announced Robinson as a moral
thinker and an environmentalist (albeit one who rarely leaves her
house). The book was nominated for a National Book Award despite
pointed criticism over her research methods by scientific reviewers.
Ten years later came *The Death of Adam*, a book of essays on Puritan
culture and the sixteenth-century Protestant Church reformer John
Calvin, as well as essays in which Robinson seeks to dismantle the
thought of major modernist figures like Darwin and Nietzsche. God
is, in her estimation, far from dead.

Since 1990, Robinson has taught fiction at the University of Iowa's
Writers' Workshop. Today she is a self-proclaimed Calvinist and has
been studying Calvin's massive Institutes of the Christian Religion
for over a decade. As a regular churchgoer, Robinson occasionally
delivers sermons to her Congregational Church. In these sermons
she radiates moral certitude, theological scholarship, and a great deal
of indignation at how the Calvinist-inspired ideas that founded this
country have been abused or misunderstood.

In September 2000, Robinson and I had four conversations
over as many days in her living room in her home in Iowa City.
Despite the insane September heat, Robinson was a prodigious
talker. My questions triggered response in perfectly composed
paragraphs of nuanced thought, made up of complete complex

sentences in which words like *toothsome* and *mirth* were used without self-consciousness.

In the spring of 2003, we spoke again by phone about postmodernism, Wallace Stevens, Moby Dick, and, of course, John Calvin. We also spoke off the record about the elusive second novel Robinson was then completing: *Gilead*. This epistolary novel set in 1955 about a dying Calvinist preacher writing to his very young son about the world and his understanding of its mysteries was published by Farrar, Straus and Giroux in 2004, and by all accounts the twenty-three-year wait was not in vain. "[*Gilead*] is so serenely beautiful, and written in a prose so gravely measured and thoughtful, that one feels touched with grace just to read it," wrote the *Washington Post Book World*. *Gilead* went on to win the 2004 National Book Critics Circle Award and the 2005 Pulitzer Prize for fiction.

Regan Good: Can you tell me about writing *Housekeeping*?

Marilynne Robinson: I was an American literature major in graduate school and I became very interested in the nineteenth century's use of extended metaphors. I felt as if that needed to be explored and that people had stopped using metaphor in that incredibly ambitious way for no particular reason. I felt that metaphor was no longer being used as a way of envisioning the world. I was working on my dissertation and people told me if you did critical work you couldn't do creative work. So I would write what to me were extended metaphors—I would write them and then put them away, and when I read them again I realized that they cohered and that they were the basis of a fiction. But I hadn't been writing them with the idea that they would be one.

RG: I read that you literally wrote the book in the dark?

MR: I wrote a lot of *Housekeeping* in France. I wrote in a little dark room at the back of the house while trying to hide from the neighborhood children fascinated by this American family living in their midst. I was trying to remember when I was in Idaho. I hadn't spent any time there for years, except for brief visits home. I was trying to remember the water and the air and the vegetation and so on. And at first it seemed undoable and then I began to realize that if I gave my mind time it would discover things. It knew things that I would never anticipate it knowing and so there was this whole rising out of the sea of this remembered landscape, which was a strange experience in itself because it was a discovery of mind about my mind that I would never have otherwise made.

RG: You've said before that *Housekeeping* was not autobiographical, though you grew up spending a lot of your time in Idaho's lonelier landscapes at your grandparents' ranch, I believe. But the description of Ruth's solitary nature and feeling of being different seems to be an echo of your own solitary nature. Do you see yourself in Ruth?

MR: Well, I was interested in what she was interested in, namely the persistence of things that perish. That fact that they reconstitute themselves, that they yield things in the mind, in the consciousness, and that the being of anything of significance cannot be said to have an end. I was sort of trying to make the argument that there's a sort of supersaturated quality to experience, that it doesn't happen once and then cease—that in a certain sense it reinvests itself continuously with a significance that rises again and again.

RG: Does it surprise you that *Housekeeping* can be found on many postmodern literature course syllabi? It actually appears on one scholar's time line alongside Blondie's "Call Me" as a major postmodern work.

MR: Well, I just received an essay in the mail from someone who was saying *Housekeeping* was postmodern. I felt very chic. But the thing is, I have been teaching *Moby Dick* this semester, which must be the great articulation of the problem of knowledge. When you show people how the novel works, they say, "Well, that's postmodern." But in fact, the nineteenth-century writers just knew that. I talk a lot about Calvin in my classes because that psychology is the product of Calvinistic theology. You know, for them the world is this amazing, dazzling phenomenon seen through a glass darkly and so on. For the nineteenth-century writers it becomes an experiment in what the human consciousness is and what experience is, which is a very beautiful question for them. People say, "Oooo, those people were so clever, they are almost as smart as we are." And that leads to the conclusion that people who are writing now don't understand that they are dealing with old, or relatively old, ideas. It seems to me the difference between nineteenth-century Americans and the postmodernists is that rather than feeling they were participating in something astonishing, the postmodernists say, "Well, we can't know the truth, we know we can't know it. All we can do is cut and paste, or something."

RG: You studied with John Hawkes as an undergraduate. What kind of teacher was he for you?

MR: He did exactly what I aspire to do as a teacher, which is that he made me sensitive to the times I was writing well. It's very difficult when you are starting out because you have the strange abstract idea of what it would be like to write without having an experience of yourself writing. So you do all kinds of crazy imitative stuff or whatever. He was always very careful to mark out for me when I was writing well and when I was doing something that was derivative or unimaginative. Even then I had a long sentence style. It has always been true for me that often I know what a sentence should sound like before I know what it should say. I wasn't particularly aware of that. He made me aware of the virtues and pitfalls of the long sentence.

RG: Explain your fascination with nineteenth-century writers like Melville and Dickinson. What is it about their approach to their subjects you find so lucrative?

MR: There was a very profound humanism in the nineteenth-century vision, which is very moving to me and which frankly seems right to me. It seems like truth. I'm attracted to it in ways I'm not attracted to other versions of human nature or personality. I love the generosity of their view of human beings on the one hand, and then the idea that is very closely related, that the whole universe exists to pass through the human consciousness. They weren't the only people to articulate it and they weren't the last, but they did it as consistently as anyone has ever done. It involved them looking into abysses a fair amount of the time, assuming that meaning was to be found at the most radical apparent limit of not meaning. They are so struck by the brilliance of human perception; the fact that not being able to know something absolutely doesn't shut things down. Who is the inquirer? What's the nature of inquiry? How amazing it is that we are the great receivers of this universe, which we certainly are, though physicists will forever say otherwise.

RG: You've called the nineteenth-century use of metaphors "real ontology" and have said that they "don't just signify, they mean." Can you explain?

MR: Wallace Stevens provides a good example. He was twelve or thirteen when Melville died and seven when Emily Dickinson died, so he was much closer culturally to them than to us. I use his poem "Of Modern Poetry" to describe how metaphors work in Moby Dick. Moby Dick has to be the great articulation of the problem of knowledge. It seems to me as if characteristically and pervasively the chapter structures in Moby Dick are "poem[s] of the act of the mind" that reach for a metaphor, encounter the limits of the metaphor, destroy the metaphor, and so forth, choosing one emblematic thing after another to be explored as meaningful. Moby Dick makes no argument beyond the display of the fact that the mind can't know what it sets out to know. It aesthetically appreciates the circles the mind makes around the question.

RG: Say more about Stevens and how he works. His lyricism seems to be generated by this constant circling and circling around his subject.

MR: Stevens himself has a way of staying faithful to objects and at the same time freeing them from context so they become transcendent versions of themselves, you know? It's as if the strategy of metaphor is to invest a given thing more fully with itself. He has such a strong degree of the awareness of the consciousness, an awareness of the operation of the consciousness, and how it gives us everything we can have and at the same time is necessarily inadequate to what it does.

RG: Why did you switch from fiction (and the obvious pleasures of working with metaphor) to nonfiction? In other words, how did you come to write *Mother Country*?

MR: There are certain kinds of problems that I solved for my purposes in *Housekeeping*—one of them being that the evanescence of things was very disturbing to me, in the way that the encounters you had with people or with the world always seemed more bleak or attenuated or disruptive in some way than the idea of these things. I was sort of pondering memory and language and other things that inhabit time—these things are not lost in the simple sense that they seem to be as time passes. Maybe that was a strange thing to worry about, but that bothered me, it seemed to me almost an insult, as if we were just being shown life. I was trying to come to terms with that to my satisfaction. I think I would have gone on to write a second novel if other things hadn't intervened, in other words, feeling that I had to write *Mother Country*. When I was doing research for *Mother Country* and writing it I really realized human nature and human prospects are not what I had imagined they were, but that the destructiveness of the human presence in the world is vastly greater. It was sort of as if the drama of reality had been recast in my mind.

RG: In *The Death of Adam*, John Calvin and the Judeo-Christian ethic are your main subjects. But in one essay you get personal. You write that you were a pious child and that you intuitively knew or felt you were part of "a vast energy of intention." How religious was your upbringing?

MR: That's a very hard thing to say. My family didn't really talk about religion much at all. I think that it was implicit. Aside from going to Sunday school, and that kind of thing, it was absolutely never imposed on me. I was more religiously oriented than other people in my family were, and more interested in the Bible. When I was in college I went to church quite regularly and continued that when my children were small. As my life developed and I had more and more time to myself, it became more possible for me to think about religion extensively. I was always interested in theology and the more my theological thinking has developed, the more essential church seems to me, so that there seems to be a sort of acceleration in my interest and my commitment over the last ten years.

RG: How much did Calvin figure in your understanding of religion?

MR: Not at all.

RG: So how did you become interested in Calvin?

MR: I think I really got interested in Calvin teaching Melville here at the Workshop. Of course, *Moby Dick* is just saturated with theological language, and it occurred to me that I should read the theology that this literature is saturated with. Of course, America at that time was deeply Calvinist. So it was illuminating in terms of reading Melville but it was also very illuminating to me because I realized I was in a Calvinist culture, and that my religious thinking was Calvinist and that I simply didn't have a name attached to it.

RG: You go to great lengths to defend Calvin, as if you are trying to rescue him from his reputation as a killjoy and a grim, punishing taskmaster. Why is it so important to you to revive his reputation?

MR: Calvinism has been significantly and persistently misinterpreted. The weird turn in his historical reputation has had enormous consequences on the one hand and on the other is simply itself such an interesting example of the oddness of collective thinking and historical interpretation. In a way, it always comes back to the same thing again: Why are we so certain that we know things that are not true and how can we live with this kind of knowledge and information as if we did not know and could not know? There's nothing straightforward in historical understanding; if you are told something is red, odds are at least fifty percent of the time it's green. My great hope is that people will read seminal texts for themselves.

RG: Some critics have commented that your nonfiction persona is strident, that you express a moral certitude that irritates? Can you comment?

MR: Well, there is a moral certitude that rubs people the wrong way. I think that if you try to talk about issues that have moral significance you simply run that risk. There are things that matter. It irritates me. We've lived in a period of moral dudgeon for the last ten or fifteen years in which it seems that self-declared morality is suspect. It doesn't have anything to do with ministering justice, loving mercy, and walking humbly with God. And the other case has not been made effectively. We depend on each other for the sanity of the culture. We depend on each other to say things that are rounded and meaningful. There's this whole froth of language that simply parrots other meaningless language. Societies go crazy, things go wrong, and maintaining the integrity of the conversation within a culture—especially a culture as powerful as this one—is not only one option among others. It's wrong to go crazy and misrepresent history to ourselves.

RG: How do you read the Bush Administration's motives in starting the war?

MR: I have to say the administration's motives are very mysterious to me. In a way, of course, they are not. I hear people talk about oil and it seems simpleminded. I think generally people see this war as retaliatory. Even though it's imprecisely retaliatory. The attacks on Washington and New York were a very direct consequence of the ways in which we are involved in the world, ways I wish we weren't. The superpower idea—there is nothing in that that appeals to me.

Our democratic institutions—the ones Calvin and Jefferson built—are not designed to survive this kind of role. Our political system depends on the free flow of information. Listening to the administration, you can feel almost instantly how much is being concealed and how many things we are excluded from having knowledge of.

RG: Have you been writing anything about the situation in Iraq?

MR: I wrote a letter to the editor—no specific editor, just all editors—but I haven't been content with what I've written. Nothing has left the house. I deeply love American civilization and I don't think there is anything more potentially disastrous when it comes from the point of view of maintaining and developing the civilization and allowing it to come to be what it ought to be than getting involved in a bunch of foreign wars. The last thing we need is empire.

A CONVERSATION WITH
BARNEY ROSSET

Win McCormack

In bestowing on Barney Rosset the honorific of Commandeur dans l'Ordre des Arts et des Lettres in 1999, the French Ministry of Culture said: "You brought writers considered marginal into the mainstream. We are still reaping the fruits of your relentless efforts and achievements, and such is your legacy that the American public is indebted to you for many of the most interesting books it reads."

The recipient of this accolade was raised in Chicago, Illinois, where his left-leaning political views were shaped in part by attendance at the progressive Francis Parker School. His later education was at Swarthmore College in Pennsylvania and the New School for Social Research in New York. He served in the Army Signal Corps during World War II, as an officer in a photographic company stationed in China.

In 1951 Rosset purchased a small publishing company called Grove Press and proceeded to turn it into what was arguably, during its heyday, the most influential alternative book press in the history of American publishing. Grove—and Grove's magazine, the *Evergreen Review*, launched in 1957—published, among other writers, most of the French avant-garde of the era, including Alain Robbe-Grillet, Jean Genet, and Eugene Ionesco; most of the American Beats of the fifties, including Jack Kerouac, William Burroughs, and Allen Ginsberg; and most of the key radical political thinkers of the sixties, including Malcolm X, Frantz Fanon, and Regis Debray. He published Samuel Beckett's play *Waiting for Godot* after it had been scorned by more mainstream publishers—and sold two million copies of it in the bargain. He made a specialty of Japanese literature, and introduced the future Nobel Prize winner Kenzaburo Oe to an American public. He published the first unexpurgated edition of D. H. Lawrence's *Lady Chatterley's Lover* and the first edition of Henry Miller's *Tropic of Cancer* in America, partly to deliberately provoke the censors. Through his legal victories in the resulting obscenity cases, as well as in one brought on by *I Am Curious (Yellow)*, a sexually explicit Swedish documentary film he distributed, he was probably more responsible than any other single individual for ending the censorship of literature and film in the United States.

Grove Press was sold in 1985; its backlist is now part of Grove/Atlantic Inc. This interview was conducted in the East Village loft where Rosset and his companion Astrid Myers live and operate Evergreen Review, Inc., a nonprofit company that manages the *Evergreen Review* Web site and the publishing company Foxrock. The long room is dominated by a pool table at its center that is surrounded by a myriad of bookshelves crammed with Grove publications, files, and memorabilia.

Win McCormack: Barney, what *Tin House* would like to discuss is your uncanny ability to spot the great writers of your era.

Let me read you something you once said: "You might not know what's going to fly into your web, but you put it where you think there might be flies. If you leave your web out long enough, you might have the option to pick only those flies that please you, and eventually you can discern a pattern or similarity in the flies that you choose, and finally you accidentally learn to choose wisely."

What was the web that you put out, and where did you put it? And who were the first to fly into it?

Barney Rosset: I don't think you can go at it quite that way. I had done a lot of reading prior to Grove Press, in high school, in college, in the army, and I had developed my own taste, for good or for bad. For example, Henry Miller's work had entered my life in 1940, in full force. There were also people like Hemingway and Malraux, and others, whom I had read and admired.

If you have a small publishing company, or a large one for that matter, many people whom you admire are published by somebody else—for example, Hemingway, or Faulkner, or Malraux. So already you're circumscribed to a degree. Your web can't catch them; they're caught. So if you, let's say, find that somebody like Miller, whom you liked, is available, you start doing something about it.

WM: When you started Grove Press, Henry James was one of the first authors you published.

BR: He certainly was, the very first.

WM: How did that happen?

BR: That happened through my first wife, Joan Mitchell, later a very famous artist. Joan's mother was the editor of *Poetry* magazine. She was the editor of it for many, many years and a poet herself. Joan was a very astute person, with very good taste for writing, just as good as for painting. She was the one who really directly got me into Grove. John Balcomb and Robert Phelps had started Grove Press and Grove Street. They published three books and quit. They really had quit. They had wanted to do *The Monk*, a gothic novel by Matthew G. Lewis. They had it almost ready. I loved *The Monk*. That was the first book we physically published. It had been published several times with changes, so we did a variorum edition, and I went to Princeton and got John Berryman, a very well-known poet at that time, to do an introduction.

The Golden Bowl was a novel by Henry James that Joan particularly liked, and she asked me to do that. I went to Princeton again and got R. P. Blackmur, who was at that time the leading writer on James, to do an introduction. It wasn't accidental that we did James, it was a direct result of being pushed by Joan. Then I went right on, did six or seven more of him.

WM: Was he out of print at the time?

BR: Not everything of his, but most. We did about eight volumes, and I got Leon Edel, a professor at NYU who was on his way to writing the famous five-volume biography of James, to do introductions to two of the books. I bought *The Golden Bowl* from Scribner's. Scribner's sent a wonderful, elderly gentleman along with Whitney Darrow, a famous editor, to my apartment on Ninth Street to see if I really existed. He walked up the four flights, and he was satisfied we were real, and we paid his small advance, and then paid the royalties to Scribner's.

WM: So you were responsible for reviving the great traditionalist Henry James.

BR: Yes. We also did other American writers such as Sherwood Anderson, who seemed to have gotten lost somewhere along the way.

WM: Was he out of print as well?

BR: Yes. I thought he was a very important writer. To me, these were the basics of American left-wing idealism, or liberalism: Carl Sandburg, Sherwood Anderson, and Lincoln Steffens, whom I didn't publish but I certainly would have if he had been out of print.

WM: You famously published *Lady Chatterley's Lover*.

BR: Yes. The only book of D. H. Lawrence we did.

WM: All of us who were boys in the fifties owe you a great deal of gratitude for that.

BR: Personally, I didn't like it that much at first. As time went on I got to like it more. I had a lot of feeling about Lawrence—to me he was, no matter what he claimed to be, a rather aristocratic Englishman, and my Irish background made me rebel against him, even though he was doing exactly what he should have been doing—trying to prevail against the industrialization of society and the sterilization of modern life. I thought he was very heavy-handed.

WM: He did not have a light touch.

BR: He didn't have a light touch at all. His descriptions of sex, I think, are ridiculous.

WM: As a publisher, did you have a strategy? I read that you said you published D. H. Lawrence so that someday you could publish someone like Henry Miller.

BR: Somebody *like* him? No, *him*, and very specifically *Tropic of Cancer*. The minute I got into publishing, that became my goal—now I can do it!

I don't know if we would have gotten away with publishing *Chatterley* or not if it hadn't been for Mark Schorer, a professor of English at Berkeley, who came up with the idea in the first place. Not for Miller, but for *Chatterley*. To him that was not a means to an end, it was the beginning *and* the end. He was a wonderful defender of *Chatterley* and of Lawrence, and I admired that and I liked it, but to me it was really a way to get to Miller. And in my correspondence with Maurice Girodias of Olympia Press I talk about how to get to Burroughs through Miller. To me, the direct line of descent was—you know, like a lineup in baseball—Lawrence to Miller to Burroughs.

WM: Henry James to Lawrence to Miller to Burroughs—how about that?

BR: I would accept that. Publishing James created a foundation to show that we were not doing what we were accused of doing by a lot of people: publishing *Lady Chatterley* as just a sensational trick. I didn't publish James for that reason. I hadn't thought about that ulterior purpose at the time, but it did not hurt. It was a good backdrop to have.

WM: Your relationship with Henry Miller goes back to your freshman year at Swarthmore College.

BR: My relationship with his writing.

WM: Did you discover *Tropic of Cancer* that year?

BR: I hardly discovered it. Somebody led me to it. Why, I don't know. It would be interesting to ask that person. He must have seen something in me that was a little different than the other students at Swarthmore. He told me exactly where to go. To a famous bookstore, the Gotham Book Mart on Forty-seventh Street.

WM: Why do you think the book had such an impact on you?

BR: I've been thinking about that a lot. First of all, it's certainly disrespectful to most of what were thought of as bourgeois American values. Two other books of Miller I read at the time were *The Air-Conditioned Nightmare* and *The Cosmological Eye*, both published by New Directions, I think. *Tropic of Cancer* actually fits right in with them. *Tropic of Cancer* isn't that different except in its overt sexual terms, which seemed to me at the time very surrealistic. Miller himself struck me as being a very unlikable person. The personality that came through, his arrogance, his foisting himself upon other people to feed him. He would plan a whole week ahead of time: "I'm having dinner at such and such a place this night, and dinner at someone else's the following night," et cetera. None of these people really wanted him, but they couldn't avoid him. That didn't endear him to me.

What I realize is this. He had an affair with a woman—I think her name is Mona in the book. She is modeled very closely, I think, on a real person. It's a terrible affair, an apparent disaster, but he's very much in love with her, and he loses her, totally. I think now, looking back at that loss, it was so catastrophic it set him free. Something like that happened to me at Swarthmore. I went to Swarthmore very much in love with a girl at Vassar, and I felt very strongly and, ultimately, correctly, that I had lost her. There was nothing to replace her. It was like Miller, who when he really lost Mona, he's free. A catastrophe that sets him free to go out and be himself, whatever "himself" is. Very obnoxious, perhaps, but free to do what he wanted to do. I think that that was what I was looking for, a way out of my own dilemma.

When I've written about *Tropic of Cancer* I've used it as a sort of an anti-American-middle-class weapon, but I think deeper down what was important to me was this catastrophic loss that you suffer and then you decide to go on living. Very existential, although I didn't know that word then.

WM: When you met the real Miller, how did he match the image you'd formed of him from reading his works?

BR: He matched up pretty well: not too friendly, very involved in his own affairs. I got to like him more each time I saw him. In the beginning he was very suspicious. I immediately coined a name for him, "The Hooded Cobra," because he had very narrow, Asian-like eyes, typically Japanese. He looked out from very little space between his eyelids, and I thought he was always being very appraising of the situation, and not really open.

At one point I had Norman Mailer write a book about him. Henry just could not understand why he was doing that. He kept figuring there was something there that wasn't there. Mailer was simply a great admirer of his writing and his life. I don't think Henry could accept that. He thought Mailer was after something that he couldn't put his finger on.

WM: You had a great deal of trouble getting Miller to let you publish *Tropic of Cancer* in America.

BR: I did for a long time have trouble. I went to Big Sur to try to convince him. I was terrified by the place. He had a couch on the edge of a cliff. I got vertigo when I looked over the side. He was living like somebody in the Albanian mountains. It was very hard to get to him. A dirt road up a steep hill, with somebody at the bottom of the hill checking you in. His wife, Eve, who was very charming, said, "When Henry arrives I'm going to pretend I don't want you to do the book, because anything I say he disagrees with." She tried playing that role, but it didn't work. It didn't work at that time, but at least he'd met me, so he knew I was interested, and that I was for real. Later his publishers in Europe convinced him to let me do it.

WM: What was his reluctance?

BR: I don't know. I can only surmise. I have the feeling he was enjoying his lifestyle. He was quite famous in certain quite large circles, among people who might read New Directions books or books from the Olympia Press in Paris. He said if this book were published in the United States, the next thing you know, it would be read in colleges as a textbook.

WM: He didn't want to be mainstream.

BR: He did not. I loved that idea, and proceeded to try to fulfill it, I might add, and did to a degree. He did not seem to understand. He liked being an outlaw, is my strong feeling. We were trying to take away his right to be an outlaw. And we did: *Tropic of Cancer* became accepted.

WM: How did Beckett fly into your web?

BR: I had actually read a little bit of Beckett in *Transition* magazine and a couple of other places. I was going to the New School. My New School life and the beginnings of Grove crossed over. At the New School I had professors like Wallace Fowley, Alfred Kazin, Stanley Kunitz, and others who were very, very important to me. I was reading and writing papers for them, and one day I read in the *New York*

Times about a play called *Waiting for Godot* that was going on in Paris. It was a small clip, but it made me very interested. I got ahold of it and read it. It had something to say to me. Oddly enough, it had a kind of desolation of scene, like Miller, though in its language, its lack of verbiage, it was the opposite of Miller. Still, the sense of a very contemporary lost soul—very interesting. I got Wallace Fowley to read it. His specialty was French literature. His judgment meant a lot to me because he was so different from me. He was a convert to Catholicism, he was gay, and incredibly intelligent. He read the play and told me that he thought—and this before anybody had really heard about it much—that it would be one of the most important works of the twentieth century. And Sylvia Beach got involved in it somehow; she was a fan of Beckett.

Waiting for Godot just hit something in me. I got what Beckett was available and published it. He flew into the web and got trapped. He had been turned down by Simon and Schuster, I found out, much earlier, on an earlier novel.

WM: In choosing writers over the course of your career, to what extent did you rely on the judgment of people you trusted and respected, like Wallace Fowley or Dick Seaver or whomever, rather than just on your own sense of things?

BR: A lot! A lot. At Grove it would have been mainly three people, Don Allen, Fred Jordan, and Dick Seaver. Each of us had different interests, but once you have a feel for the other person's mind, what they are thinking—if Fred, for example, brought up a German writer and said, "This is really good, something we should publish," I would not have been very inclined to say no. I found out after a few years that he had a very strong sense of what he was saying and feeling. Not necessarily that I always agreed with him, but a certain sensibility echoed.

WM: When you first met him, how did Beckett match the image you'd formed of him?

BR: I liked him immediately. Unlike Henry, he was very warm. I know some people thought he wasn't. He made me think, ultimately, of a great psychoanalyst, in the way he treated people. If you were Freud's patient, I would imagine Freud listened to you very carefully, with great intensity, and made you feel, while you were with him, that you were the most important thing. Beckett had that same facility, which some people would misinterpret as meaning he was cold. Because he just listened. He was very sympathetic to whatever you had to say, was very warm, but it could be with very few words. I never discussed it with him, but I think he knew a lot about analysis. He was very irascible and unhappy in the younger journals of his that I've read. I introduced him, reintroduced him, to Miller. They had known each other slightly in Paris in the thirties. We three had lunch together, and afterward both of them said more or less the same thing to me, separately: "My, how he's changed! He's so much nicer than he used to be."

WM: Maybe it was true. In both cases.

BR: I think it's true. My feeling is it was true in both cases.

WM: You said somewhere that Miller was intriguing but not as loveable as Beckett, and that as a person Beckett meant a lot to you. It seems to me that he was the greatest of the writers you published.

BR: Absolutely.

WM: It also sounds as if he was the greatest human being among your writers. Do you think there's any connection there?

BR: I hope so! I certainly think that was true. Also, there is an odd connection between Miller and Beckett, something that may be common to most human beings, I don't know. In Beckett's writing it seems to me there's an echo that keeps coming back of a terrible, catastrophic love that he had.

WM: *Krapp's Last Tape.*

BR: *Krapp's Last Tape*. And in many other things as well. He told me about it a little. He was very, very much in love with the girl. She was English. Her father was a teacher, a professor, and they were living in Germany, on the Baltic. He talks about that in *Krapp's Last Tape*, you see elements of the Baltic, the North Sea.

When he wrote *Krapp's Last Tape*, whether I had anything to do with it or not, I don't know, but I had asked him, "Why don't you write in English?" Why wouldn't he type his letters and why wouldn't he write in English? And the first thing that came out, right after that discussion with me, was *Krapp's Last Tape*, written in English.

WM: Why do you think he wrote almost all his later works in French?

BR: My feeling is that it had partly to do with what had happened to him as a very young man being published in England. Although he wasn't anti-British anywhere near to the degree of, say, O'Casey or some of the other Irish writers, nevertheless he was anti-British. He had a real grudge against his British publisher, Chatto and Windus, who took him on and then abandoned him. The British had proved themselves to him by their treatment of him.

More than that, I think of French as being a much calmer language than English. I think English is a very emotional language, and writing in French would be a way for Beckett to put himself in a straitjacket, to a degree. I really, really do. I think maybe it got him away from that sadness that he felt.

WM: He made statements to the effect that English was too beautiful, too poetic a language for the things he wanted to say.

BR: Yes, that fits, that's the way he would put it, but . . . that's putting it very mildly, actually. The first books, *More Pricks than Kicks* and *Murphy*, were written in English. *More Pricks than Kicks* foreshadowed many of the later things. *Waiting for Godot*, though, brought out a lot of things that I believe. More and more, it's obvious to me that a strong element in that play is the reflection of him and Suzanne, his wife-to-be, and their boredom with each other in the Vaucluse during the war, when they were hiding from the Nazis. Just utter boredom. What can we do? What the hell is going to happen? Hoping that something would happen to excite them, but nothing ever did.

Pozzo, in *Waiting for Godot*, to me, was Joyce. I never got the feeling that Beckett was enamored of Joyce. I mean, as a writer, yes, but as a person, no. Pozzo doesn't treat Lucky very nicely.

WM: Joyce as sadist . . .

BR: Yes. Beckett was Lucky, but he was only one of the models, I think. Lucky was put together from a mélange of several young Irish devotees like himself whom Joyce used very cruelly.

WM: If it was Beckett's time in Provence that led to *Waiting for Godot*, his breakthrough work, that period would be the most crucial of his life, those years of boredom down there.

BR: I think they certainly must have been very important ones, in terms of getting him to write. In terms of emotional involvement, I think that was in the Baltic. *Krapp's Last Tape* is pretty straight-out emotion. It's not like *Waiting for Godot*, or *Endgame*. It's not French! It's far and away my personal favorite.

WM: Did your publishing Beckett lead the Beats to your door?

BR: No, not to my door, to Beckett's door. I thought American Beat writers were very, very good in one sense: they were much more outgoing toward other cultures, toward French, Italian, and German literature. Whereas the Europeans were not very outgoing toward Americans at that particular time. People like Ginsberg and Burroughs recognized Beckett early on. They really did, and they wanted him to accept *them*.

WM: But Beckett was not a Beat.

BR: He was not a Beat. He was not a Beat! I think he was particularly disturbed by Burroughs's cut-up theory. He did not like to do things by accident. If there was going to be an accident, it was going to be one that he planned. To take a text and cut things out and put them next to each other, that was not his idea of how to write.

WM: There's a story I've read about how Beckett, when he was acting as Joyce's secretary, was taking dictation for *Finnegans Wake* and somebody came to the door and said something and Joyce immediately incorporated it into the book, and Beckett was absolutely appalled at the randomness of that.

BR: Yes, that would be similar to Burroughs. I would personally applaud it. I would disagree with Beckett about that. Maybe when he was much younger he could have been more open to that.

WM: How did he regard his earlier work?

BR: He constantly put it down, all the time. Didn't matter which thing it was. I was reading the other day a letter from him about *More Pricks than Kicks*. He hated it! He wrote to me and said, "I don't know how I ever allowed you to . . . the idea of publishing it is terrible. It's loathsome. I'm sorry I put you in this trouble and, and send back the contract."

However, as the years went by, he would change his mind and insist on publishing the earlier things. And would be giving out ideas on how to do it.

WM: How did you get to the Beats? The second issue of the *Evergreen Review* was devoted to them.

BR: I would say that Don Allen was the leader in that. He was very aware of them, and brought to us the writings of Allen Ginsberg. Allen Ginsberg couldn't have been more different from Don Allen. Burroughs might be a little closer to Don, in his ascetic, Puritan exterior. Don wasn't enthusiastic about anything. The worst thing you could do—if you tried to get him to be enthusiastic, that would turn him off forever. If you just went by what he turned up, however, he was very important to me. Kerouac, for example, whom he brought to us, was to me immediately in line with Whitman and Miller and

Sandburg, a loosening up of those figures, of that tradition. Things from Kerouac that came much later, I did not like too much. I thought he began to lose it. Don was very involved with Zen Buddhism, but not me. When Kerouac seemed to immerse himself completely in Zen Buddhism he lost it, in my opinion.

WM: Did you bring any of the Beats together with Beckett?

BR: I did once. I had a dinner at Maurice Girodias's restaurant in Paris with Beckett and Burroughs. I've told the story so many times I'm beginning to wonder if it was real or if I made it up or somebody else did, but my memory is that Burroughs tried to get Beckett interested in cut-up. And Beckett, who was extremely polite, really polite, said, "That's not writing; that's plumbing." That's my memory. Whether he ever said it or not, that's the way he felt.

WM: What about Ionesco? Did you have a relationship with him?

BR: Yes, much less but real, and very amusing. Ionesco lived in the same absurd way as a character out of *The Bald Soprano*. Beckett and Ionesco shared a lot. They admired each other, I might add. They didn't really know each other well but they were very aware of each other. They were both expatriate writers. Really unusual, both took French to be their language to write in, one from English, the other from Romanian. To me they were both refugees living in Paris, but the French liked that so much they adopted them. Beckett is now considered a French writer. Ionesco is considered a French writer. I don't think they are, but a lot of the French literary community obviously thinks they are.

Ionesco was the bourgeois character carried to its ultimate absurdity. He wanted to be accepted as a bourgeois, and of course at the same time he was making fun of it. Not as engaging as Beckett, or Miller, for me. I was a little more at a distance from him. I got closer to Jean Genet.

WM: Talk about Genet.

BR: Jean Genet could have come right out of the slums of Chicago, my home city—a tough city. When the Democratic National Convention was held there in 1968, to my eternal discredit I did not go to it. I was afraid. I literally was afraid. I thought, If I go there, I'm gonna get killed. Since before the convention I had been anticipating, more or less, what happened. But Genet went, and Dick Seaver went, and Burroughs went, and Allen Ginsberg went, and Norman Mailer. A lot of people went. I felt too close to Chicago. I had reserved a room a year in advance, and I turned it over to CBS. My childhood companion Haskell Wexler not only went, he made from it his film *Medium Cool*, a great creative success.

Genet fit right in there. He made a speech in the park, under the hail of the tear gas, which Dick Seaver translated to the crowd. Nationality didn't much matter to him. I don't think he knew where he came from. He was a wanderer by himself. He was a Henry Miller with more overt emotions.

WM: You've said elsewhere that he was quintessentially a thief, a criminal.

BR: He was! He was sentenced to life in prison for various crimes. To the great credit of the French, all these famous writers gathered together in a committee and appealed his sentence and won. There was no point in continuing to arresting him. He was going to steal till the day he died. So what?

When we first met Genet, my second wife, Loly, had beautiful earrings on. He took us to the top of a building in Montmartre and pointed out the window, saying, "Look what's going on down there!" Loly had one hand on her ear, and Genet had his hand out to get the earring. It was beautiful. Nothing happened. He didn't shove her hand away, she didn't take it away. She kept her earring. She liked it.

WM: How did you get your connection with Editions de Minuit in Paris and publish not only Beckett but also the French nouvelle vague writers?

BR: It started with Beckett. Then I met Alain Robbe-Grillet there; he was an editor. I liked him very much, as a person and as a writer. He was the important one to me there, next to Beckett.

I liked Robbe-Grillet so much as a writer that I tried to imitate him. It was the getting rid of overt emotion to me—not showing emotion directly, but by description—cold, flat, you could almost say medical description that conveyed, to me, an enormous amount of emotion . . . by describing objects, the slightest change, the slightest shift of position of a piece of rope, or the way a bicycle wheel was turned, and describing exactly how it was turned—but not telling you anything about a person's emotional reaction to what was going on. But you knew.

WM: Have you read his autobiography, *Le Miroir Qui Revient* [translated as *Ghosts in the Mirror*]?

BR: No.

WM: He says in it that the idea he put forth at the time of objective, neutral writing, of purely objective description of the physical world, was a deception, a ruse, and that what he was really writing was his own subjective fantasies, particularly his sexual fantasies.

BR: Sure! Absolutely! "Ruse"? Call it whatever you want, but that's the way I read it from the beginning—as his sexual fantasies. But by doing it in that way he was able to convey them very powerfully. He is, I think, one of the most sexually charged writers I've ever read. And his wife, too, who is also a writer under the name Jean de Berg.

WM: Nabokov, you know, was a big fan of Robbe-Grillet, and I read once that the Nabokovs invited Robbe-Grillet and his wife to dinner in Paris, and she came dressed as Lolita. I guess she is quite a bit younger than her husband.

BR: That's her! She looks like Lolita. Very tiny. Very tiny, but very tough, boy, let me tell you, underneath that Lolita appearance.

WM: What other writers whom you've published have been important to you, as writers and as people?

BR: Kenzaburo Oe became very important to me, as a writer and a human being.

WM: Did you tell me a story once about how you flew to Tokyo to meet Oe and decided, based purely on your meeting with him, to publish him?

BR: No, no. We had already decided to publish him. I got interested in Japanese literature because of the war and because of Donald Allen, who knew a great deal about it . . . I saw a sensibility, a taste there, and so we put a web up to catch Japanese writers. They were available. Even though Knopf had made quite a specialty of Japanese literature. Very strong. Most interestingly, when Oe came along, he was going to be published by Knopf, and he switched to us—which said something for him, or for us, or against Knopf, I don't know. I wasn't even aware of it at the time, that he had made a conscious decision to do that.

We'd already made our mind up to publish him when I went to Tokyo and had hired John Nathan, probably the best translator of Japanese in his generation, as his translator. I hadn't met Oe and was very curious to know what he was like.

WM: What was he like?

BR: I'll give you an idea of Oe's character: He greatly admired Norman Mailer. He was asked to come to Harvard, I think by Henry Kissinger, who was holding international seminars there and inviting people like Oe. Oe went. He sent me a letter saying, "I met the great Norman Mailer yesterday, but he didn't meet me." That's Oe, very self-effacing, very. Mailer, whatever else, is pretty filled with himself. Oe said, "Unfortunately for me, he didn't meet me." I believe that was unfortunate for Norman, that he missed something, really lost something there.

Oe came to East Hampton and stayed with us, as had Beckett. I remember watching a film with him about Che Guevara. Oe and I both saw Che as a great hero, the hero who ultimately failed. Oe and I were both taken by Che's heroic persona. This guy from the CIA had chased Che all over the world and finally caught him in Bolivia, and he said, "With these little guys"—meaning Bolivian soldiers— "we caught him," and that was a great triumph because he was a great soldier. His enemy was the one best able to appreciate him. Oe and I were both crying.

WM: What about his writing?

BR: Oe, like Beckett and Miller, wrote beautifully and hauntingly of a romantic disaster in his life. He handled the situation in a different way. It's treated in his book *A Personal Matter*. The protagonist is very, very much in love with a woman and is planning to leave his wife for her. Then the wife gives birth, and the child is born with a faulty head, its brain literally cut diagonally. The child should die, the protagonist thinks. But the child does not die. This was also the case in real life, because I know the child! The protagonist tells the doctors to let the child die, but they don't. The baby keeps on living. It doesn't die. It keeps on living, and then, as the days go by, the character changes his mind; he realizes that the child's going to survive and decides that he's going to go back to his wife. He gives up the big romantic adventure of his life to do that, to return to his wife and help raise the child. To my utter amazement, the real child grew up and became a famous composer! He doesn't speak very well, but he can compose like Bach, and is more famous in Japan than Oe.

Miller and Beckett found themselves by losing someone and going off on their own. Oe found himself by going home and dealing with the situation, in a very existentialist and beautiful way. He reversed it. He reversed the dynamic.

WM: In designating you a Commander in the Order of Arts and Letters, the French Ministry of Culture referred to your "conception of publishing as an art." Do you have any final words for us on the practice of that art, on the spinning of your web?

BR: Why do you like one girl better than another? You can make up reasons, you know. You can make them up. But ultimately, you had the answer before you made up the reason.

These things are not done by the numbers. You won't find her, or the great author, or the secrets of a painting, in a mathematical equation or a sociological treatise—but when it happens, you can sometimes say, "Ah, sweet mystery of life at last I've found you." Then go with it. Don't ask the whys and hows of it. Just go with it. Your very own mystery.

A CONVERSATION WITH
JAMES SALTER

Chris Offutt

I met James Salter in 1989, when I was completing my MFA degree at the Iowa Writers' Workshop. He was a visiting instructor, one of the few times he has taught. It was a glorious season, the air crisp and chilly, brilliant leaves scattering along the streets, pigs browsing the harvested cornfield at the edge of town.

Jim enjoyed contact with all the students and was particularly loyal to those of us fortunate enough to be in his workshop. He joined us at the bar after class, invited us to his house for supper, and played softball and football on the weekends. Jim was like an officer who rolled his sleeves up and spent time with enlisted men. Above all, he was a terrific workshop instructor.

Jim spoke little in class, but when he did, the only sound was that of a dozen pens transcribing his words. His editorial comments burrowed into the flaws of a manuscript, revealing a way of thinking that would allow you to improve it. Jim had a knack for guiding young writers into challenging themselves.

Once during conference, he zeroed in on a line I'd written that didn't fit with the tone. "Too much like Mickey Spillane," Jim said. I told him that I'd lifted the phrase straight from Faulkner, proud that I had stolen from the master, and that my teacher had somehow missed it. Salter nodded patiently, his voice calm. "Where," he said, "do you think Faulkner got it?"

Chris Offutt: I was casting around, trying to figure out how to introduce you, and I know that you hate the long-winded introductions about being a decorated combat pilot, so I didn't want to mention that; or, how you published your first novel before I was born, but I won't mention that; or other topics you don't like to mention: the wars, living abroad for years, getting married in Paris. So I talked to people and said, "What should I bring up?" They said that I should just open with the fact that you had written the greatest anal sex scene in literature; however, I didn't want to bring that up.

James Salter: This is like a famous thing in rhetoric, where you say, "I won't speak of his deceitfulness, I won't mention his vices," and so forth. So now you haven't mentioned those things. Thank you. I was introduced once by someone who said that I was a member of a generation rapidly disappearing. I sometimes think of that; I think of myself as rapidly disappearing. Although I've been writing for a long time—my first book was published in 1957—and I've been writing more or less all that time, I don't seem to have a long list of books that have been published; but it so happens that at this particular period of time, I have three coming out within twelve months.

CO: What are those books?

JS: The first book is called *Gods of Tin*. It was written by me, but not assembled by me. An editor took parts of three books I had already written, sections of them that had to do with flying—I was at one time an air force pilot. The editor put the material from those three books together in narrative, chronological form, to make some sense of it in that way, and added to it some material that had never been published. I was a fighter pilot in Korea, and I had kept a journal. I had never published any of it, and there are excerpts from it in the book. Then I have a book of short stories, recently written. Following that is a book that my wife and I wrote together. It's a nonfiction book, and it's like a book of hours, except it's really a book of days. There's a page for each day of the year, and on each page, there's an entry or two. The title of the book is *Life is Meals*, and the entries all have to do with eating, drinking, food, cooking, the table, and so forth. It has some recipes in it, but it is not a book of recipes. The material is historical, anecdotal, informative, et cetera. I've read this book a couple of times, and what makes me think it's good is that every time I read it, it's as if for the first time. I can't remember having written that, and even the facts seem new and fresh to me. We wrote it in a terrific way, which is, she went off somewhere and wrote some pages. I went off in an entirely different place and wrote some pages. Then we traded them and edited them. She edited mine, and I hers. We never had a single argument. The style of the book is such as to make it relatively seamless anyway.

CO: When you first started publishing, you changed your name to a nom de plume. Why did you make that choice, and how did you come up with the name?

JS: The principal reason was I'd written a book, and I was a regular air force officer at the time, and regulations in those days were that anything that you sent out for publication had to be vetted, passed by some general in some office. I didn't want to do that, for a couple of reasons, the most important of which was that though I thought I'd written something wonderful, everybody feels that, and I knew that might not be true, and I didn't want to jeopardize my career. So I decided to disregard regulations and publish it under a pseudonym. I cast around for a name that was going to be completely remote from mine, that didn't use the same letters, or I was going to keep the James, I don't quite remember. I had a long list of them, just the way you name characters in fiction, and I kept crossing them out. You're a little—I don't want to say pretentious—but you're a little silly when you're young, and I had a name, Psalter, which of course is the name of a group of psalms. I liked the sound of that, and I thought it would be perfect, but somebody wisely talked me out of it and said, "You can't do that. It's too precious. People aren't going to accept it. You've got to drop the P." So that's what I did.

The other reason is that, after that book was published, I resigned my commission and became a writer. I was changing my life completely. Everything I had done for sixteen years I was pitching out, and I was turning into someone entirely different. I thought that it was appropriate at that time to start out completely fresh and start out with another name and another person. I didn't invent myself. I am who I am; but in a sense, I discarded the old snake skin. It was time to get rid of it and move on.

CO: You were in the military sixteen years?

JS: Yes. At first I thought it was just going to be an episode.

CO: Did you ever regret resigning the commission?

JS: No.

CO: Never?

JS: It was the most difficult act of my life, I would say, and I regretted it immensely at the time, and probably for a few years after, but you get over that. It was like a divorce, when you really have put everything into it, then you say, "It's over," and you're going to have to start again.

CO: Did they try to talk you out of it?

JS: No. I didn't confide in anybody. I wrote about this in *Burning the Days*. I went to the Pentagon to do it. I was in Washington at the time, and I went to the Pentagon, and I met a guy I knew, a colonel named Berg, who was in personnel, and I told him I was going to resign. He didn't bat an eye. There was nobody around to say, "Stop before you do something you'll regret forever."

CO: I know you went to West Point, and then you went to Korea, but before that, you'd gone to a high school with another guy who went on to become a writer.

JS: Yes. Can we name him here?

CO: Yes.

JS: I was at prep school in Riverdale, and I think two classes ahead of me was John Kerouac, who was there as a ringer. They used to give an athletic scholarship for the final year of high school to gifted athletes, and he was one of them. He was a football player. I was on the literary magazine, among other things, and one day we had a submission from him. It was unheard of, really, to have one of these thugs turn in a story. We all said, "What is this? Let me see it!" It was pretty good and we published it. I don't remember what the story was, some sort of detective story. Then years later, in Pensacola, I was walking by a bookstore, and in the window, there was a book called *The Town and the City*, displayed both front and back. I recognized the name immediately, John Kerouac, and I recognized his photograph as well. I bought that book and read it, and it was pretty good. It's very Wolfe-ian, Thomas Wolfe. I read it with both admiration and envy, and I thought, Well, I'll be—as they say—damned. Look at this! That was in about 1950. It certainly acted as a spur for me. I thought, If he can do this, what's wrong with you?

CO: Were you writing while you were in the air force?

JS: No. At that time, it was before Korea. I was writing, but, nothing, just junk that you write when you're young. I was not writing stories. I was trying to write a novel, actually. I was attempting to. I had, latent within me, I suppose, some urge to do this, and I was trying;

but I certainly didn't have the background to do it, and I was completely on my own. I never talked to anybody about it.

CO: Your influence has been profound on me, as well as on many other writers. Who are the writers who influenced you, besides Jack Kerouac?

JS: He wasn't really an influence on me. His achievement was an influence on me. I didn't read anything more of his until *On the Road* came out, and that must have been seven or eight years later.

CO: So who did you read who had an impact?

JS: In 1948, I was in the hospital in Honolulu with blood poisoning. It was great, actually. The hospitals were not crowded then, and I knew what was wrong with me, and they were very solicitous. I sent a friend out to buy me a couple of books. I told him which ones I wanted, and they were two or three books by Thomas Wolfe: *The Web and the Rock, Of Time and the River*, and I've forgotten the name of the other one. I devoured them. I read all three while I was in the hospital, and they were very influential. Why do you write? Something in you makes you want to write, but also the whole, shall I say, image of it is important, and Wolfe had a very powerful, romantic image. I presume you're familiar with him, although he's not much read now. He was a big—and when I say, "big," I mean both physically, and in terms of reputation and readership—a very large figure in prewar literature. He had the most famous editor at the time, who was also a large figure, Maxwell Perkins. Wolfe was a very poetic, very lyrical, very unbridled writer . . . he's off there somewhere, just going and going. I was influenced by him. Plus, I was influenced by a lot of junk that I read, the normal, sugary diet of young people.

CO: Such as?

JS: I can remember I was tremendously influenced by a book called *My Son, My Son.* I don't remember who wrote it. It was a big best-seller at the time, a dramatic story of two families and their sons and what happens to each of the sons. Of course I still, just like your early telephone numbers, I still remember passages, or at least lines, from that book. That's one of the bad parts about not being careful about what you read when you're young. It's probably better to stick to a very healthy diet at the beginning. But there is no "way." There are ways, a lot of ways, and writers have different ways, and there are writers who've read the most horrible trash and gone right through and swept it aside, so to speak, and gone on to write wonderful things. In my case, I don't think it crippled me, but it didn't help me to read all that.

CO: Do you still read contemporary fiction?

JS: Not so much. I don't read for pleasure anymore.

CO: What do you mean? Then what do you read for?

JS: I get some pleasure incidentally. Reading is not an entertainment, or something I do to enrich myself. I read because I want to see how they did it, and to fill in certain gaps. You die with huge gaps. Even Harold Bloom is going to have a lot of gaps. So you can't really catch up completely; but there are some books and some writers that are very important to you, that become essential to you, and I often read and re-read the same writers. It's too late—well, I don't want to say it's too late—but, fortunately, I am past the point of being formed by those writers and following in their tracks. I said there is not a way, there are ways: James Jones, who wrote an exceptional book, *From Here to Eternity*, went to a writers' colony in Illinois, and the woman who ran it had a particular idea about how to teach writing. She sat every student down for two or three hours in the morning, and had them copy out, in longhand, paragraphs from her favorite three writers, who were Hemingway, Fitzgerald, and Thomas Wolfe, or maybe it was Faulkner. I laughed about that. My God, I thought, there is ignorance operating at full speed, but I'm not so sure of that now. I'm not sure that the mimetic approach of copying and copying isn't, at a certain stage in your career, something that can be beneficial. Churchill, in his autobiography, said that he was a poor pupil, that he was left behind for a couple of years. While the brighter boys were going on studying Greek and Latin, he was obliged to take English again, over and over. That way, he had fixed in his mind the exact grammatical structure, and the tone and the lyric, of an English sentence.

CO: Did you ever do that?

JS: No. I heard this much later.

CO: When you write, do you write in longhand?

JS: Yes.

CO: And then you type it?

JS: Yes.

CO: So in a way, you're transcribing your own work.

JS: It's a bit different from copying another writer.

CO: Does it change from one draft to the next?

JS: Of course. It certainly changes when you see your galleys, doesn't it? It has some authority then, and it reads differently, and you see things in it that you didn't see in the typescript. First of all, time has passed, so the fog of creation has lifted. I think it's definitely true that in each form, you see things a little differently. Here, again, I wouldn't recommend writing in longhand to anyone. I think for me it's a question of never having adopted newer methods.

CO: What do you mean?

JS: I presume that almost everybody writes on a computer now, for a lot of reasons, not the least of which is that publishers don't want a manuscript; they want your disk, so that puts you in the position of having to work on a computer.

CO: You use Wite-out. You may be one of the few people who are keeping the Wite-out manufacturers in business. I'm interested in this idea of writing it out in longhand, and then transferring it into a different form.

JS: I feel too silly talking about this. It's like saying, "Do you move the fork from your left to your right hand after you cut the meat?" I personally find it very satisfying to put a pen to a piece of paper and make marks and write. I don't know why that is. Maybe it wouldn't be satisfying for someone else, or maybe it would be if they tried it. I like it. I also like the convenience, the utter convenience of being able to write at any time; that is to say, at night, you're lying in bed, and you think, Jesus, that's an interesting name, isn't it? Or whatever comes to you, you don't have to get up, you simply scribble it on a little piece of paper, or while you're traveling, or walking, or doing one thing or another, you can't carry your laptop with you, but you can simply reach in your pocket for a piece of paper. I think convenience is an important thing. My method of writing is that I write on scraps of paper and keep accumulating things I think might be useful; then with those things, at least I go in with something. I don't have to look at a blank page. I have something in advance.

CO: Do you organize those scraps of paper, or type up the notes?

JS: I usually just organize them by marking them up in ink: A, B, C, or 1, 2, 3, or whatever. Then I make an outline, trying to find a place for them, and of course a lot of them have no place. They're wonderful; I think they're wonderful or I wouldn't have written them down, but they turn out to be not so wonderful, and after a while, you say, "Get real." But some of them are interesting, and the ones you can use, you use. Evelyn Waugh once said something like this: "People think that one writes books by standing behind a screen in a room and writing down the clever things that people say." It is true, unfortunately, at least for me, that if I don't write down something that somebody has said that's particularly right, or memorable, I'm not going to find it again. I can know what they said, but the order is lost. So I write down a lot of things as quickly as I can. Going back to Waugh, he said, "People think you stand behind a screen, but that's not it at all."

What you really do—it's like working in a huge rubbish heap and you're just sifting through a lot of terrible rubbish and suddenly you come across something. Ah! There it is! It's dented, it's tarnished, but if it were polished up a bit and straightened out somehow, it might be a nice candelabra. So you are going through what amounts to a rubbish heap of your own ideas to find what works.

CO: It sounds as though the way you work is never ending. There is no break from being a writer.

JS: Well, why would you want a break?

CO: Exactly. Why would you want a break? *Arm of Flesh* was your second book, and I don't know if it was experimental, but each chapter is from a different point of view. That book was out of print, and remained so for a while, and I assume that was your decision.

JS: Not really, but who would want to print it? The first book I wrote was a success. It sold far more than the publisher expected, which is to say, twelve thousand copies. The reviews were good, and all that business that was important to you when you're starting out. They said, "We're very eager to see another book from you," and of course, everybody has this story about the second book. So I wrote and wrote. I was under the impression at that time that if I took a book like Faulkner's *As I Lay Dying* and simply lifted the whole concept of it, nobody would notice such a thing. That's what I did, but he was a masterful, a great writer, and I simply didn't have that kind of stuff. I wrote not a very good book. My editor at Harper and Row said to me after he read it, "I don't really understand it, but it's probably good, so we'll publish it." They did, and it vanished immediately. It didn't sell at all, and got very little notice, and that was it. Decades, about forty years later, a publisher who had published a number of my things, Jack Shoemaker at North Point Press, said, "I'd love to republish *The Hunters*"—that was my first book—"and also this other book, *The Arm of Flesh*." I was not enthusiastic about either of those notions and especially about the second one. I said, "I wouldn't want to republish *The Hunters* unless I had a chance to make revisions," and he said, "Fine," and I said, "As for the other one, I don't want to republish it at all." He said, "I'd like you to think about it." After a while and the conversations and the letters, I said I would only do it if I rewrote it completely, from start to finish. He said, "That would be fine." So, not having anything else I was doing, I said I would do it. I did rewrite it, and it was republished. Is it any good? I don't know. It's better than the first one.

CO: I don't know if this is precedented in American letters: to not simply revisit, but to rewrite a previously published novel.

JS: I don't know if it's such a brilliant idea. I worked from the other book as one works from a translation. I crossed out a lot of things. I made a lot of derogatory comments in the margin and worked on it as an editor might with somebody who—I don't want to say, "showed promise"—but somebody who would have to do a lot to pull this thing together.

CO: What was the biggest adjustment or biggest change from one version to another?

JS: The first thing was jettisoning the form of *As I Lay Dying*, which had been fatal. So I simply threw that away and started again as a book written in the third person. I also changed the structure somewhat, and so on and so forth.

CO: One of the stories in your other book of short stories, *Dusk*—recipient of the Pen/Faulkner award, which is without doubt the award that has the highest esteem among the literary world—is about going to a West Point reunion. Do you still participate in those?

JS: I've been to some of them, yes. The story was inspired by one particular reunion, but a lot is made up, as you know.

CO: Do you have any relationship at all now with the air force?

JS: Both my roommates were killed. There were eight hundred fifty people in my class. Of those, perhaps two hundred went into the air force and became pilots. Of those, a lot of them got killed early on. There were a lot of accidents. Those I had as real friends, maybe a half dozen, for some reason, they're all dead.

CO: Of that generation, the ones who were your friends, isn't that the first generation that began flying space missions?

JS: Oh yes. Buzz Aldrin was in my squadron. He was a flight leader. Ed White was in the same squadron. He was one of the three astronauts killed in the capsule fire in 1967. Virgil "Gus" Grissom, as well, was in my wing in Korea. Yes, I've been very close to greatness.

CO: If things had gone differently, you could have been an astronaut. Did you ever think that?

JS: I don't think so. Test pilots were a big romantic thing, but they were not the road to advancement. The people who went into test pilot school and became test pilots were famous, a bit, but never advanced very far. Advancement went to those on staff and in command, and when the astronaut program first came out, it was affiliated with the test pilot program, and you had to go to test pilot school to become an astronaut. Who ever thought they would go to the moon? That was just a pipe dream.

CO: You mentioned that Thomas Wolfe occupied a certain figure in the world and that you've seen the writer's position in the culture shift drastically. What is a writer's place in the world now?

JS: It's like a big bus, this culture. It's going a mile a minute. I'm on it, and I don't even know why I'm on it or where it's going. New people are getting on every minute, just raising hell, and with all kinds of baggage; a lot of them have run marathons. You say to yourself, "what's going to happen here?" I don't have the faintest idea. Is it important that a culture be elevated, or move upward, so to speak? I doubt it. I'm not persuaded that that's essential. Proceeding from that, the loss of the eminence of literature doesn't strike me as being something tragic. I feel that most people are missing a lot. They just don't know. They're not going to know. They're perfectly happy; probably happier than I am, but they just don't know. That's the way it is. I don't know what you can do about it. Every writer I've ever known who's addressed this has said the same thing. Books and reading are down a few steps. Anything except the most time-killing junk—a terrible expression, "killing time"—but that is of less interest to the country as a whole. What are you going to do? Live with it.

CO: Now you're finishing a new collection of stories?

JS: Yes, it's the most fruitful period in my life. My daughter is a publisher in France, and she had just started her own publishing house about two years ago. She asked me if she could publish something of mine to help her get started. I said yes, but I didn't have anything except some stories. She said that would be wonderful. I already had a French publisher, but we cleared it with him, and she published six of these stories in Paris. In France, for some reason, like Jerry Lewis, I'm treated differently. People often say that the French have done nothing culturally for forty years, and that it's a backwater and they're always admiring and praising the worst American writers. That's the only thing I feel a little uneasy about, but she published it there, and it did very well, so I wrote some more stories for it, and Knopf is publishing it here.

CO: The last time we talked, you hadn't completed it, and you had to write a story.

JS: I still am short one. I know exactly what it is, if I ever—I need a little quiet to sit down and focus on it.

CO: It's amazing to me that you can write stories to fulfill the book.

JS: I'm not writing them to a prescription. They're stories that I would like to write, but I never worked at this feverish pace. It used to take me a decade.

CO: Why has it changed? How did you find yourself in this fruitful period?

JS: At my back I always hear Time's wingèd chariot.

CO: You're a senior writer in this country, and you're publishing stories in *Tin House*, which some might consider a hip, young person's magazine. That has to be gratifying.

JS: There's always the chance that you're going to do something good, right? The chance may be slim, but there's always a chance. I like writing, and I like reading, and you reach a point where there wouldn't be much of a life without it. As to what's happened to me, and what I think about writing, and what I did: it's like going up and building a house somewhere, and suddenly there's a terrible cracking, and it turns out you're on an ice floe, and the thing is drifting away from the main continent, and it's melting. That's what's happened to writing—and here you have a house on the place!

A CONVERSATION WITH
MARJANE SATRAPI

Heather Hartley

Among stanzas by eleventh-century poet Omar Khayyám, screaming children, the Angel of Death, obese Iranians in 1980s California,
opium, whirling dervishes, a hairy daughter-in-law, prayers, late-night
buses, cigarettes, unrequited love, and Sophia Loren's breasts, you
will find Nasser Ali—a virtuoso of the *tar* (a stringed Persian instrument). Marjane Satrapi's graphic novel *Chicken with Plums* portrays Ali
in the last eight days of his life—a man resigned to die because he has
lost all pleasure in life. No more eating, no more sex, no more family
or friends, and, most tragically for Ali, no more tar.

The only child in a privileged, intellectual family, Satrapi grew up
in Tehran and studied at the Lycée Français. During the upheaval
that followed the 1979 Islamic Revolution, she moved, alone, to
Vienna at age fourteen for her personal safety and her studies. Her
parents stayed behind in Tehran. Almost overnight, Satrapi went

from being an adored, pampered child to an exiled, confused, brilliant, and miserable adolescent. This is the story told in *Persepolis*, the first Iranian comic book in history—a chronicle of Iran during and after the revolution, as well as a compelling narrative of adolescent rebellion depicted in Satrapi's seemingly simple yet powerful black-and-white style.

After *Persepolis* came *Embroideries*, also a graphic novel but with a somewhat different approach: it is an intimate, humorous, and occasionally sarcastic story of Satrapi's female family members, friends, and neighbors, who drink tea while conferring about love, sex, clothes, and, of course, men. If the artist's country and her family are the main subjects of these earlier books, *Chicken with Plums* explores a new theme—the portrait of an artist.

Though the book is set in 1958 in post-Mossadegh Tehran, politics is not its main focus but rather serves as a framework for the story, as do scattered references to Islam. As to politics, religion, child care, or salary earning, Ali couldn't care less: he's just obsessed with finding a new tar. In a fit of rage, his wife breaks his beloved instrument and eight days later he is dead. In the intervening week, some things still rouse Ali's desire: his favorite dish, chicken with plums; his adored daughter, Farzaneh; Sophia Loren's heaving chest; and, most significantly, his search to find a new tar. The stories of his life fence to and fro in time between the present and the past—often differentiated by a simple change in background color from white (representing the present) to black (representing the past). Although the subject matter is one of despair and renunciation, a sense of humor runs throughout the book—even the Angel of Death is a little bit funny. In 2005 *Chicken with Plums* won the Prize for Best Comic Book at the prestigious Angoulême International Comics Festival—one of the few books written by a woman to receive the award since its inception in 1976.

Satrapi eventually moved to Paris, where she joined l'Atelier des Vosges, an artists' cooperative with many well-known French cartoonists, including Christophe Blain, Emmanuel Guibert, and David

B., author of the highly acclaimed graphic novel *Epileptic*. There is more than one connection between David B. and Satrapi: not only have they masterfully depicted their respective childhoods in graphic novel form, but they are also both represented by the same pioneering French publishing house, l'Association, formed in 1990 by a group of French cartoonists including Jean-Christophe Menu, Lewis Trondheim, Stanislas, and David B. In this short time, l'Association has transformed the European comics market with its innovative approach to subject matter, format, and style. Satrapi has found a home both with her publisher and at l'Atelier des Vosges, as well as in Paris itself—a city where you can smoke absolutely everywhere. She spoke with Heather Hartley, *Tin House*'s Paris editor, on the phone from the studio where *Persepolis* was being made into a film.

Heather Hartley: In an earlier interview, you speak of the image as an international language. In terms of your work, would you say that an image translates more easily and more powerfully than language, and if so, how?

Marjane Satrapi: Absolutely. I have a pictorial way of thinking—I like to express myself in images. Whatever the facial or corporeal expression is, it looks the same in every culture—a sad man, a screaming woman, a baby crying. It's an international language—like a pictogram. Images are a bridge between my culture and the West and that's what has given me the power to assimilate.

HH: You've also said that you don't come from a culture of comics.

MS: That's right. And I wasn't in love with comics growing up. I never had any dream of becoming a cartoonist. I'm still not a big reader of comics. But what I do read is mostly American—I prefer American cartoonists much more. Like [Art] Spiegelman.

HH: What are you reading now?

MS: A book about religion by an Iranian author who destroys every myth of religion one after the other. And I'm also reading one hundred fifty film scenarios in the next nine months—three scenarios per day.

HH: Your books have been translated into more than twenty-four languages. How do you think your work—and words—translates?

MS: Words are words and we speak the way we think. When you have a language without masculine and feminine [grammatical gender], like Persian or English, there is a culture that goes with it. In French, I always have to find rules as to why the masculine object always takes over the feminine. [In French two singular nouns of dissimilar gender always become masculine in the plural.] And the smaller object is often feminine and the larger object is masculine. Like *la bite* [dick], *la merde* [shit], or you've got *le cerveau* [the brain], *le corps* [the body], *l'esprit* [the mind]. [laughs]

Language goes into culture. Sometimes words don't exist in another language—like the word *fun* in French—in French they have no *fun*. Or *excited*. Because in French you can't say you are excited about a book, because *excite* is always sexual. With images you don't have that problem.

HH: Why did you choose the graphic novel form to tell your stories?

MS: I wrote *Persepolis* to teach people what Iran is. *Embroideries* is like a conversation—more open on the page and one image flows into other ones. *Chicken with Plums* is about the life and the death of an artist. It's dense and short—eight pages of a life.

HH: When did you start drawing?

MS: I've been drawing my whole life. I can't remember a time when I wasn't drawing. I was drawing before I was writing and reading.

HH: And have you followed any specific training?

MS: Yes—lots. I went to art school in Iran and then in France to l'Ecole des Arts Décoratifs for seven years. But you know, everything is related in the arts. Comics is just a medium between other media. I've already made a big mural in Barcelona and we are now turning *Persepolis* into a movie.

HH: Your publishing house, l'Association, has a unique, independent vision in the world of French comics. It represents a wide variety of authors and has original distribution procedures, diverse book formatting, and a strong preference for black and white—tenets that seem to complement your work in its vision and scope. How did you find each other?

MS: Coincidence. Coincidence and luck. I was sure no one wanted to publish *Persepolis* but l'Association took it right away.

HH: And it was at l'Atelier des Vosges, the studio where you now work, that it all began. What's the connection between l'Atelier and l'Association?

MS: I knew people who knew people and there was an open space in l'Atelier des Vosges and we were sharing rent. They were all cartoonists. "Oh," I said, "it's so boring and so obsessive." In each frame, you know, there is an obsessive quality, and just one page is made up of something like six to twelve frames. I didn't want to do it then—not like my friends . . . They told me I could write about my childhood.

HH: Did you grow up listening to stories?

MS: Absolutely. I was involved with old people a lot—I love old people. What bores other people is that old people's stories are long and they repeat them two or three times and that is what I love about it. I spent lots of time with old people in my family. I have a good oral memory. And what makes old people's stories interesting is how one story moves into another one. Like with Nasser Ali.

HH: What role did stories and storytelling have in your family life?

MS: My parents were obsessed that I become an intellectual. I watched Bergman films at seven and eight years old and I was reading Emily Brontë when I was eleven . . . I could have as many books as possible in my house.

I didn't read children's literature so much—all those abused, working, depressed children. Not Mark Twain. Agatha Christie was more fun. But I read everything—philosophy, novels, Iranian poetry too—it's so rich.

HH: Poetry is directly integrated into *Chicken with Plums*. The book is framed by the poetry of Omar Khayyám—Nasser Ali quotes him at the beginning and the Angel of Death quotes him at the end. There's also Rumi and *Romeo and Juliet*. With all of these direct references to poetry, what influence would you say that poetry has on your work?

MS: Poetry is the basis of language. The role of poetry is to not close down a culture. The whole basis of a culture is in its poetry. In *Chicken with Plums* there's Khayyám and Rumi. Sufism was the basis of my education.

HH: Throughout *Chicken with Plums* there are also a lot of stories contained within other stories, like a *mise en abyme*. For you, what makes a story work?

MS: One of the biggest masters is Vittorio de Sica with *The Bicycle Thief*. It's the importance of the anecdote. Otherwise it's just a story about a bike and nothing else. The small anecdotes describe the whole drama and catastrophe in *The Bicycle Thief*. If the anecdote is well treated, then the story comes through.

HH: In France, *Chicken with Plums* has been called a book about absence in many forms (absence of love, of food, and of music at the beginning of the story). You countered that the book is a portrait of an artist.

MS: With this book it's the story of an artist and maybe of myself . . . It's me behind Nasser Ali.

I censor myself a lot . . . When I draw a woman I'm much more aware that it will be compared to me. When I draw a man I'm more at ease—it's much freer.

It's not a true story. My uncle died for some strange reason. He was very good-looking. I chose him because he was a man and good-looking and as a plastic artist I'm attracted to beauty. Nasser Ali is an unbearable, complete asshole and also a sensitive, nice man. I have never been as honest about myself before as with Nasser Ali.

It's important to talk about who an artist is—the basis of an artist is narcissism. Think of publishing. You have these books the public must like, plus they have to buy them and then applaud and love you. It's a nice kind of creative narcissism. You're in love with yourself. But egocentrism—*that* is bad.

HH: Humor runs throughout *Chicken with Plums* and often in the details—the look on a character's face, a well-timed one-liner. What place does humor have in art?

MS: Humor is subversive and against all hating. The highest level of understanding is laughter. We laugh at something when we understand it culturally.

HH: The idea of pleasure is also central to *Chicken with Plums*.

MS: Absolutely. Eating is the last pleasure. You will die if you don't eat. It's not the same with sex or some other pleasure. Nasser Ali starts really dying when he's not eating. Lack of pleasure is a symptom of a conservative culture . . . I wanted to underline pleasure in this story.

HH: Exile has shaped and informed your work. Why have you decided to make France your home, and Paris in particular?

MS: I grew up in French schools from the time I was four or five. I can smoke here anywhere I want. I've become very French myself and I don't really like it . . . I'm an exiled person. I would go to the States except for two things: number one: smoking [not as accepted], and number two: George Bush.

Iran is my mother: psycho emotional blackmailing, and I would do everything for her. France is my wife: I have children with her, I can be unfaithful to her, divorce her. The U.S. is my other wife . . . or maybe my lover. [laughs]

HH: What do you make of the riots in France this past fall [2005] and the rising political right?

MS: I started laughing when people were so surprised. What do you expect? You colonize a country: now you are French, now you are not. Now you are Arab. All the soccer people are French. Everybody else isn't. This is a secular country with Catholic holidays. Excuse me but Sarkozy is a motherfucker. [Nicolas Sarkozy is the president of France.] Thank God that a government doesn't represent the entire people of a country. I mean, look at George Bush. You must fight stereotypes all your life and cannot give up.

HH: Yet racism in France seems to be on the rise.

MS: Democracy is extremely fragile. You see how politically correct we are now in Europe—there is so much racism in that. You have to call people one thing, then call them in another way. Censorship and racism are so related. Why do we make jokes about the Americans but not about the Arabs? Because Americans have money. Arabs don't and that means they are not considered equal.

HH: There's a lot of discussion in *Embroideries* about sexual mores in Iran, and sex and sexuality appear in both *Persepolis* and *Chicken with Plums*. Could you speak about the differences in views of sexuality with regard to Iran, France, and the States?

MS: Sex is always a problem in all religions where women are objects of attraction. In my culture, sex is not related to something dirty. It's a macho culture, much more macho than in France. In my culture there is the taboo of virginity, and where virginity is important it means a patriarchal culture and a patriarchal culture is the biggest enemy of a democracy. In France it's definitely better. And in the U.S.

the men have big necks and muscles—the U.S. can be macho in a very different way than my culture. Mine is a taboo culture and there's lots of frustration. In the U.S., it's dental floss and no germs. The States are more open about guns [than sex]. There's a love of weapons and you can have all you want and then sex shops are forbidden. More masturbation and fewer guns.

A CONVERSATION WITH
GEORGE SAUNDERS

James Schiff

George Saunders's work is a whirlwind of verbal energy, inventiveness, and, most importantly, humor. His short stories, which have appeared in the *New Yorker*, *Harper's*, and *Esquire*, can reduce a reader to uncontrollable laughter. When teaching his volumes of short fiction, *CivilWarLand in Bad Decline* (1996), *Pastoralia* (2000), or *In Persuasion Nation* (2006), or his novella, *The Brief and Frightening Reign of Phil* (2005), I often feel the urge to read aloud long passages. This is fiction you want to share with others and a voice that seems to want to get off the page and fill a room.

At the heart of Saunders's success is his talent for depicting the internal lives of his characters, capturing the mind as it speaks to itself: fantasizing, strategizing, countering, reversing, worrying, doubting, and continually vacillating. Sometimes described as "losers," Saunders's characters have cruddy jobs, live in "dangerous crapholes" with their demanding mothers and parasitic relatives, yet they fantasize about changing their lives through dreams of fame, wealth, and sex. While failure and pathos color his fictional world, compassion and humor work to balance his vision.

During a 2002 visit to Cincinnati, Saunders and I sat down before an audience at the University of Cincinnati to discuss his writing.

James Schiff: Let's go back to the early 1980s, after you graduated from the Colorado School of Mines and before you enrolled in the MFA program at Syracuse. Were you sending out stories, and what were you hearing from publishers?

George Saunders: I went to the School of Mines in Colorado, which is a geophysics and mineral engineering school. They didn't have an English department and not much of a library, and I had never read anything published after 1950. After college, I was working in oil fields in Asia. I had gone there with this romantic idea of experiencing some really cool things and then writing about them, but the only models I had were Hemingway and Somerset Maugham. It was the oil boom, and all these white-trashers like myself were over there making more money than we ever should have, and there were lots of drugs and just really exotic things. But I didn't have the voice to do anything with it because the most beautiful moments were when this New Age MTV culture was intersecting with people on mushrooms who were dating transvestites while dressed like punks. When I tried to write about this in Hemingway's language, I couldn't even start. I was writing in that mode at night in this camp and not sending anything out. Then I got sick, came home, and went into this Kerouac phase for a few years, which was equally unproductive. At that point I was so stupid—I didn't know that there were creative writing programs. I didn't even know that there were literary magazines. I just floundered, working a bunch of jobs. Then one day I decided to find out about contemporary fiction, almost as a way of getting it done with, so I could go back to writing like Tolstoy on Quaaludes. I went into the Chicago library and came across this story called "Hot Ice" by Stuart Dybek. It's a beautiful story, set in a neighborhood that I knew. That was the first time it occurred to me that you could use a contemporary idiom to get effects that hadn't been gotten before. Until then I was always trying to update the Nick Adams stories, taking the same emotion I'd felt while reading those stories and trying to re-create it using details from my own life. Reading that story was like having the top of my head blown off, because I suddenly realized that not only could you use contemporary material and language, but the effects you would create would be new and unknown even to you. At that time, though, I wasn't sending out stories. I was actually in the apartment of a stripper, where I picked up a copy of *People* magazine and read an article about Raymond Carver and Jay McInerney . . .

JS: The apartment of a stripper?

GS: Yes. Not a furniture stripper but an actual stripper. She had this magazine, and that was the first time I realized that there was such a thing as creative writing programs. Being the imaginative guy I was, I applied to Syracuse and got in the next year. Until then I was just blundering around. I didn't know anything about contemporary fiction.

JS: What kinds of things did you learn at Syracuse and with whom did you study?

GS: I studied with Tobias Wolff and Douglas Unger. To get into the program, I wrote this one really crazy story that was in the *Northwest Review*; it was a bit like "CivilWarLand" but was only three pages long. I got into the program on that story, and once there I repented of that story. I thought, Oh, it's so goofy, and I want to be a realist writer. Whatever energy there was in that story, I didn't trust it. So I started again doing the Nick Adams thing, or actually imitating Toby Wolff and Raymond Carver. But what they did so beautifully, I had no talent for. So I had two years of writing pretty lame realist stories in which there's a pop at the end, a thinly veiled metaphor: "And he saw that the bush was complicated yet simple." And you say, "Oh, yes, like his marriage." At the time, my composition process involved reading a story I loved, noting the effect that it had, then trying to jury-rig that effect on the reader, which is an impossible thing to do. I don't know what to compare it to. It's like trying to have sex while you're anesthetized—you're just watching the video over there, trying to imitate it. But there's not going to be any spontaneity or feeling. So there were two years of that in the MFA program, with really dismal stories. It was a big step backward from that early piece. I had three good pages when I entered, and for the next two years of grad school I totally stunk up the place.

JS: How many stories did you write during that period before you starting gaining acceptance?

GS: I had written one book of stories after coming back from Asia that I didn't even send out. Then I wrote three stories, all of which got published while I was living in Texas. I wrote them in four weeks—I was in the mode. Then I went to Syracuse and wrote at least four hundred pages of stuff, none of which got even the slightest interest. After that, I got married and wrote two other books that I also didn't send out. It's embarrassing, but there were probably fifteen hundred pages of shit that even I knew weren't anywhere near good enough. It was a case of suppressing all of the things that were my obvious gifts, saying, "Well, that can't possibly be art, because it's too easy. It's got to be something that I can't really do. It's got to be a prose that's so exalted that even I can't write it, until once I do write it." So that was just bad news, and it went on for about four years. I was writing every day, as many hours as I could.

JS: You must have written thirty or forty more stories there. Did you believe you were getting somewhere?

GS: Not really. In my heart, I knew they sucked. When I wrote that three-page story in 1986 or whenever it was, it was so much fun and it felt like it was going directly from the heart to the page, and I was ecstatic. I knew that I wasn't having that experience anymore, and I also knew somehow that you can't fake it. I was trying, and I think I was learning about structure and was maybe learning something viscerally about the way you put a story together, the way that you build up to moments of pathos. The stories weren't good, and I would do the thing that we all do, which is to think, Oh, this is so great, it's the best thing I ever wrote! And then a day later say, "Well . . ."

When I was thirty-three I went to a wedding in Mexico (we had two kids by that time), and I felt that, if I was going to claim to be a writer, it was time for something to happen. This wedding was great, with mezcal and a wild cast of characters: a guy who had just gotten out of prison, a radical Catholic priest, a surfer, and everything you could possibly want. So I thought, This is it. I'm going to make this into a novel. When I came home—I had just started working a new job—I would help my wife get the kids to bed, drink a pot of coffee at about ten, write for three or four hours, get up for work at seven, and so on. I did this for six months and had this four hundred-page "masterpiece." I then made the mistake of sleeping for a week, just to catch my breath, and when I went back and read it, it was incomprehensible. Even I couldn't understand it. I thought, Oh, God. This must be *really* brilliant. I then gave it to my wife, and I had made a lot of this book, saying that this would get us out of our misery, and I remember her face as she read the first couple of pages. You know how when you really hate something and you're trying not to show it? Her jaw stiffened and I said, "Aw, you're kidding!" And she said, "This is terrible." And it really was. At the time, this was huge—to work six months, sacrifice your health to do it, and the book just didn't make any sense. It was like this encoded language—Joyce on stupid pills. But as a result, right after that, I had a breakthrough of sorts, as if in reaction or revulsion to that book.

JS: Was the breakthrough related to discovering your voice?

GS: Yeah, it was literally during a conference call at this job I was working. I was a lowly tech writer-photocopy operator. It was an environmental engineering office. I was the cover guy—there was a format for the covers that you had to use. There was nothing to it: three times down for the title, then go into eleven-point font, and so on. But I was the "Cover Man." They would invite me to these conference calls to take notes. It was a professional courtesy they were extending to me, but not one anyone would want extended to them. Like being allowed to sit there watching while somebody did a proctological exam. I was sitting there, and I started writing these little poems, almost like a Dr. Seuss imitation, just dumb little rhyming couplets, and I drew little pictures near them. I did that for the duration of this very long conference call. At the end I had eight pages of one-page poems and corresponding pictures. It was fun, and when I brought them home and threw them on the table, my wife picked them up, and I could hear her from the next room laughing. I thought, Ah, that's kind of cool. She said, "This is the best thing you've written in four years." It was like a dam opening, this kind of permission giving. Whatever I was doing there, it was good. Or at least better. I went back and consciously imitated that three-page story from years before. I said, "I'm just going to knock myself off." That became a story in the first book called "The Wave-maker Falters," which is almost a direct structural knockoff of that earlier piece. Suddenly it was so easy—the technical questions were answerable. When I got to a place where I didn't know what would happen, suddenly now there was always an answer, and that answer had to do with playfulness. If you didn't know, just throw some shit in there, then that would become self-justifying if you carried it through with conviction. Before, it was always up here in the head: "Well, since he represents patriarchy, he's got to have a beard, and the beard will . . ." As soon as I let go of that and let it be more about language and humor, even if it went off track, it was somehow okay. I've been reading Randall Jarrell's short-fiction anthology, and in the introduction he quotes Rabelais's advice to writers, "Do what you please," which I hear as "Do what pleases you."

JS: It's interesting that you mention your wife laughing in the next room because with your work the audience's reaction to the humor is so strong. It must be a wonderful feeling when you give readings to hear the audience laughing, and I wonder if that affects you as you sit down to write the next story.

GS: When I was younger, I always had this idea that if you weren't very smart, humor was a fallback. Life, of course, was earnest, real, intellectual, and very serious, but if you're a moron, then go ahead and get your laugh. As I get older, I find that I believe with all my heart in the comic approach to life. I mean, we're all sitting in this room very seriously, we all selected clothes, but in X number of years, we all will definitely be rotting in the ground. Which is hilarious when you think about it. Or at least humbling. The pretense, all the elaborate stuff we go through to bolster our egos, and the truth is that nothing—none of this—will last. That's very funny. When you hear anybody in any context talking, including me right now, and think that he's just a corpse in progress, it's kind of hilarious. The other side of it is that it argues strongly for kindness and human compassion. For me, that's the root of comic writing, and that's what I want to get to at some point in my life. In that respect, the laughter is great; it's not cheap and it feels like a spontaneous expression of who I am.

JS: Closely linked to the humor in your stories is the voice, which is mostly internal and gradually accreting. I'm thinking of this passage from "The Falls," in which we follow the thoughts of a man named Morse as he walks home from work. The passage has a long and extensive reach, yet it's all contained in his head. The interior of the mind is your canvas. You depict characters worrying, doubting, vacillating, and reversing themselves. Would we find that in the fifteen hundred pages of manuscript you came up with early in your career?

GS: Not at all. As I remember those pages, they were completely bereft of humor. Also very controlled. If, for example, I knew that Character A was going to need to kill someone for cutting him off in traffic on page twelve, on page six I would have him internally philosophize on the evils of losing one's temper. That way, I thought, when it happened, it would be Subtly Meaningful. Whereas in, say, "The Falls," I didn't start the story by deciding that Morse was going to be a worried neurotic. I just started typing, and in the process a pattern emerged. Once I noticed it, I highlighted and even exaggerated it. The fun is to start typing, find a voice, then realize that there's actually a character implied by the voice. If you listen to your own patterns, you can find out who the character is. That's much more about discovery than imposing your will on a character. So when he thinks something, there isn't any motive for it at all because at that point in the story, I don't even know what's going to happen. That, in turn, generates plot, in a funny kind of way.

JS: If we examined an early draft of that story, would we see anything close to that final version?

GS: On that one, you would, actually. I wrote the initial two sections of that story right after I sold the first book. The first book is all first person, very terse, so I was reacting against that. I wrote it at work as an exercise in longer sentences. So those two sections are very close to what was written earlier, but I'm always trimming because my thinking is that you want it to mimic real thought. If I'm sitting here, and you get up and walk away for a minute, I have a certain amount of time to have a thought stream, but not infinite. My idea is that you have a thought that's appropriate to the time that passes. Also, the thought should follow itself in a way that's realistic. The common thing is to make the thought do something that you need it to do. So, those sections were originally longer. At some point you say, "This is too much, this joke has already been done once before, or this moment builds better if I cut this little lump off here."

JS: So your pattern is to go back and keep compressing?

GS: Pretty much. It's a stripping away. We have at our house one of those glass-topped stoves—the only way you can tell it's hot is that it glows red. With writing, it seems to me, you have your eyes closed, and you're passing your hand over the stove, trying to feel where the hot spots are. My thought is that you trust the hot spots. Don't even think about anything else. Look for the place where the prose energy is high. Cut away the other stuff—be brave enough to do that. This accomplishes two things: it compresses the piece, and it creates little places for new text to join. My model is that the story already exists in your mind perfectly, though not in your conscious mind. In writing it, you're kind of klutzy. Pieces fall and break and get out of order, and stuff that doesn't need to be there gets there. But if I revise in a certain spirit, in time that story puts itself back together the way I think it maybe was originally. It's mostly looking at the story and saying, "These three pages don't do anything—they're boring," so I cut them. Don't worry about what's going to happen—just cut it. Don't worry about how much you loved it when you wrote it—cut it. Sometimes you have fragments lying around, and you don't know how they're connected. As long as you trust the hot spots, you'll have in time a bulk of text that doesn't suck, and the plot comes out of that. How do these three non-sucky parts fit together? For me it's great, because you don't have to worry about it. You just have to maintain your standards, keep cutting, and in time the story will reveal itself.

JS: You said that with your story "Sea Oak," you had something like two hundred pages of manuscript and several abortive albeit polished endings. Can you take us through its composition?

GS: I was talking to my sister in New Orleans, and her daughter, I think, was studying for the GREs. That got me thinking about studying for GREs while having two jobs, a real hardscrabble thing. Also, I was at the mall in Syracuse and these girls were talking in that freaking way, you know: "Aw, fuckin' shit." So I thought it would be fun to do dialect. I don't remember where it started, but I was on a plane and wrote something about the strip bar, Joysticks, with the idea that if the world was run by women, what would Hooters look like? If there was a strip-club restaurant, what would the guys wear? Okay, it's going to be an air-force thing, and I started riffing on that. What would their uniforms look like? What would their routines be like? That was a couple of pages. Then I wrote some dialogue between two sisters. This is what I often do—if two things are interesting to me, I'll put them in the same story by whatever corny mechanism I can come up with. Then I went through the text every day, cutting out what was weak. If there was a three- or four-line riff about the place where somebody works, then a new line would spit out and I'd put it in. Suddenly one section turns into a scene. I got the whole first part written that way. I don't remember many of the details except that it was easy and fun, and it mostly focused on those two girls talking. Much of it involved cutting out the weaker manifestations. Sometimes you'll have a page of dialogue with really only one joke, so you get rid of the rest. The story started remaking itself into scenes, and I remember being very open to stuff I was seeing on TV or hearing about. In one of these stories I had heard of an elderly woman who was frightened to death in her apartment, so I just put that in there. At this point, it had only been about a month, and I was having a lot of fun. Coincidentally, a friend of mine's husband had died, and we went to the funeral, and there was material I lifted from there—the setting, the graveyard, the terrible sadness.

JS: So you really didn't know where this was going?

GS: No, no idea. Sometimes you get a scene ending that's so strong you don't want to lose it. That locks it in. Aunt Bernie died—it wasn't anything conceptual, but just the way that ending comes off when the paramedics arrive seemed about as good as I could do, so I thought, okay, let's make that reality. She's dead, and that's where I got in trouble, because one, I liked what I'd done so far and started clinging to it, and two, structurally she was the most interesting thing in the story and now she was dead. If you think of a story as a juggler juggling six balls, at some point he has to catch them all, which becomes the end of the story. Aunt Bernie was one of those balls, so to speak, and she was important, so her death had to be the story. I went off on a tangent about them getting out of the apartment complex—it became a class story—but then somehow, with her dying like that, it seemed boring to go in that direction, anticlimactic. I polished it all the way to the end. Until she died, I liked it, but after that it seemed like your garden-variety class-consciousness story— boring. I tried infinite variations, and I always have to polish it to the end to see if it's working. Every time I would get to the point where she died, I'd feel a drop in energy. I thought that she had to be in there, so I did this cheesy thing where she was coming to him in dreams and urging him to go find her killer. That seemed too made-for-TV movie—you know: "Avenge me!" If she could come back in a dream, why not just have her reveal the killer's name? The story itself had already dictated the ground rules, and I couldn't violate those. Finally I said, "Maybe it's not going to work," and I went on vacation. On my very first day back, I thought, If she has to come back, just let her. Somewhere along the way, I'd read this book by Alvin Schwartz, *Scary Stories to Tell in the Dark*. One of the stories was an old African American myth about a woman whose husband dies. The day she starts dating again, the husband comes back as a skeleton and sits in a chair watching this other guy court his wife. Finally the woman and her date tear the husband apart, throw him out in the yard and get down to it. So that was in my mind, and I thought, Of course! That's the easiest solution. From there, it was another two weeks until it was all done.

JS: I'm curious about the way you described it. You said you were having fun, particularly at the beginning, but that it became more difficult. I assume we're talking about this going on for several months. When you sit down and move a narrative forward, then realize that those thirty pages aren't going to work, how do you deal with the frustration?

GS: I think I have something wrong with me. I'm really passive in all other aspects of my life, but in writing it offends me that something would be shitty, or not as good as it could be. When I was a kid in Chicago, a neighbor took us to a Bears game, which was a big deal because they didn't have a lot of money. So we made this epic trip downtown: me, my friend, his father, and his uncle. We were at the gates of Wrigley Field and his father said, "Now boys, I gotta tell ya, the thing is, we only got two tickets." I was a Catholic altar boy, a real straight arrow, and his father said, "But don't worry. I've got a plan. What we do is, you guys are gonna ride on our shoulders." They had these big overcoats, and the deal was that you were to put your foot down the overcoat and they would walk by the ticket guy. "They never check, they never look up," he said. I was torn. I didn't want to disobey him, but I also didn't want to do this. First of all, you're on your friend's father's neck, which is gross, touching him. Second of all, he's telling me—me, an altar boy and future Catholic saint—to lie. He said, "If you get caught, don't worry—all you gotta do is act retarded." Then he said, "Show me how you're gonna do it." So I'm up on his shoulders and I have to pretend to be retarded in front of this massive crowd of people at Wrigley Field. Something about writing is like that moment, because for all of my moral rectitude, my main impulse is: I am not going to get caught. That's the first rule. You can deal with morality later, but don't get caught. When I get to the place where I have thirty pages that stink, I feel just like that: I am not going to get caught. No way. I have to start over. There's a despair in the morning, and in the afternoon there's a feeling of being liberated from the shitty stuff that you somewhere in your heart knew wasn't up to snuff anyway. Once you do it a few times and realize that there is a solution, always, and that when you hit it, you'll feel good and believe in it, there is a difference between the stuff that didn't work and the stuff that did. You have to be patient. It goes back to the idea that you can't be attached to the story because it won't yield itself to you until you give up. When you give up, it'll walk right in the door.

JS: Does it get any easier?

GS: No, it's getting harder because now I'm conscious that that's part of it. You get to this point in your life when you think, I'm forty-three years old. I teach writing, so I should know how to do it, but that just isn't the case. The only thing I've learned is that you have to be comfortable with not mastering it, ever. And that's the mastery: when you know it's going to suck, when you know it's going to be hard, when you know the solution is going to be something you didn't expect, and you have to resign yourself to that. Which is kind of a drag. But also thrilling.

JS: Many fiction writers today are generating very funny stuff: Lorrie Moore, Dave Eggers, yourself. However, when you look back at, say, the modernists—Hemingway, Faulkner, Fitzgerald—there is relatively little humor. In contemporary American fiction, particularly the short story, humor seems pervasive. Why do you think that is?

GS: My guess, from my own experience, is probably TV and movies. If you've been a kid and sat through *The Brady Bunch* and cared, it's hard not to be ironic. I also think—though I'm not smart enough to articulate this and wouldn't dare try to write it—that the seriousness of the modernists isn't unrelated to fascism. That is to say, it's not an accident that these two things were in the world at the same time. You could see them as two manifestations of the same impulse—a God urge, maybe; or an aversion to ambiguity and humility. The fact that these people could have had such a humorless dedication to aesthetics and were of the same generation as Hitler are somehow related in my mind. Humor makes the door bigger. If you write in a comic vein, anyone can get into your story—any person, any place—whereas drop Hemingway in Wal-Mart, and what is he going to do with that material? Hunter S. Thompson said he thought that that's why Hemingway went crazy. As the world became more complicated, his style couldn't accommodate it. Gogol, on the other hand, you could put in Wal-Mart and he would do fine. Also Shakespeare, although he'd probably catch grief for the pointy shoes. For me, humor is a way of making that front door bigger. The great thing about modernism is that it can be so breathtakingly technical, so physical and gorgeous, and so formally complicated. But the tradeoff is that it's a very tiny door. To be a Hemingway character, you have to have one of eight occupations and one of three mind-sets, and if you don't, you're just out of luck. For me, having lived through the seventies, it's hard to be serious about human potential. I don't have much reverence for anything. I have love for things, great interest in them—but not much reverence.

JS: You've published mostly short stories with one novella in each collection. The novellas were originally longer works, planned as novels but then compressed. I'm curious about what you think are the differences between the various forms.

GS: The one trick I've learned is compression. I know how to compress. The ideas I have aren't three-hundred-page ideas. What humor there is, it's quick. I don't think "Sea Oak" could be one hundred fifty pages. There's not enough there. All I've learned is to trust stylistic density and tone. Get the tone you want, then whatever length it is, that's fine. I had this piece called "Jon," which I thought was a novel, about one hundred sixty pages, and it seemed okay, it looked like a novel. It wasn't overt, but every time I would get to page thirty, some part of me withdrew from it. Finally, a couple of weeks ago, I had the guts to say, "It's not a novel, dumbass. It's a story." As soon as I did that, it felt so much easier. My sense is that novel writing has to do with elaborating, and that's not something I'm good at. I'm content to be a compressor and not worry too much about how long the final product is.

JS: Do you feel any outside pressure to write a novel?

GS: Not really. I don't get any pressure from my agent. I'm so slow that they don't bother me. It's more like, "You still living?" I have internal pressure because part of me feels that you're not a real writer unless you write a novel. My wife, though, has been great by saying, "If you can write stories, that's good, just do that." So not really, no. I'm always thrilled just to get one more story.

JS: Do you ever feel like pulling back and getting away from that humor and voice you're known for? And does audience play a role in how you write?

GS: Not so much. At this point, I feel like I have a subtly internalized audience, but it's always getting away from me. Out of ten writing days, I probably have half a day where I'm writing something that I'll keep. I would love to sit down and just be funny, but more often the writing is off-voice or too smarmy, or I'm trying too hard, and then titrating it back over many iterations. That's what is so great—if you go over a piece of writing three million times, you're getting the benefit of all your different selves: your anal-retentive self, your anal-expulsive self, your intuitive self, and so on. By going through it many times it becomes purified to where it's more like you than anything else you do. I have days when I'm stupid and really insulting to the audience and other days when I'm suddenly channeling James Joyce, but if you do it enough times, it'll become purified in some way.

JS: There's a very strong pathos in your work, which would almost be sentimental if it weren't cloaked in humor. How do you skate close to that without falling into sentimentality?

GS: To get to the originality in ourselves, we often have to confront some essential—and false—duality that we've imposed internally. Somewhere along the line, young writers set up Traits in Opposition, then throw in their loyalty with one or the other. Shall I be Earnest or Jocular? Dostoyevsky or Tolstoy? Hemingway or Faulkner? These are self-generated and, of course, artificial. But something about the way we develop seems to require this. When I was younger, I was soppy sentimental—a fan of John Denver, Dan Fogelberg, and Kahlil Gibran. For a working-class kid, it was really artsy to be involved in all that. So that was one extreme. My affection for Hemingway and Kerouac fit into that too, that extreme lyricism. On the other side, there was the reality I was living in, which was much tougher and sometimes even brutal. All emotion was conveyed in sarcasm, and any truth was conveyed in smart-ass remarks. Any time you showed that other side, you were completely ripped apart. The way my writing evolved, it seems to me now, was by accommodating both of those in the same package, whereas for years I thought you had to choose

one or the other. I really feel the pathos, that sense of social awk-
wardness. I remember once I was dating this girl who was way above
me and brought her home to Texas for Christmas. The girl and I
were having this little Kahlil Gibran make-out session in my parents'
apartment; it didn't go too far, but it was nice and bookended with
all this Gibran-inspired sentimental love talk. She dozes off on the
couch and I'm on the floor, being a gentleman, and the door opens.
My brother-in-law, who's wasted, comes in, goes right to the corner
and starts pissing for a long time, a real waterfall. Who knows where
he thought he was? She sits up, I sit up, it's very quiet except for the
sound of running water, and in that moment, what do you say? It's
funny, but at the time it was heartbreaking because I wasn't sophis-
ticated enough to see it as a complicated literary moment. It was just
a direct contradiction of everything I liked about myself. I didn't see
myself as the guy whose brother-in-law pisses in the corner. That
kind of pathos is real to me; probably the deepest emotions I have
felt are in that mode. But the only way to get at them is to dress them
up in this silly stuff. It's like having two hand puppets—this one is
smarmy and sentimental, and this one is vicious. You can distract
with this one while you're pinching someone with the other one. All
I've tried to do in writing is to accommodate those two things in a
way that isn't inconsistent or cheap.

JS: You've said that it took a long time to figure out how you write
and what is easiest for you. Now you're the teacher and people are
studying with you. Just as you imitated Toby Wolff, people are now
imitating you. How do you feel when you see that, when you come
across a George Saunders story?

GS: I don't see those stories, though I know people who have said
they exist. When it's your work, you think, No one else even vaguely
resembles me. But the great question is how do you teach writing?
I'm having a hard time with it this semester. Before, it was easier. I
would just say, "I will tell you what's wrong with your story." That's
not very good because you've said it in *your* vocabulary, not neces-

sarily the writer's. Did you help him? I feel like I'm finally getting old enough that I realize that's not a good approach. To guide somebody to find his own voice is an incredibly hard thing, and I don't quite know how to do it. The one helpful thing, I think, is to ask a lot of questions. I've been doing that more. For example, I notice that many writers tend toward avoidance; when there's a pregnant moment in the story, they write around it. I've been finding lately that those moments are the ones that are very good to direct somebody back to—the place where there's a missing scene, or a scene ending seems to be going in one direction and suddenly truncates. It's an incredibly hard job. I don't quite have the knack for it that I'd like to have. I assign exercises. I have them write a two-hundred-word story, but they can use only fifty words, so that it's by definition an exercise in repetition. It's amazing how many people find a voice doing that for some reason. I don't know why.

JS: You mentioned early influences being Hemingway and Maugham. What do you read now?

GS: Because of teaching I'm reading mostly student fiction. I used to read a lot, but now I'm down to a book every couple of months, sadly. Ben Marcus is a favorite writer of mine. Brian Evenson, who is teaching for us this semester. I always go back and read Gogol, since I love him. The main reason for a writer to read is to get fired up, and I feel like writing when I read him. He's also the one I go back to when I'm feeling depressed. Shakespeare I still read a lot, believe it or not.

JS: You spoke earlier about television being an influence upon your narrative structure and humor. Are there aspects of your writing that you could point to and say, "Television did that"?

GS: I was thinking that when someone asks you about influences you can give them the first-order answer, which is the lineage you hope you're in: Gogol, Shakespeare, God. But when I wrote the first book, I'd read only one Gogol story. The second order of influence is the things you've actually read. And the third order of influence is the stuff you don't even realize, like television, which I watched end-lessly as a kid. You and I were talking about how there is no way, since it was the primary narrative experience, that television could not affect my work. I've been recently thinking about how it might have affected where a narrative break comes in the story, which is like a commercial break. As I approach what I feel should be a section break, I start trying to get certain things to happen, which I'm sure is related to television. Also, Monty Python was a huge influence when I was young. I felt that it was sarcastic and tongue-in-cheek, but at the same time deeply satirical. For everybody in this room who grew up with TV, it's got to have an effect on structure and form. If you read memoirs from the 1700s and 1800s, young men and women were as obsessive about literature as we are about music. When I was growing up in the seventies, a whole hierarchy of bands represented different parts of the human condition. On the low end, there was Aerosmith and Foghat, and up here was Yes. We probably work out our intellectual ground in a different way than other generations, but that stuff is real and rich.

JS: When I heard you read from your fiction last night, I became even more aware of the importance of verbal energy and voice in your writing. Before you found that as a writer, would you have identi-fied that same kind of verbal energy and voice as being part of your speech pattern? Would your wife or a friend have recognized that as being you?

GS: Yes, definitely. One of my friends said early, "This sounds just like you." When I was a kid, if you could make somebody laugh, that was very powerful. In our world in Chicago, a kid was not visible unless he or she was funny. Then you could sit at the big table. I played on the basketball team in the eighth grade and was not very athletic, but there were only fifteen boys in the school. A friend and I would sit at the end of the bench, and our self-appointed job was to make fun of the other team. We developed these mythologies about each one of the guys. There was one team where the guys were older than us and had body hair. One guy even had a light beard in the eighth grade, which was really freaky; he was called "Hero of the Beach" and another guy was "Louie the Lizard." Whenever they would run by, we would say, "It's Louie the Lizard!" After a while, even our own teammates hated us and would say, "You're embarrassing us! You're so femme!" But for us that was fun, and when I finally got around to it, I think that's the energy I was using, that kind of verbal play.

JS: Before the interview today, students were debating the merits of various stories from *Pastoralia*, arguing as to which is their favorite and which is most successful. Do you have a favorite story in that collection?

GS: "Sea Oak" I like because—this sounds strange—it was the most autobiographical story. Autobiographical in terms of the emotional space, that feeling of being surrounded by mayhem. Also, the fact that that story took so long, and that the breakthrough was kind of dramatic. But I don't really like any of them that much. I feel like that's the best I could do at that time, and it's made a certain amount of hay for me, so I'm fond of them, but if I go back now I think about what I could change. The one thing about that book is that each story is important—there weren't any throwaways. I was really in them as I wrote them. I like them all right, I guess. I heard Vonnegut say that when he looks back at his ninety-seven books, it's just like looking back over a slope and being able to see your tracks: that's where I was at three o'clock, that's where I was at two. It's not so much that they're particularly great tracks, but at least you made a track.

A CONVERSATION WITH
WALLACE SHAWN

Denis Johnson

There is too much in Wallace Shawn's list of accomplishments to name them all, but here are a few: He has won three Obies, for *Our Late Night, Aunt Dan and Lemon,* and *The Fever,* and his other plays include *The Hotel Play, A Thought in Three Parts, The Designated Mourner, Marie and Bruce,* and a translation of Bertolt Brecht's *Threepenny Opera.* I think of him chiefly as a playwright, but I first became aware of him, as most of us outside the theater scene in New York did, as an actor, who first appeared in the movies as Diane Keaton's ex-husband in Woody Allen's *Manhattan.* By now, of course, he is a familiar face on TV and on-screen. But it was when *My Dinner with André* came out that I became riveted by Wallace Shawn. I didn't know it was possible to make a film about two people talking for ninety minutes and make it so fascinating. Sometime after that I wondered, Who wrote that thing? And it was Wallace Shawn. I like to tell everybody who asks me that *My Dinner with André* is my favorite movie. I thought it was a great bargaining chip when, in arguments with producers about my own scripts, they'd say, "Eighteen pages! All dialogue! What are you doing?" And I'd say, "Haven't you seen *My Dinner with André?*"

In recent years I've tried to become a playwright and that has made me more appreciative of Shawn's writing. *Marie and Bruce* is a play that was written in the seventies, but was recently made into a film. Also, *The Fever*, which is a wonderful, slender volume of writing, has been made from a play into a film, though it hasn't been released yet, and *The Designated Mourner* has also been made into a film. In July 2005, Shawn gave a reading at the Tin House Summer Writers Workshop and we were all very honored to have him there.

Denis Johnson: I think the voice of Jack in *The Designated Mourner* is Wally, the same Wally that was in *My Dinner with André*, and it's the voice that's in *The Fever* too. In fact, hearing you read that passage I was reminded that we have met a couple of times. The first time was in the lobby at the Intercontinental Hotel in Nicaragua. I believe we were there for the ninth anniversary of the Sandinista takeover.

Wallace Shawn: Yes, we were visitors to the seekers of a better world, I suppose. Looking to see if the Sandinistas had come up with one, which I thought they had, really. I mean, yes, I personally had gone through most of my life not imagining that there could be anything different from what there was, and yet those people thought there could be.

DJ: Was that an inspiration for *The Fever?*

WS: Well, yes. Although I was already writing what turned into *The Fever* before Debbie [Eisenberg] and I went to Nicaragua, but yes, it was. There is a great autobiographical element in that play. Just the very idea that maybe things could be done differently, and maybe the degree of justice in the world, and even the degree of happiness, could be adjusted. Very exciting.

DJ: Did you think they were making it?

WS: I did. But I did know that one could hardly make a judgment about it, because it lasted such a short time. It was an experiment in a much more cheerful form of socialism, with a lot of music, partying, drinking—it was so unlike the Eastern European model, and yet—they taught people to read, and the health care was better than under the old dictatorship, and they were wonderful people trying to do something, I felt.

DJ: I thought it was working, too, but when I talked to people, it seemed that people were having some problems trying to adjust the economy—they were trying to have a mixed economy and it was difficult. It was supposed to be free market in some areas and controlled in some parts and it was a difficult evolution there.

WS: Well, it was a tiny moment—they didn't have a chance to get very far because the Americans squashed them, really, and presented them with an unwinnable game. I mean, rules that made it impossible for them to win.

DJ: It's true. They were kind of like Cuba, only they didn't last. Our stance toward them was similar to our stance toward Cuba.

WS: It was. With Cuba it was very personal—always trying to kill the leader. In Nicaragua, it was more violent. They actually killed a large proportion of the population. I mean, proportionately, it was a hell of a lot of people.

DJ: My understanding is that you were a history major in college.

WS: It's true.

DJ: I got that off the Internet.

WS: It's true!

DJ: We don't know what's true and false on the Internet, but I just read that the other day, and now I'm wondering what went wrong.

Where did you jump the track? It would appear that by the time you got to Managua you had a foot on either track, or a wheel on either track. Apparently, you were studying history and then you got into the world of drama.

WS: My senior year of college, I decided I would try to spend the next year in India, because at that time India was like what Africa is today—the place that you'd think of as the poorest place in the world. And, as I thought I would be some sort of civil servant in my life—that was my plan—I thought that was the thing that I should see. I had a privileged upbringing. I had barely seen poverty in my own city, much less what I thought would be the greater poverty in India. So, it was in India that I—well, this becomes the story of my life, which is not too interesting, but—when I was a teenager, thirteen or fourteen, I was literary-minded in a vulgar sort of way. Up until the age of fifteen I was very into books and art, and had romantic ideas about life. Then I became very harshly rigid and actually was against literature and tried to discourage others from reading it! That was the way I was all through college. I had contempt for literature and all artistic expression.

DJ: Because it was decadent?

WS: I felt that privileged people who were getting an education should devote themselves to making the world better, and personal happiness was not important. Then I went to India, and it's a long story, but President Kennedy had only recently been assassinated, and I was a Kennedy-minded type of a guy, with the idea that—I don't know if anyone in this crowd remembers Walt Rostow's book *The Stages of Economic Growth?* I guess not. Well, that book was kind of an inspirational manifesto that said that people could go through these five stages of economic development and then they would go through this incredible moment when they'd become like us! And be in our incredible stage of economic development. It said that without going through the evils of Communism, people could still go through the stages of economic growth and become like us. That was the frame of mind I was in when I went to India, and when I got there I kind of fell in love with India, and felt that I had been completely wrong about everything, because I was more amazed by how happy I was over there than I was upset by the poverty that was indeed there, as I had expected. I felt no impulse when I was there to try to make India be like the United States. I thought, Well, then I can be a writer! Because I don't need to try to make these people be like us. On the contrary, there's something intellectually, culturally wrong with us— we should be more like them! So I thought, if I feel like it, I should be a writer, and I would be justified in working in those vineyards.

Then over the years I flipped back. So by the time I was writing *The Fever*, I was writing with almost as much contempt for literature, art, and writing as when I was a college student, and it's really basically saying something not unlike what I said as a college student, which is that injustice can't be allowed to go on, that we have to devote ourselves to fighting it. But now I've slightly flipped back again, particularly in the Bush period. It's obvious, obvious to me that part of the problem with people like Bush and Rumsfeld and Dick Cheney is that they are not—their human sensibilities have not been developed by a wider cultural reference. They're provincial. And I do feel that if you presented them with a more truthful analysis than the one that they hold, then they would be incapable of grasping it, partly because of an insensitivity that can only be ameliorated by a wider cultural experience, in other words, literature, art, places where people have developed more of the human spirit. So I think there is a kind of role—I mean, you and I don't know that we are among those whose writing is valuable, but I do think writing in general is. So, I've rocketed back and forth.

DJ: Was it a conscious choice to make pieces that you'd perform yourself? Because the prose is as distinguished as anything you'd want to read on a page, and to me it's as thrilling to read it as it is to have it performed. Why did you end up making these things for the theater?

WS: Well, that's psychological and I can't fully explain it. My father was a famous editor. He edited prose. If I had written prose, I would have had to submit it to him! So there's a psychological element there for me.

DJ: That doesn't sound psychological at all—that sounds practical!

WS: I'm also one of those people who has always had an abnormal interest in theater. Even as a kid, from the very earliest days—I mean, when I was nine years old, I saw Paul Newman play a criminal in a play called *The Desperate Hours*. It was later made into a film. I remember Paul Newman's performance as if it happened yesterday. I remember most of the plays that I saw unbelievably well! I mean, the plays that I saw as a kid—and I don't remember the events of my own life half as well! And as a kid, I was in plays when I was nine, ten, that type of age. I wrote plays, I did puppet shows, my brother and I put on theatrical events. It's a showing-off thing. My grandfather was a peddler who then went to carnivals, where he would sell his wares by attracting attention and, I suppose, saying entertaining things. It's just—

DJ: So it's a calling, it wasn't a conscious choice.

WS: Well, I remember a poster the year that I'd come back from India. The poster said there was a play contest. For some reason I thought, Oh well, if there is, then I will enter it. Of course I knew nothing about theater really. I didn't know the things that I now know. I mean, who is going to be watching the plays? That never occurred to me. It turned out, sadly, that the people who go to plays don't like my writing! So it was all a kind of very odd choice, as it turned out. But I didn't know about that. I just liked theater! I still do, actually. I still enjoy watching actors act in almost anything, really.

DJ: When you see something made from a play into a film, is something lost for you? I'm trying to get you to say yes, by the way, but you don't have to.

WS: Well, it's so hard to compare because the standard of plays is very, very low; I mean, most plays that I have seen are somewhat sloppily thrown together. There's not much time to rehearse them, and plays have deadlines—except for the stuff that Andre Gregory and I do, where Andre doesn't really care if it's ever performed. He doesn't decide in advance when it will open. It opens when he feels like it, but almost all regular theater has an opening night set before the actors even meet, so, are they ready? It doesn't matter. The play opens. That's not a very high standard! I mean, a writer wouldn't do that! I mean, sometimes they do, there are deadlines, but it's on a low plane, whereas films—in every department except for the script, the standard is high. The standard of makeup, even on a low-budget film, is unbelievable. The hair standard is unbelievable! The people who do the hair are incredibly talented and skilled, and in every department they are, except the script department! So in a way, it's hard to compare the two. And in the way a film is edited, the acting can be brought to an awfully high standard. But yes, film is a kind of flat medium, and can be very shallow. The whole essence of it is terribly clumsy, that really you can only look at one person at a time, or two people. That's so crude in comparison to theater, where you can watch five people at a time. Its essence has got a kind of subtlety to it.

DJ: Was *Vanya on 42nd Street* ever done live?

WS: Well, we did *Vanya on 42nd Street* live for twenty people.

DJ: Did you do it on a regular basis?

WS: We did it many times. We rehearsed it for a couple of years with no people, and then we started bringing in five people, ten people, twenty. But we never performed it for more than that. So we never projected our voices. We just talked like regular people.

DJ: It was very filmlike.

WS: Right. Our acting style was like film acting.

DJ: It's a fantastic play. It's the best Chekhov I've ever seen, frankly.

WS: Thank you.

DJ: I think Chekhov would really love it. People are murdering Chekhov everywhere. That's the only one that even comes close to doing it right, I think.

WS: Well, Chekhov is very, very subtle. And very, very prone to clichés, and the clichés that attach themselves to Chekhov are particularly boring, so that it's unbearable. In other words, the point to rehearsing for as long a time as André Gregory does, is that if you stick with it long enough, you do hear what the author wrote and you realize that some of what you thought he wrote was actually your own stupid clichés that you've imposed on what he wrote, so there's a lot of sentimentality and self-pity that people rather automatically add to the Chekhov cereal bowl, which aren't in the original package, but it takes awhile to see that.

DJ: How do you feel about people who say they don't like plays (or literature or film, et cetera) that deal with politics? People often say that writing about politics is boring, and to be avoided. But your work certainly addresses it.

WS: The history of literature is obviously full of political commentary. Certainly, starting with Homer and Sophocles, Euripides—you could say political commentary came first and everything else continued from there. The way that society is organized—politics, oppression, justice—these are important themes of literature, and it's ridiculous to say that they have no place in drama or literature. That's absolutely unbelievable. People say these are improper themes—that you should really only write about intimate things. Well, that's ridiculous because there's nothing so intimate that it isn't affected by the society you're living in—that's just ignorant! Even if you're writing about the relationship of, let's say, the three sisters who want to go to Moscow, the political life around them is determining the problems that they have. So if you think that Chekhov wasn't aware of the world, that's ignorant! But it is true that you get harshly criticized for mentioning political subjects in literature or drama. A lot of people do criticize you, and if you even mention something political, people say that you have been standing on a soapbox, to use a somewhat outdated idiom, and that your writing is dishonest. It's ridiculous.

DJ: *The Fever* deals with class and economics very directly—you have that monologue about a rich character mulling over the inevitable problems of having a poor friend, while Anne Marie, a character briefly mentioned in the play, talks about rich and poor living side by side. Can you tell us a bit about how this play is wrestling with class, whether your own background informs the characters in this play? And is a play like *The Fever* part of your questioning the value of art in a world with many more immediate, economic needs?

WS: Of course, I've never actually met anyone who literally said, as Anne Marie does, that the rich and poor should live side by side as friends. But in a way, that is what a lot of people hope for.

I was writing it as mockery, because actually by the end of the piece the character does figure out that to be poor is a destiny that you don't choose, but to be rich is kind of voluntary. So the character is someone who at first says, "Hey, it's not my fault that I was born with a little money and privilege, and I've worked hard, and I still have a little money and privilege—I didn't steal it from anybody," but by the end, the character realizes that he did steal it, that no one is forcing him to actually keep for himself the money he happens to have. It's sort of a choice. So, I myself am a bourgeois person to the core of my being—I mean, I can't remove that from myself although I would like to. I was raised in a privileged way and I was taught that I was special. I was taken to schools where the teachers said I was special, as opposed to going to schools where the teachers said, "You are not special and you are a dog." I didn't go to that kind of a school. I have made an attempt in my life to try to root those things out of myself, but you can't ever fully succeed, and I am poisoned by that. So that's what I am. At the same time, I'm trying to write my way out of it, and by trying to write my way out of it, I am exposing myself, and exposing others who are like me, and admitting the things that are there. So the horrible passage about the fear of getting involved with the poor friend is me, the conscious writer, trying to show something nauseating about the human being that is partly me. It's a self-contradictory activity that I am involved in. It's just what I have done. If anybody out there is wondering why anybody would want to be rich, you should read *Cruising Speed* by William F. Buckley Jr., because he really paints the picture of how enjoyable it is, more than any other picture that I've read. I do also think it is true that there can be beautiful things in the life of a poor person, and there are certainly many bourgeois people to whom very little that is beautiful happens.

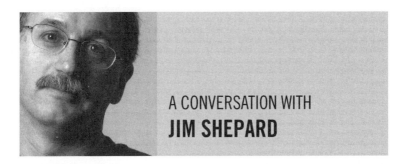

A CONVERSATION WITH
JIM SHEPARD

Ron Hansen

I first met Jim Shepard in 1981 at the University of Michigan, where we were both teaching in the English Department. One glorious autumn Friday afternoon—football weather at its finest—he phoned and asked, "How'd you like to toss around the ol' oblate spheroid?" And so we got to know each other and our mutual interests in literature and film and *The Honeymooners* while running hitch-and-gos and post patterns. We've been friends and editors of each other's fiction ever since.

James Russell Shepard was born in Stratford, Connecticut, on December 29, 1956, the second son of Ida and Albert Shepard. Jim got his BA in English from Trinity College, with Stephen Minot as his thesis advisor, and his MFA in fiction writing at Brown University, working primarily with John Hawkes. Upon completion of his graduate studies in 1980, Shepard took a three-year job at the

University of Michigan, and then was hired as an assistant professor at Williams College, where he is now the J. Leland Miller Professor in the English Department.

Shepard is the author of six novels: *Flights* (1983), *Paper Doll* (1986), *Lights Out in the Reptile House* (1990), *Kiss of the Wolf* (1994), *Nosferatu* (1998), and *Project X* (2004). His short story collections are *Batting Against Castro* (1996), *Love and Hydrogen: New and Selected Stories* (2004), and *Like You'd Understand, Anyway* (2007). With me, he edited the anthology of short stories *You've Got to Read This* (1994); with Amy Hempel, he edited *Unleashed: Poems by Writers' Dogs* (1995); and all by himself he edited *Writers at the Movies: Twenty-six Contemporary Authors Celebrate Twenty-six Memorable Movies*. He lives with his wife, Karen, and their children Aidan, Emmett, and Lucy in Williamstown, Massachusetts.

Ron Hansen: When did you first realize you wanted to be a fiction writer?

Jim Shepard: In third or fourth grade I found myself writing stories, almost exclusively about monsters: mostly variations on the Universal monsters or silent-film monsters, all of which I'd seen on TV by that point. My family tended toward very lax supervision. The nuns—I went to a Catholic school until junior high—were happy to allow me to write, and write about anything, as long as I did it on my own time. So in English I'd finish diagramming sentences way before the time allotted was over, and I'd go back to chapter three of whatever I was working on. I drew the covers, too. I remember Sister Justine looking bemusedly at one entitled *All That Blood*. I never thought I'd be a writer, necessarily; my secret plan was that I would write and people would give me food. My ambition was to be a veterinarian, until I realized that they have responsibilities beyond playing with puppies or giving old dogs treats.

RH: Some of your early stories and the novels *Flights* and *Kiss of the Wolf* describe an Italian, Roman Catholic upbringing that is less apparent in your later fiction. To what extent is your religious background still influential in the subjects you choose and the ways you write about them?

JS: My Catholic upbringing was, and still is, absolutely central to my writing. Catholicism prepares someone for writing literature in all sorts of crucial ways, I think: one of the foremost being the earliest possible initiation into the appeal of mystery, and the power of wonder, as well as an early—critics like to say too early—initiation into the notion that one must always be looking inward and holding oneself accountable. In other words, Catholicism beautifully teaches a precept that Aristotle claimed is central to all literature: the idea that flaws of character produce flaws of judgment for which the character must take responsibility.

RH: One of your first undergraduate short stories was published in *Redbook*. Soon after that another story appeared in the *Atlantic Monthly*. You sold your first novel, *Flights*, to Alfred A. Knopf before you reached the age of twenty-five. Were you surprised by that initial success? Was there then a pressure that made it harder to write your next fiction?

JS: I was too clueless to be surprised by almost anything. My undergraduate teachers were both delighted for me and aggravated, I think, that I didn't seem to realize what a big deal it was. Given that kind of cheerful vapidity, I felt very little pressure.

RH: More than most American fiction writers you have demonstrated an ardent and informed interest in science, technology, warfare, and history. Some of that is clearly due to your father's job at Sikorsky Aircraft, which influenced your first novel, and his wartime experience in Europe with B-25s, which formed the basis for *Paper Doll*. But a good deal of your unusual subject matter seems to emanate from your wide, even encyclopedic, reading. Why do you think you're attracted to that material as a reader and writer?

JS: I think I'm attracted to historical and/or scientific material because, first of all, it's a way of enlarging my contact with the world, and secondly because it's a way of enlarging the arena of my autobiographical obsessions. It's a way to fiddle with and expand what we might call the ground: that element in our work that proscribes all our choices. I guess I'm looking to complicate my memory, and to complicate the categorical narrowness of my intellectual discipline.

RH: Why do so many contemporary writers seem to avoid that material?

JS: I have no idea. If I had to guess, I'd say that they worry about the issue of authority, forgetting, perhaps, that that issue—the issue of the essential chutzpah involved in trying to imagine any other kind of sensibility—is always with us. Really: where do we get the authority to write from the point of view of anyone, other than ourselves? The whole project of literature is about the exercise of the empathetic imagination. Why were we given something as amazing as imagination, if we're not going to use it?

RH: I'm especially intrigued by the uses of history in your fiction, as in your novels *Paper Doll* and *Nosferatu*, and many of the short stories in *Love and Hydrogen*. Some people—we'll call them idiots—consider it an unethical cheat: that you've been given characters and a narrative that you have no rights to and just have to reword things to avoid plagiarism. What are the chief pleasures and encumbrances for you in writing historical fiction? How faithful to the facts do you feel compelled to be?

JS: Most historical novelists, I'd bet, would call it a wash: on the one hand, you're given characters and a situation; on the other hand, you're provided with all these constraints. I think those fiction writers who deal with history the most effectively—and let me add, while we're engaging in mutual back-scratching here, that you're certainly one of them—have an understanding that A) fiction about real events needs to respect the facts and B) as our politicians have taught us, facts are malleable things. The trick, I guess, is to do everything possible to honor A as you understand it, while taking full advantage of B to shape your material into something aesthetically beautiful.

RH: With *Nosferatu* you wrote a stunning and very sympathetic fictional biography of the German director F. W. Murnau. You edited an anthology of film appreciations and have regularly contributed film criticism to the Sunday *New York Times*. You often write about film for *The Believer*, and at Williams College you often teach huge and hugely popular lecture classes on film genres and great directors. Has film influenced your choices or methods of fictional narrative? Are you torn between your love of literature and your love of film?

JS: Like a lot of people of our generation, I grew up on movies. We watched movies all the time in my house, so I'm sure that kind of model had a fundamental effect on how I construct narrative. There are all sorts of ways in which film has directly and indirectly showed itself in my fiction, besides *Nosferatu*. I remember conceiving the end of *Paper Doll*, which involves the massive and catastrophic Eighth Air Force attack on Schweinfurt, in cinematic terms: What would you see at this point? Where would the camera be placed for this? There's a way in which film pushes you toward both the visual and the kinetic, as opposed to, say, the intricately expositional, or ruminative. At other times—a story like "The Creature from the Black Lagoon," for example—film has given me not only my governing metaphors but also my protagonists.

RH: Did you ever consider a career with a more direct, hands-on involvement in filmmaking?

JS: Coming out of college, I did consider going into film, even going to a film school like USC or NYU instead of getting my MFA from Brown. I didn't, I think, principally for two reasons. One was the independence fiction affords as an art form: it's solely my work, and not the product of a hammered-out compromise. The other was the sense I had that I'd be pretty lousy at raising money. And raising money turns out to be a large part of your job in filmmaking unless you're very, very lucky.

RH: Which of your books have been optioned for the movies?

JS: Only two of my novels—*Flights* and *Kiss of the Wolf*—and a few of my stories: "Eustace," "Batting against Castro," probably a few others I'm forgetting. Nothing came of it, except a little money. Over the years I've gotten lots of calls from people who claimed they were *about* to buy something. As H. L. Mencken said of Hollywood, "You can die of encouragement out there." By far the biggest thrill I've had regarding the film world was a phone call from Robert Altman telling me how much he loved *Paper Doll* (and he'd flown in B-24s during the war). But naturally, as far as my luck with film has been concerned, at that point in his career he was in no position to make anything.

RH: A good deal of your fiction is voice-driven: first-person narratives in which the author adopts the persona of his characters and demonstrates his pitch-perfect ear for the nuances and inflections of various speakers, as in *Kiss of the Wolf* or the stories in *Batting against Castro* and *Love and Hydrogen*. Some writers—me, for example—find first-person narratives frustratingly difficult and limiting, but you seem to relish the challenge of them. What else is going on in these Actor's Theater improvisations of yours?

JS: Who knows what's going on in my head? It's like rush hour in Naples in there. A good deal of my fiction *is* voice-driven, and I'm sure part of that comes from my family background. On my mother's side we're a big extended Italian family—the Picarazzis—and everybody does voices when telling stories: "So Auntie Ida says to me, 'Aw, go take a shit for yourself.'" And so forth. It makes you associate telling stories with doing voices.

RH: John Gardner felt that all fiction writing was genre writing, or a form of playing with genre. *Paper Doll* is a literary variation on any number of air war novels. *Lights Out in the Reptile House* is a kind of Orwellian nightmare that's partially indebted to the surreal fictions of J. M. Coetzee and Jerzy Kosinski. *Kiss of the Wolf* is a novel of suspense that Alfred Hitchcock would have loved to adapt. Your story "Batting against Castro" seems to pay homage to Ring Lardner and the genre of the naïve, tobacco-spitting, baseball autobiography. Any comments?

JS: I guess at times, like a lot of other writers, I'm especially galvanized by the usefulness of such literary and not-so-literary models. Sometimes the impulse to play off such works is generated by a kind of awed sense of wanting to do something like that—that's partially the way *Lights Out in the Reptile House* relates to *Waiting for the Barbarians*, for example—and at other times, the impulse is generated by a more ambivalent reaction. "Batting against Castro" is both an affectionate gesture toward that baseball genre you describe and a way of subverting it, a way of getting at that genre's insistence upon a kind of American naïveté that I often find to be willed and disingenuous, especially when it comes to politics.

RH: I find that a common element runs through much of your fiction. Forgive my oversimplifying: A sudden malaise or accident or threat of violence causes a keenly alert and sensitive juvenile to hide and watch out for other betrayals (*Kiss of the Wolf*), desperately seek escape (*Lights Out in the Reptile House* and *Flights*), or execute some compensatory violence of his own (*Project X*). A number of your stories also feature a version of this kid—the first of his kind was in your story "Eustace"—and his vexation over the dissolute ways of the world. We never hear Patsy Cline singing "I Fall to Pieces," but we do detect a heightened sense of awareness and melancholy, even cynicism. Is there some Ur-event behind all these stories? Beyond it being a great device for generating plot, why do you think this explosive theme has been such a powerful force in your work?

JS: I think I'd add to your analysis that with all of those adolescents I've been very interested, thematically, in the ethical costs of passivity. I haven't wanted to suggest that they're merely victims, set upon by a disappointing world. As for the sudden accident or threat of violence, I suppose that's been, first of all, as you say, my way of getting the story up on its feet and moving and, secondly, a means of reflecting the way I've experienced the world around me. There was certainly plenty of run-of-the-mill violence in my childhood, both in my neighborhood—I lost my last fistfight when the guy who had me pinned took off his shoe and beat me with its heel—and at home. My older brother, whose undiagnosed mental illness became a tormenting problem when he was about fourteen and I was about nine, was always capable of going off, with me being thrown over the sofa or down the stairs as a result. But if there's a single Ur-event behind all of my writing, I've successfully repressed it.

RH: Where did the idea for *Project X* come from? Some would say the Columbine High School murders, but the novel feels newer and far more personal than that. To what extent did your experience as the father of two sons contribute to your portrayal of the boys and the dark maelstrom of that novel?

JS: *Project X* came from my remembering, in the face of all sorts of recent school violence, just how radically and frighteningly disaffected my friends and I were for long stretches in our schooling. And we were not the ones the administration would have singled out for particular worry. I found myself very impatient with pundits who, after whatever most recent act of violence, pontificated about how impossible such a thing was in the old days, when everyone had values. I'm quite certain that one of the reasons no one did a Columbine-like thing at my junior high was that they only had access to, say, their dad's hunting rifle. And even the least imaginative and most frustrated realized that at best they'd get one or two good shots off before they were put out of commission. I'm fascinated by the way in which that kind of disaffection can't be traced to any one source: bad parenting, MTV, a gun in the closet, et cetera. And, of course, being a parent makes that kind of understanding all the more terrifying.

RH: *Love and Hydrogen* contains several of what I would call "found stories," such as your poignant, romantic retelling of "The Creature from the Black Lagoon," the bitter reminiscences of a member of The Who in "Won't Get Fooled Again," and your satire based on the autobiography of our present attorney general, "John Ashcroft: More Important Things Than Me." Are these responses to pop culture? Are they ways of making fiction more familiar and relevant? Or are they born out of a frustration with the wan and evasive interpretations of contemporary life by some journalists and cultural historians?

JS: Wan and evasive is right. A long time ago I read an interview with Allan Gurganus in which he said that it is the writer's job to take the world personally. I think that's true. When I read about The Who or John Ashcroft, I'm reading, I suppose, in a way that energizes not only my imagination but also my emotions, and when I'm engaged by what I'm reading in a particular way, I find myself starting to construct a combination of what I intuit about such subjects and what I project upon them. If I didn't find some odd and plangent emotional resonances with what I discover about these figures, I would never write fiction about them. They turn into personae, figures who both are and are not that actual public figure. What I've done in such a case is stumbled upon a shared emotional genealogy that research has helped more fully uncover.

RH: When you take on a subject for fiction, are you fairly certain of its final length, or do some stories grow into novels for you?

JS: I've had only one story become a novel: *Nosferatu*, which originally appeared in *TriQuarterly*. But in that case I should've known from the start that something was up: the finished story weighed in at thirty-three pages, which made it far and away my longest up to that point. After I'd sent it off, I found myself with still more questions about aspects of Murnau's life, and especially aspects of early filmmaking and the challenges and excitements that he faced in this new art form. So I pursued them. With most of my other projects, I've known very early on which was a novel and which was a story. I suppose out of some dawning sense of the scope of the subject? The extent of my interest? Some combination of the two?

RH: Your wife, Karen Shepard, is also a fiction writer, the author of the novels *An Empire of Women*, *The Bad Boy's Wife*, and *Don't I Know You?* You share the same home office in Williamstown and comment on each other's pages. Are either of you ever worried about giving too much input too soon? How do you make such an intimate arrangement work?

JS: Other writers arch their eyebrows dubiously, or shudder involuntarily, when they see our shared study. It isn't as weird as it first sounds. We face away from each other, each looking out windows into the woods, and rarely are we both writing fiction at the same time in there. The other question, though, touches on something more fundamental: our shared intimacy as readers, an intimacy unprecedented for me, in terms of the speed with which we share things. I think it only works because in the very earliest stages we're only looking for some evidence that what we're producing is intriguing and for feedback about what sorts of associations are raised by such material. So reactions can be helpful without being inhibiting. It's also not as though I write a sentence and then lope across the room to see what Karen makes of it. It is wonderful, though, knowing someone you trust is so looking forward to seeing what mess you've made today.

RH: What are your habits as a writer? What does an ideal day look like?

JS: I write fiction in the mornings; do busy work in the afternoons. If I'm doing well or at the end of a novel I might return to the fiction for a few hours in the evenings. An ideal day would involve all of that and basketball, and romps with the kids, and hours of lovemaking, and getting an inordinate amount of reading done, too—too much sharing, I know. Anyway, as you can tell from the list, an ideal day is impossible. Mostly I stare out windows, my mouth ajar.

RH: In terms of intelligence, variety, humor, depth of feeling, and sheer mastery of craft, your fiction is among the finest being produced in America, and yet many of your books are scandalously out of print and you're not even close to being a household name. I wonder if this deplorable situation isn't the fate of being a writer's writer. What gets in the way of your popularity? Why ain't you famous, kid?

JS: Ha! Why so parsimonious with the praise? I'm not even sure I *am* a writer's writer. I mean, a lot of writers that I respect have told me that they admire my stuff; on the other hand, I've won fewer literary awards than Charo. I suppose one of the things that gets in the way of a bigger readership is something that countless reviewers have mentioned, occasionally with surprising peevishness: how different all of my fictions are; how hard it is to decide exactly what kind of stuff I do. It may be that without that kind of categorization it's hard for book buyers to know what they're getting. I'm not the Catholic Guy or the Postmodern Guy or the Satirical Guy or the Historical Guy or the Whatever Guy. Other than that, who knows? I lament reaching—as you so deflatingly point out—so few people. But I also remind myself how fortunate I am: every so often the world leaves me alone, and lets me do the thing I want most to do.

A CONVERSATION WITH
MARK STRAND

Christopher Merrill

"Waste makes haste. I hurry to the dump," Mark Strand writes in
The Sargentville Notebook, one of his many unclassifiable works probing
the border between poetry and prose, philosophical speculation and
stand-up comedy. But there is nothing wasted in his writings, and
no sense of hurry in his description of our walk in the sun. Between
presence and absence, desire and plenitude, memory and oblivion,
the lyrical and the tragic, this is the shifting terrain of his literary
work, a world predicated on nothingness and charted with an exact-
ing—a twinkling—eye. There is indeed no one like him—one reason
why he has been so richly honored for his work, with a MacArthur
Fellowship, the Poet Laureateship, the Pulitzer Prize, and, for a poet,
the greatest compliment of all: legions of imitators. He himself has
followed a singular course through ten collections of poems, a volume of short stories, a book-length meditation on immortality titled

The Monument, children's books, translations, anthologies, and monographs on the artists Edward Hopper and William Bailey. What Strand discovers at every turn is how, as he writes, "one word after another erases the world and leaves instead the invisible lines of its calling: out there, out there." What is *it*? Let me try to explain.

I had the good fortune to take Strand's graduate seminar on Wallace Stevens. He had his students make presentations about poems, and one week we heard a tedious lecture about "Like Decorations in a Nigger Cemetery," which, according to the student, was the subject of a fair amount of critical debate. Was the poem successful or not? The student recited arguments for and against it, and after about an hour Mark interrupted him. He didn't know if the poem was successful, he said. But he did know that one summer he was living in Maine, and every afternoon he would make himself a pitcher of martinis, which he would take down to the lake. There he would sit on the dock, drinking martinis and reading "Like Decorations in a Nigger Cemetery" until he dozed off. Upon awakening, he would write down the lines running through his mind—the first draft of *The Sargentville Notebook*, which may or may not be a critical success but which has inspired countless readers and writers. What is *it*? Whatever it is, Mark Strand finds it somewhere between the dock and the dump, and we are the luckier for his discoveries.

At the 2004 Tin House Summer Writers Workshop, Strand gave a reading in an outdoor amphitheater on the Reed College campus and then the two us sat down to chat.

Christopher Merrill: I think we should begin by acknowledging that you *do* have a beautiful body.

Mark Strand: I don't know, I haven't checked. It's been years since I've seen it.

CM: We had some people in the audience wondering if you would remove your shirt before the night is over.

MS: It's getting too cold for that.

CM: Yes, and dark.

MS: You know, I'm only joking about my body. I wasn't the old man in that poem I read. I'm not that old. And, um . . . Well, let's forget about my body.

CM: Well, Mark, you mentioned that it takes you a long time to finish a poem. I wonder if you could talk a little bit about how a poem begins for you, and how you write a poem, what the process is for you, how it starts.

MS: It happens in different ways. I sometimes get an idea for a whole poem, and sometimes I just get two words that I want to write down. I was reading Borges—I taught Borges's stories this spring at Chicago—and there was a line in one of his stories: "How easy it is not to think of a tiger." That line jumped out at me and I thought, Hey! What do you put after that line? It became a challenge. That was several months ago, and I'm finally moving through the poem, but it will be several months before I'm finished. I never know where a poem is going. That poem I read, "Mother and Son," I'm not sure, it's probably not a very good poem, but I had the beginning, and I had the moon appear at the window, and I wanted the moon to speak, to say something. I thought that would be my way out of the poem, but I couldn't think of anything. I spent months, writing lines for the moon.

CM: Doesn't it make you crazy when the moon won't talk?

MS: Well, I wrote down, "What would the moon say if the moon could speak?" And then, clearly, the next line came: "The moon would say nothing." If the moon could speak, it wouldn't say anything. So I sort of interrogated the poem to come to the conclusion of the poem. But it happens different ways. Very often I'll get ideas from things that I read. Very often I'll see something. The idea for "Man and Camel" just popped into my mind. I thought, How wild to have a man and a camel singing together. If I did that in a poem how could I treat the poem so that it would be both absurd and deadly serious at the same time? How could I keep it from being over-the-top yet not ordinary or mundane? I mean, just the notion of a man and a camel singing, and to be the image for all uncommon couples, strikes me as so absurd. And yet, you know, it's different; it has a kind of weird authority. I don't like saying things just for the sake of saying them. They have to have a kind of edge. When the man and the camel come back, they say together, "You've ruined it. You've ruined it forever." Because in the middle of the poem I interpret what they mean, and so I made a poem of that. My authorial intrusion into the movement of this poem became a way of concluding it. Does that make sense?

CM: Yes.

MS: It happens different ways. I write on yellow lined paper with a ballpoint pen, generally, or on white sheets of paper. I write as slowly as I possibly can. I don't like to rush. It's so fun to wake up in the morning and have something you're working on, something you really want to get to. Sometimes when you write, you'll write a whole page, and it has some promise, but usually you spend your time dismantling it, or figuring out what the hell you're saying or where to go. Not that you really know what you're saying when you're writing a poem. I think the writing of the poem is an effort to discover what it is that you have to say, and the working out of a poem is a process of figuring out what you're saying. You can write a poem and not know what you've said, not understand the poem. You can follow certain formal imperatives that don't indicate meaning, that indicate whether you're on the track or off the track, in terms of sound, of tempo, or of other things, but not in terms of meaning. What Wallace Stevens called "the rightness" of a poem can reveal itself without the poem telling you what it means. You sometimes write something, you don't know what the hell it is, it's just right. That's it. It may take weeks or months or years before you realize what it is that you've said. But you have to trust language—you can't trust your own consciousness, because you don't know that much. Language has much greater resources, and knows a great deal more than you do, and you just have to sort of give in to it.

CM: You've also said that if you get too many words in a row, a cluster of words, you're inclined to distrust that because you feel that you've heard it from somewhere else, or maybe you've read it. So it's more of an excavation for you, isn't it?

MS: I think that when you get an adjective-noun together, the chances are it's a cliché, or something you've received from somewhere else. We tend to think in clusters, and if you want to be original, you have to sort of . . . For example, if a phrase like "black sheep" comes to you, you don't want to say, "blue sheep," but you might want to say, "slack sheep," or "slick sheep." I can't write a poem here, but I think when words come in combinations, you have to mistrust them. Chances are they're coming from something else that's already been written, unless you're a genius and everything you say is original. But there aren't too many of those.

CM: You mentioned Stevens; I know that he has occupied a large part of your imagination, almost from the beginning of your writing life, as an inspiration, as a kind of guide. Could you say a word about him?

MS: I've read him since I was a teenager and am terribly influenced by him. It was the worst and the best thing that ever happened to me. He was my introduction to poetry, and I had an intuitive grasp of a lot of what he talks about. Not the most difficult poems, that took years. But the influence was so powerful that I've had to stop reading him because I found myself slipping into his diction. It's best to read many different people. I wouldn't get stuck on one writer.

CM: So how does a poet read? Are you reading to steal? Are you reading for inspiration?

MS: Oh, you always read to steal. But you have to disguise your thefts.

CM: What are some of your favorite thefts that never got caught? You once said you stole an entire poem, and no critic has ever figured out what that was. Every line was stolen. Maybe you no longer remember.

MS: Well, I did it deliberately when I wrote a cento after Virgil, after reading *The Aeneid*. I picked lines from *The Aeneid*, and I wrote this Virgilian cento, but there are lines like, [searches pockets] I think I may have them here . . . Oh, I don't know, I don't think I've stolen *that* many lines. I think it's rather rare. Now people just make collages—they steal lines left and right, and they call them their poems; I think that's very unfair to the original poets. The original poets did all the work and you go along picking a line here, a line there, and then you put them all together and say it's your poem. I think that's terrible. Like that line, "How easy it is not to think of a tiger," I'll give Borges credit for that line.

CM: When you're writing—you have that line from Borges, which comes from a story—how do you tell if this is going to work out as a poem or as a fiction or as a parable?

MS: Well, I'm a poet, and I don't write any of the other stuff anymore. I never was a very good story writer. Or children's author. All those other things that I did, the reason I don't do them now is that I was never any good at them.

CM: They were important to you, right? You've said that *Mr. and Mrs. Baby* made it possible to bring your sense of humor into your poems.

MS: If it can be called humor, yes. I mean, I was poor. I was living in New York. I didn't have a teaching job. And I talked to my editor—he was an editor at the *New Yorker*—and he said, "You ought to write fiction, you can make some money doing that." So I started writing fiction, selling these humor pieces to the *New Yorker*, and I thought, Hey! This is great. They bought the first four pieces that I wrote and I thought I had another career; and then they didn't buy one and then they didn't buy another, and then they did buy another, and I thought,

This is too risky. But if I were Philip Roth, I would be writing it. Or if I were Alice Munro or William Trevor, I'd be writing it. But I'm not. You do what you can.

Yes, writing fiction was useful to me because I always thought I was a funny guy and my poems struck others as unbelievably gloomy and dark. Everybody said, "You're so gloomy. You're so dark." But I remember I'd always start out trying to be humorous. There was an earlier poem called "The Accident," which begins with a line I think is hilarious and difficult to follow a poem after: "A train runs over me." I gave it as an assignment to a class: write a poem using this as the first line. Of course, nobody got anywhere. Because what do you do after a train runs over you? I thought it was a hilarious line, and I think I said, "A train runs over me. I feel sorry for the engineer who kneels down and whispers in my ear that he is innocent." And it goes on like that. For me, writing is interesting because when I don't know what I'm going to say, I make discoveries along the way, and I'm always surprised. Otherwise it would be terribly dull to be yourself, if you were entirely predictable. Here I am again! It's another day and I'm me. All over again. And I'm going to write another poem, by me. Dreadful.

CM: So is it safe to say that in writing the stories you learned a little bit about timing in humor?

MS: Clearly, I did. [laughs] Except now I read the stories and I don't think they're so funny. I would love to think that they are still funny, that they are timelessly funny, but the truth is, they're not.

CM: How about a poem like "Elevator"?

MS: Oh, that I think is just—

CM: —timelessly funny.

MS: Nobody had ever done that. Part one, and then part two is exactly the same. But I realized part one changes when part two is read and part two is not heard the same way as part one. It wouldn't be a poem, it wouldn't be complete, if one half of it was there. And it happened quite by accident. I was writing it and I started rewriting it, and I was about to cross out some words, and I saw, yeah, they're exactly the same, and that's the poem. It's a poem that took five seconds to write. "Orpheus Alone," the last poem I read tonight, took over a year.

CM: Did you write a third part to "Elevator"?

MS: No. I thought two was enough.

CM: If the fool would persist in his folly . . . You know, in "A Poet's Alphabet," in a very interesting entry about a poet's apprenticeship, you talk about the fact that as a young poet, you have to learn to distinguish between what is derived from your reading, what you've picked up around you, and what is actually yours, and what might come out of your own quirkiness or your own weakness. How do you do that?

MS: That's a good question. I really don't know. I think one of the problems with workshops—I don't teach workshops; as a rule, my job is teaching literature—is the poem becomes a poem by committee. Someone says, "I don't like this line." And suddenly, the poem veers toward clarity and something that everybody can agree on, that makes sense, so the teacher can say, "Now you've said what you intended to say." When in fact, the most valuable thing in the poem may be its idiosyncrasy.

CM: The second section of "Elevator," for example.

MS: Yeah, take that to a workshop and see what happens. There wouldn't be any poem left. I think the thing is to be surprised by what you do and to say, "Did I say that? Did I have that in me?" It's better to be a hundred people in one, than just one dull person in one, again and again.

CM: Especially if you have a beautiful body.

MS: Yeah, well, it doesn't last.

A CONVERSATION WITH
GUS VAN SANT

Todd Haynes

Portland is incredibly lucky to lay claim to two such accomplished, uncompromising, and important filmmakers as Gus Van Sant and Todd Haynes. In different ways, and through sometimes parallel methods, each has managed to blaze trails into the landscape of American cinema. Van Sant began in 1985 with *Mala Noche*, based on a novella by a writer named Walt Curtis, which he followed up with *Drugstore Cowboy* and *My Own Private Idaho*, along the way establishing what has come to be known as American independent film. Haynes started out in 1987 with *Superstar*, a movie that is now banned, which he followed with *Poison*, *Safe*, and *Velvet Goldmine*, and along the way established something called "New Queer Cinema." Both have since made successful forays into Hollywood—Van Sant with *Good Will Hunting* and *Psycho*; Haynes with *Far from Heaven*—somehow without sacrificing their fundamental artistic vision or basic creative identities.

There are other interesting similarities between them, too: both are visual artists, accomplished painters in their own right, and huge music fans—Van Sant is also a musician himself. They are both writers. And you may have heard they are both gay. Yet it's their dissimilarities that make the following conversation interesting. Whereas Haynes's practice is a study in control, obsessive art direction, period-precise costuming, and camera moves, Van Sant pursues an increasingly organic and improvisational method, shooting long takes of unscripted scenes and collaborating intensively with his crews. So, by very different methods, they've both managed to channel the passion and intelligence that they continue to bring to their work.

This conversation took place in July 2004 at the Tin House Summer Writers Workshop.

Todd Haynes: When I was thinking of things to ask you, I thought, Oh yeah, I'm a director too. I could probably ask him these really interesting questions that nobody else would ask. These are questions I'm asked, kind of basic questions that I would just love to know. My first instinct is to talk about the more recent films that you've made because they're so extraordinary, and they also mark such a change from your earlier films. And yet, the earlier films are so different in and of themselves.

You have done comedy, personal cinema, bigger-scale films that have been Hollywood productions, independent films that have been taken into the Hollywood world and influenced it. You've also done shorts, written novels, and kept a real diversity and fluidity and almost a playfulness about the role of feature-film maker. That's so unique, very difficult to pull off so successfully, for how many risks that demonstrates along the road. One of the most dramatic changes in your evolution is the change from *Finding Forrester* to *Gerry*. They are just such different films that come out of such different influences, I think. I'm curious, what happened to motivate that switch?

Gus Van Sant: After doing *Psycho*, which was a literal copy of Alfred Hitchcock's *Psycho*, I thought I would try to copy *Good Will Hunting* with this screenplay by a guy from Portland, Mike Rich, who had constructed *Finding Forrester* with *Good Will Hunting* in mind. On a whim—most of the films are done are on a whim—I decided to say yes and go ahead and do it. The story of *Finding Forrester* is pretty traditional, like *Good Will Hunting*, and it was a way to kind of lose yourself, and lose your identity or your individuality, within the story itself and the storytelling. It seemed like it wanted to be a particular type of story that didn't have a director's spin on it. It was the first black film I'd ever made—or maybe ever will make—so it was an area I'd never worked in before. Having done that, working with all the powers that be and a big star like Sean Connery as the star and one of the producers, I'd reached an end in how far I could go in this type of work. There were so many different opinions included within the production of the film.

Later, I was in Toronto, where a friend, Harmony Korine, had shown Fassbinder's *Why Does Herr R. Run Amok?* And one of the things he said about *Herr R.* was that Fassbinder needed not to worry about being boring. He felt like, Who cares, I'm telling my story the way I want to. That somehow clicked with me, and making *Gerry* was a way to be completely independent of something I had been part of for ten years, which was a dependence on financing. And even if it was a movie like *My Own Private Idaho* or *Drugstore Cowboy*, still there's this community of people making the film. You can never really get away from that, but I wanted to try and get as far away as I could. And I wanted to play with different ways of constructing a film. In *Finding Forrester*, you had a very strict 118-page screenplay. I think the word has always been they're supposed to be 108 to 118 pages, for some reason, for it to be an honest screenplay. So I wanted to do something that didn't really have a screenplay in the ordinary form, something that was somehow made while you were shooting the film, so when you got up in the morning, you tried to develop ideas, storied ideas that you would shoot that day, and react to them, and build your film as you made it. That was the original idea. And not really go through the screenplay situation, which I started to think of as a road map that you plan out so far in advance that by the time you get to shoot it, you're just copying these roads you've already driven through many times in screenplay form. You've worn them out already, so by the time you're shooting, you're trying the best you can to force the film or the scene into what the screenplay is dictating to you, which I found confining.

TH: *Gerry* is really cool in its relationship to writing—the way that you were really trying to strip away the systematized way of thinking about storytelling that has so much to do with a script being a blueprint for an attitude—way beyond a story or a setting where this character meets this character in this scene. It becomes almost a justification for the enterprise of filmmaking that's going to make sure that all these people who get paid this much money are all going to be at this place on this day at this time. The level of money that's spent on films creates such anxiety and fear that it's all imaginary until the film is done—so the director's role is to be this cheerleader of a non-existent form—like the Iraqi government-to-be. But so you were simultaneously challenging that system, starting with, most importantly, the way it was financed, where you really took control of it yourself, which is already such a radical thing to do, but also with the way it evolved with the relationship between two actors and the idea of the two boys, one of whom was killed by the other after they got lost while mountain climbing in the desert.

GVS: It was based on a news item about the two guys, best friends, in Calabasas, who were basically taking a small hike but couldn't find their way out, and at the end of three days, one of them killed the other one. And in the end, there was really only one witness, so it was a black hole of what really did happen, whether he was delirious or whether there was actually some reason that he had to kill his friend. We started out in Argentina to shoot, and we went into a desert without a screenplay partly to deprive ourselves, as you would be deprived of water or food. We were going in there to relive the situation to graft it onto this film. Or make it grow into this film.

TH: Did you work with Harris Savides, the director of photography, before *Gerry*?

GVS: We did a little commercial once, but *Finding Forrester* was the first film I did with him.

TH: You also carried that relationship from such a different experience and context to *Gerry*. The camera work in both *Elephant* and *Finding Forrester*, and *Last Days* as well, is as if the trajectory of the camera is the defining shape. It's as if the story is forming around a certain curiosity or tendency the camera is taking. It's very specific to each film. Because you're stripping down all of these commercial expectations about filmmaking, and trying to free yourself from the studio control and opinion-making, you'd think that would mean you'd keep it as simple and bare-bones as possible. On the contrary, you were following really radical ideas about how to use a camera, how to set up a scene, how to tell a story with the camera by stripping away information, even stripping away dialogue.

GVS: We started the project by heading into this journey where we were all going to have no screenplay and we thought we might improvise, and it would maybe appear to be like a John Cassavetes improvised film. Matt Damon and Casey Affleck were my two stars, cowriters, and conceptualizers, and the first thing we all did was panic that we wouldn't be able to pull it off, because we didn't really know what we were doing. Like the guys going into the desert were unprepared—they didn't really know how to survive after a few hours. We wrote a screenplay in about five days that none of us could agree was any good. At least Matt and Casey were positive it wasn't anything they actually wanted to film. I was reminding them, "The whole concept is that we can do whatever we want, we don't need the screenplay, so let's just put it away and forget about it," even though I really liked what they'd written. Somehow I was unable to persuade them.

It was getting very cold in Argentina, too cold to be shooting. We didn't know this desert was so high in the mountains that it was going to be snowing, almost. We started having fires in the cabin where we were working, and because we were so positive we weren't going to use the screenplay, we used a few pages at a time to start the fire. After that fire burnt out, we got cold, and we were looking for some newspaper, but there wasn't any, so we just kept saying, "We're not using the script, right?" So by the time we were ready to shoot, five days later, we panicked again because we had no screenplay. We still had it in our heads, though, so it was kind of part of the game.

TH: You had an ending. And you had a beginning!

GVS: Yeah. Two guys go on a little day hike, and in the end one of them kills the other, so how to get there? It was very contained, and it was also going to be shot in order. And it was also one location, even though within the desert there are lots of different places. I think the first discussion was when we started shooting in a particular area—Matt said that he wouldn't have gotten lost in that area because you could see the red rocks on the side of the hill. And I said, "Yeah, but you eventually venture away from the red rocks, that's how you get lost, because you can't find the car, you cut your losses, you think there's a road down there." By the time you get where you think the road is, you can't see the red rocks any longer." So we had to go find sagebrush because he was refusing to shoot near the red rocks. It became a very physical activity of these very graphic images of hills and rocks and walking, and in the end not very much dialogue. Casey and Matt had their own way of speaking because they've known each other since they were like ten years old. I had thought they would speak all the time. So, without really intending to, we were subverting another thing I've grown to dislike in our cinema, which is that everyone's talking all the time.

TH: That implies a kind of looseness, an improvisational approach to filmmaking where the structure is being decided on as it goes, even if it has a beginning and an end. But actually the end result is so formally assured, minimalist, but exquisite. What's so funny about you talking about Fassbinder not being afraid of boring people is that in *Gerry* I was on the edge of my seat. Part of it is the sustained shots. They are lengthy; they are incredibly beautiful; shot in thirty-five. The final decision to commit to the beautiful medium of thirty-five stock forced this strict series of decisions about where and how the scenes would unfold, and a lot of silence, but because the shots are long you're suspenseful about when they will end, and what they're telling you about this friendship—tensions are just starting to seep into it that you can't quite understand. What's not said is probably as important as what is, because a lot of it is playful talk. They're getting scared and getting irritable with each other. And little pranks, or little games, start to take on more forbidding implications as they start to realize that they're really getting lost and they have no food and stuff. And then it comes to the end. The result does not feel that improvisational.

Similarly, with *Elephant*, visual strategy structures that film. It has a lot to do with following kids through a day at a high school and moving through these corridors from behind in these hypnotic long takes that connect to each other. You realize that you're seeing the same progression of kids and traffic in the school from different points of view, leading up to the penultimate moment of the shooting. Again, I felt that the visual strategy was conveying something way beyond a formal experiment. It would put me back in that strange hypnotic state of being in high school, where you are in your own bubble-head, and you're walking in these corridors, and there's this silence, and kids are passing. Then finally, after minutes seem to pass, one guy goes by, and you say, "Hey man," and that's all you've heard. You never see that in a movie. In films a high school is filled with events and activity and conflict. This really puts you back in that strange boredom, that out-of-body experience. It's also pitted against this terror that's about to happen.

I'm really curious to hear about *Last Days*, the film you just shot and are finishing a cut of. Could you talk about the way some of those ideas actually started with *Last Days* but you applied them to *Elephant*?

GVS: *Last Days* was an older idea from about 1995 that was inspired by the death of Kurt Cobain. It's about what happened in the last couple days of his life, which seem to be a mystery. Nobody could really come up with any kind of account of where Kurt had been or if they had seen him or not. So it was another gray area, kind of like *Gerry*, with only one survivor with his one story. In this case, no survivor and no story.

I wanted to do an alternate-universe version of his last days, and I had wanted to use a house as the single setting, again as the desert was in *Gerry*, also as a way to have a low budget. It was, for whatever reason, very, very important to me, and mysterious to me, and it kept my interest. I devised this idea of the camera going through the house and following him doing mundane things, because I assume those last days were pretty uneventful. Other characters' journeys within the house would overlap with his, and the story is about those overlaps, which aren't about a traditional conflict that holds your attention. It is a different way to hold an audience's attention, a different kind of "amusement," a way of transfixing the audience while you're busy feeding information to them. Generally the job of narrative is to somehow get the conflict in a way that it succeeds in transcending the time that you're reading or watching the piece. So the overlaps are the actual device that is doing that rather than the conflict.

Then I got worried about it; everybody was always afraid of Courtney, basically. Everyone was afraid of something going wrong with the estate and people getting mad, and we were also playing with an icon, so we were nervous about how we were going to do it. And at one point I wanted a fourteen-year-old boy to play Kurt, though the character's name's not Kurt, it's Blake. But it somehow stalled out at the same time that we got a go-ahead on another project that started out as a response to the Columbine shootings. I had initiated it but it was now about three years old. JT Leroy had actually written a screenplay, but I was trying to get out of it because I wasn't really interested in that particular screenplay.

Plus, after three years it was not as interesting. So I had this very bizarre meeting with the executives at HBO, in LA, and I was in the mode of trying to get out of the job. When you're trying to get out of something like that, it never works. Usually you're trying to get the job but that's not working either.

So I was trying to tell them that I didn't want to work with the screenplay any longer, and that they obviously wouldn't be interested in that, so naturally we would have to abandon the project. And they said, "No, no, that sounds great, we like that." And I said, "Well, it's going to be very long and very boring, too." And they said, "That sounds really good, because an unconventional approach to this material is what we want." And I said, "Well, we want to shoot it in black and white," which I thought would be a big deal. And they said, "Well, that one we can talk about." And then I thought, Well, you know what, if they really are serious, if they really want to help with this project, then that would be great. I went ahead and did *Elephant* before we did *Last Days*. We were using very similar ideas; all of a sudden my ideas for *Last Days*, which had been roaming around in the cross sections, were being adopted into this new project. We made it very quickly, a year and a half ago. And cast kids from Portland,

We shot it at Adams High School. While *Gerry* still has a three-act structure and a pretty traditional, linear approach, *Elephant* is kind of retracing the same piece of time. I had seen it done before—it wasn't particularly new—but it was just using a different device than I had ever used to tell a story.

With *Last Days*, one of the questions is how the cinematographer works into the situation. Harris Savides has become a very important collaborator, the arbiter of our ideas. He's the kind of solid one who can tell me when things may be gratuitous. He's often asking, "What are we saying with this shot?" A lot of times you're not saying anything. There are a lot of things that, starting with *Gerry*, we just stopped doing. Like reverse angles, over-the-shoulder dialogue scenes—we decided those were meretricious or gratuitous and they didn't deliver what they were promising. Over-the-shoulder shots were about coverage of action, rather than committing to particular action.

TH: With coverage, the whole idea is to take one scene, shoot a master shot, which is a shot of the whole room so you see everybody enter and exit. Then you shoot a shot of the star lady, then you shoot a shot of the star guy. Then if the actor is bad in the scene, you can stay on the lady, and then if she trips and falls in the master you can cut to the guy's expression. It gives you all the options. But it also gives you the same language of filmmaking that we always see. And what I think Harris says is that you stop thinking why, and you're not looking anymore, because you're seeing the same exact style of shooting telling any story. It's as if what you're telling, and how you're telling it, are mutually exclusive terms. So when I first saw *Elephant*, I thought I was seeing something for the first time, because it wasn't relying on a staid, automatic formula of storytelling.

GVS: Another thing about "coverage" in a film is that in writing it would be like writing a few different drafts, and letting the editor decide which draft to go with. You're working very hard to get your wide shots and close-ups and details just right, which takes a lot longer than if you commit to a particular shot, but you're also passing the buck to the editing room. You're saying, "Well, we'll figure it out later." The powers that be really want it to be like this, because then by the time they get to the film, they can help out and be a part of it. They can say, "Why don't we stay on the shot of our star longer than this?" Partly it's a control thing, where the film is made later, when you're done, as opposed to being made while you're shooting it.

TH: When you choose to just shoot a tracking shot that goes on for five hundred yards, parallel shot with the guys walking, that's it! That's the only way the shot has been covered for the film. If it doesn't work—

GVS: You can cut it shorter.

TH: But that's about all you can do. So that does terrify the financier, obviously. Fassbinder would make arbitrary rules. He would say, "We're only doing one take. We'll set up all the lights, and the camera's gonna move over here, and she goes over here, then she gets on the bar and sings her song, and then they fight, and then they go off—but one take only!" The actors would talk about it after the experience, and what they said it would do is give a rush of adrenaline—it's like being in a play. You get this amazing spontaneity, even in this less-spontaneous style of filmmaking. It pushes things into different directions and the outcome can be really startling.

GVS: I guess with all three films, *Elephant*, *Last Days*, and *Gerry*, we didn't ever know what we were doing until we started to do the first shot. You talk about lots of things and watch lots of things, and then it gets to that first day and without even talking, almost, you do something. It's like a sentence almost, the next sentence or the next piece of film will relate to the first piece. And the third one will relate to the previous two and the fourth one will relate to the previous three, and you're just building it as you go.

TH: How do you now feel about *Last Days*'s closeness to the Kurt Cobain story?

GVS: I've never discussed it. I have an agreement actually that I don't have to do press on this one, but I probably will. It's not really trying to show a real thing. I guess in its imagination it's trying to get as close as possible to something like the last days of Kurt's life, but it's not supposed to be "this is the way it was." We don't know how it was.

TH: *Elephant* is not Columbine, but we know it's informed by Columbine. And really in all three films, it's about a known, final, tragic ending.

GVS: Death.

TH: Death, in all three films, really. But different kinds of death.

GVS: Death by the hand of somebody you know, death by a stranger, and death by your own hand.

TH: And what your films are really concerning, in all three cases, is that uncertainty—what precedes those known moments, being explored and plotted out in different ways, in all three cases.

On another topic, when I was in New York starting to make films in the late eighties, independent film hadn't quite defined itself yet. It really belonged to the nineties. But the film that was so definitive in defining that term, *independent film*, was *Drugstore Cowboy*. And it had a lot to do with the fact that it was the first use of a star, Matt Dillon in this case, a star whom you usually think of as being part of Hollywood films, being in this small film. He was doing something really different, low-budget, a kind of character in a kind of setting you would not associate Matt Dillon with. And usually, because this is a pattern that we now take for granted in independent films, you get this amazing performance from somebody you've never seen that way before.

And I'm just curious about how that happened initially, because it wasn't something that people were doing.

GVS: Well, *Drugstore Cowboy* was made by Avenue Pictures, and it was their technique to offer good material to big actors who don't really get to play the good stuff because Hollywood, even back then, was more concerned with making less risky stories. And you get a big star for very little money, too.

TH: And that was not the typical mentality at the time.

GVS: It wasn't typical, perhaps, but it was happening. I guess most people would just say, "Oh, we would never be able to get that star." Maybe it just wasn't as prevalent as now.

TH: But they'd benefit, because their career would look good.

GVS: Yeah, both sides would win. That was actually why I was working with Avenue Pictures.

TH: Did you worry you weren't going to get something really great from a movie star?

GVS: I think I was worried. I had never worked with a movie star. I remember feeling that I was just handling an image. I wasn't used to that. I was used to your actor being your actor, but not somebody whose previous films you'd seen. I tried to ignore that. But he was game to do everything. It was also the first time I'd ever worked with a big crew, so all of a sudden I was besieged with moving big trucks around and stuff like that, which I had never experienced.

TH: The movie just doesn't feel that way, you know. Again, I felt like I was seeing something I hadn't seen before. I felt the same way with Nicole Kidman in *To Die For*.

GVS: In *To Die For*, you really don't like this character. You like disliking her, because she's very divisive and very manipulative and dishonest. Nicole called me directly and she said that she knew she wasn't the first on our list, and I tried to say, "No, no, that's not true," and she said, "Well look, I just know. You don't have to say one way or another, but I am destined to play this part." By the time I hung up, she pretty much had the role. She was married to Tom Cruise, and I assumed that within the household there was a competitive something going on, and she would work very hard. This would really be something she could call her own.

TH: I want to ask about New Queer Cinema and *My Own Private Idaho*, which will always be one of my favorite movies, period, because that's when I got to know you. You were ahead of me and of other film directors who started to be lumped into the "new queer cinema" category. How was that for you? Did you feel at all affected by that "queer" label? I wonder if it made you think about gay themes in your work in any different way. Or even just the success of that film, because critically it was so cherished at that time.

GVS: I was and still am interested in making a different kind of gay-themed film. You know, *My Own Private Idaho* was quite a tragedy, although it was a fanciful tragedy.

TH: It was such a love story, even if it wasn't.

GVS: But it was a downer.

TH: But the best love stories don't end happily! You make us feel all the yearning for the characters. No one will ever forget the campfire scene, and that performance. It's so full of vulnerability and tenderness. It's really indelible.

GVS: Yeah, I felt connected to the scene, which is different now. It was a period in time. I think my big gay-themed film was about Harvey Milk, but it was so overburdened and heavy that it fell apart. It was right around the time of *Even Cowgirls Get the Blues*, like '93. The script that we had was really bland and the two lead characters, Harvey and his boyfriend, kissed on like page fifty-six. Later we rewrote a story where they had really hot sex on the first page, that kind of stuff. You could tell that, even today, there's just not a way to make the big studios happy. If you're gonna make it like *Queer as Folk*, maybe, but otherwise . . .

TH: Not that you would want to do that.

GVS: No. I was trying to capture San Francisco in the seventies and it was hard to really capture Harvey Milk without including lots about everyone's sexual orientation. It had to permeate everything, and I think the studio was more interested in why Dan White shot Harvey Milk instead of why Harvey existed.

TH: What is it like using nonprofessional actors and what is the motivation for using them?

GVS: Well, in art school, at Rhode Island School of Design, at one point I used a lot of people who were faculty and friends. I think I could relate to the nonactor because I wasn't an actor. So I knew what was in their head. And one of the main things in a nonactor's head is, first of all, they don't know what is going on. They may be nervous, sometimes they're not, but there's a common ground. A professional actor, especially a stage actor, there's a history to how you're supposed to be working, but it's not something I've ever studied. I've always worked with both actors and nonactors. There are ways to cast people who really are the character. Say you're looking for a guy who walks onto the scene for even just a little while. Maybe he's a plumber. If you really look around for real plumbers, these guys have got the tools and they know how it all works. We cast a real FedEx man in *Elephant* in the role of the FedEx man. They know how to make small talk at the door and stuff. I can ride with a FedEx man, study what he does, write it down, and then get an actor and tell him how it was, or I can just go to the source.

TH: Except that so many real FedEx men would get really self-conscious about being real FedEx men. I insist that there's something about your personality that must make them feel comfortable.

GVS: A lot of times the people working on a film, including the director, are very anxious about what they're doing. Everything is so very important, we forget that we should relax on the set, and so a lot of times I'm just acting like it's okay to be relaxed. For instance, during a take you can talk. You can almost small talk, and during the take it lets the actor know that it's not that big a deal; you don't have to be that rigid. We can talk, and then we can actually resume the scene. You make it seem like it's not that big a deal. The camera isn't running the show, it's filming you, and you're the important thing. It's a trick, or a way to work, is the best way to put it.

TH: I remember the *Nation* did an issue in 1990, and they asked people—they asked me—"What do you think gay film will be like ten years from now?" I don't know why I thought this then, but I remember saying that I thought gay cinema could very likely become what black cinema was in the sixties, which was that in the future it would be this Sidney Poitier version of the sixties, in that flat gay characters would have to be perfect. It would be a kind of liberal rewrite of how they've been depicted in the past, which is definitely a kind of Hollywood trend, this kind of masking over. There were also these incredibly ambivalent feelings, to say the least, about what was going on in the world, in America in particular. There were these movies of the perfect black man, the overqualified gorgeous perfect flawless whatever—and then the Rupert Everett character became frequent: the perfect handsome best friend to the girl character, with no sexuality and no real story of his own. He was just charming and handsome—kind of the way sitcoms talk about gay people now. There's still violence against gay people and real ambivalence about homosexuality in this country. It's hard to know what's going to happen when it seems like we're in the midst of an incredibly reactionary time politically. There's also this gay-marriage thing, which seems at the very least something like our Bill of Rights, our Constitution. It's moving in its own internal logic, probably toward an inevitable situation where gay marriage will be hard to contest. But that opens up so much shit, and you wonder what the shit will do in response. We're seeing a little of it now, but that isn't necessarily a resolved issue. Do you think queer cinema will continue and become a nonissue, in terms of gay characters in films? Or do you think there might be a return to a genre specific to gay themes?

GVS: It's like telling the future. All you can do is look at today, compared to where we were twenty years ago. I used to go to Vista Theatre on Hollywood Blvd. To the gay-film festival, which at that time was brand-new. That was like, '78? '77? There were like three Tennessee Williams films, which were great. And there was a Dutch film and an Australian film. Now you have OutFest, which has tons of gay-themed films made everywhere, and there were groundbreaking films along the way. There are more gay-themed films that play in theaters. I guess it just depends on the actual success of the film. I'm sure that a mainstream film can be about a gay relationship. I think it can be that way, or it can be a genre, or can be ghettoized in a certain way. I'm not sure. I assume that it will be part of the landscape of human existence.

TH: Your recent films have been based on news stories. What other things have interested or influenced you to work in an ultrarealistic fashion?

GVS: With *Elephant* and *Last Days*—and I guess *Gerry* works this way too—the method the movie works on is that it expects the audience to come with some information about the topic. That's how it usually works the best. It's okay if you don't know what you're going to go see, but when you see it, particularly with *Elephant*, you have your own opinions about what you're watching. A lot of the time the film is actually not telling a story to the audience, it's trying to pull a story out of the audience. There are little indications, little buzzwords and buzz-incidents happening in front of you, and your thoughts about those things are what is making the actual story experience happen. It's not being thrust on you or dictated to you. You're part of it, you're participating in it, in the creation of the story. I think in *Gerry* it works because you may have been lost yourself at times. *Elephant* is hoping that you have an opinion or have read about high school violence. *Last Days*, which is a little more out on a limb, is expecting you to know something about rock stars and their tragic consequences, in some cases, like Kurt Cobain. That's the reason that I am drawn to it.

Contributors

Claribel Alegría was born in Estelí, Nicaragua, in 1924 and grew up in El Salvador. She has published over forty books including many volumes of poetry, a number of novels and testimonies, and a book of children's stories. Ten of her books of poetry and fiction have been translated into English, including *Ashes of Izalco*, *Luisa in Realityland*, *Family Album*, *Fugues*, *Thresholds and Sorrow*. Her home is in Managua, Nicaragua.

Sherman Alexie has published eighteen books of stories, novels, and poetry, most recently the novel *Flight*, and is the recipient of numerous awards and honors. The *New Yorker* named him one of twenty writers for the twenty-first century and *Granta* magazine named him one of twenty best American novelists under the age of forty. His work has been included in *The Best American Short Stories 2004*, *Pushcart Prize XXIX*, and *The O. Henry Prize Stories 2005*. He lives in Seattle with his wife and two sons.

Tracy Chevalier is the author of five novels, including *Girl with a Pearl Earring*, *The Virgin Blue*, *Falling Angels*, *The Lady and the Unicorn*, and *Burning Bright*. She lives in London.

Charles D'Ambrosio is the author of two collections of short stories, *The Point and Other Stories*, and *The Dead Fish Museum*, and a collection of essays, *Orphans*. His writings have appeared in the *New Yorker*, the *Paris Review*, *Zoetrope All-Story*, and *A Public Space*. He lives in Portland, Oregon.

Lydia Davis, a 2003 MacArthur Fellow, writer, and translator, is the author of *Varieties of Disturbance*, *Samuel Johnson Is Indignant*, *Almost No Memory*, *The End of the Story*, and *Break it Down*. Her work has appeared in *Conjunctions*, *Harper's*, the *New Yorker*, *BOMB*, the *Paris Review*, *McSweeney's*, and elsewhere. Among other honors, she has received a Guggenheim and Lannan Literary Award. She lives in upstate New York, where she is on the faculty of SUNY Albany and is a fellow at the New York State Writers Institute.

Anita Desai was born in Mussoorie, India, in 1937 to a Bengali father and German mother, and grew up in Delhi. She is the author of fourteen books, three of which—*Clear Light of Day* (1980), *In Custody* (1984), and *Fasting, Feasting* (1999)—have been nominated for the Booker Prize. Her most recent novel is *The Zigzag Way*.

Roddy Doyle is an internationally best-selling novelist and screenwriter. His works include *The Commitments*, *The Snapper*, *Paddy Clarke Ha Ha Ha* (1993 Booker Prize winner), and, most recently, *Paula Spencer*, and for younger readers, *Wilderness*. A collection of stories, *The Deportees*, will be published in January 2008. He lives in Dublin.

Rikki Ducornet is a writer and illustrator. Her novels include *The Fan-Maker's Inquisition* (an *L.A. Times* Book of the Year), and *The Jade Cabinet* (a finalist for the National Book Critics Circle Award). In 1993 she received the Lannan Literary Award in Fiction. She is novelist in residence at the University of Louisiana, Lafayette.

Deborah Eisenberg is the author of four collections of stories: *Twilight of the Superheroes*, *All Around Atlantis*, *Under the 82nd Airborne*, and *Transactions in a Foreign Currency*, as well as a play, *Pastorale*. The recipient of many awards, including a Guggenheim Fellowship, a Lannan Literary Fellowship, a Rea Award, and a Whiting Writers' Award, she lives in New York City and teaches at the University of Virginia.

Ellen Fagg, a graduate of the University of Iowa's Nonfiction Writing Program, is the editor of a collection of fiction, *The Way We Live*. She has written and edited for Web sites, magazines, and newspapers, and currently reviews theater for the *Salt Lake Tribune*. She has taught writing and literary journalism at the University of Iowa, Portland State University, and Westminster College.

Nuruddin Farah is the author of ten novels; he lives in Cape Town, South Africa.

Abbie Fields has lived in Nicaragua since the mid-1980s, working as a producer of documentary films, a translator, and a writer. She is currently teaching psychology at a small liberal arts college in the town of San Marcos.

Ben George has been the editor of *Fugue* and associate editor of *Tin House*, each of which has published his interviews with writers such as Rick Bass, W. S. Merwin, Margot Livesey, and Peter Ho Davies. He is at work on an anthology of essays about fatherhood.

Regan Good is a poet and writer living in Brooklyn, New York. A graduate of Barnard College and the Iowa Writers' Workshop, her poems have appeared in the *Paris Review, American Letters & Commentary, Exquisite Corpse, Fence,* the *Literary Review,* and other journals. A chapbook, *The Imperfect,* was published by Westown Press in 2005.

Tom Grimes is the author of four novels and two plays. His fiction has twice been a finalist for the PEN/Nelson Algren Award. It has also been a *New York Times* Notable Book of the Year, an Editor's Choice, and a New and Noteworthy Paperback, as well as a James Michener Fellowship winner. One of his plays, *SPEC,* won three *Los Angeles Dramalogue* awards. His essay on preserving the Katherine Anne Porter house appeared in *Tin House.* His essay "Bring Out Your Dead" appeared in *Tin House* no. 25 and was named a Notable Essay in *The Best American Essays 2006.* He directs the MFA Program in Creative Writing at Texas State University.

Ron Hansen's latest novel, *Exiles,* is forthcoming from Farrar, Straus and Giroux in May 2008. His other books include *Isn't It Romantic?: An Entertainment, A Stay Against Confusion: Essays on Faith and Fiction, Hitler's Niece: A Novel, Atticus: A Novel,* and *Mariette in Ecstasy: A Novel.* He has received fellowships from the Michigan Society of Fellows, the National Endowment for the Arts, the John Simon Guggenheim Foundation, and the Lyndhurst Foundation, and was presented with an Award in Literature from the American Academy and Institute of Arts and Letters. He is now the Gerard Manley Hopkins, S. J., Professor in the Arts and Humanities at Santa Clara.

Tin House Paris Editor **Heather Hartley**'s work has appeared or is forthcoming in the *Los Angeles Review, Post Road, POOL, Smartish Place, Mississippi Review, Web del Sol Review of Books,* and the anthology *Food & Booze: A Tin House Literary Feast,* among other publications.

Todd Haynes's films include the forthcoming *I'm Not There, Far from Heaven, The Velvet Goldmine, Safe,* and *Poison.*

Denis Johnson is the author of five novels, a collection of poetry, and one book of reportage. He is the recipient of a Lannan Literary Fellowship and a Whiting Writer's Award, among many other honors. He lives in northern Idaho.

Anna Keesey teaches at Linfield College. Her work has appeared in *Grand Street, DoubleTake, Tin House,* and *The Best American Short Stories,* among other journals and anthologies.

Ken Kesey's books include *One Flew Over the Cuckoo's Nest, Sometimes A Great Notion* (both made into films), *Caverns, Demon Box,* and *Kesey's Garage Sale.* He also wrote, directed, and performed plays including *Where's Merlin?* and *Twister.* Kesey's cross-country trip with a group of "Merry Pranksters" was chronicled in Tom Wolfe's *The Electric Kool-Aid Acid Test.* Kesey died in 2001.

Tracy Kidder graduated from Harvard, studied at the University of Iowa, and served as an army officer in Vietnam. He has won the Pulitzer Prize, the National Book Award, and the Robert F. Kennedy Award, among other literary prizes. The author of *The Soul of a New Machine, House, Among Schoolchildren, Old Friends, Home Town, Mountains Beyond Mountains,* and *My Detachment,* Kidder lives in Massachusetts and Maine.

Heather Larimer lives in Portland, Oregon. Her work has appeared in *Tin House, Swink,* the *Sun, Open City,* and *Jane.* She is a cofounder of the Loggernaut Reading Series, writes a style column for the *Portland Tribune,* plays in two rock bands, and is currently taking a year off from teaching writing in order to join 12, an experimental advertising program at the ad agency Wieden + Kennedy.

Win McCormack is the founder, publisher, and editor in chief of *Tin House.* His work has appeared in the *Nation,* among other publications.

Christopher Merrill's books include four collections of poetry, *Brilliant Water, Workbook, Fevers & Tides,* and *Watch Fire,* for which he received the Peter I. B. Lavan Younger Poets Award from the Academy of American Poets. He is also a translator of numerous works of poetry. He now directs the International Writing Program at the University of Iowa.

Rick Moody is the author of *Garden State, The Ice Storm, Purple America, The Ring of Brightest Angels Around Heaven, Demonology, The Black Veil, The Diviners,* and, most recently, *Right Livelihoods: Three Novellas.*

Chris Offutt is the author of the story collections *Kentucky Straight* and *Out of the Woods,* the novel *The Good Brother,* and two memoirs, *The Same River Twice* and *No Heroes.* His work is widely translated and has received many honors, including a Lannan award, a Whiting award, and a Guggenheim Fellowship. He has also written comic books, screenplays, and teleplays. He has taught at several schools, most notably as a four-time visiting professor at the Iowa Writers' Workshop, where he was a student of James Salter in 1989.

Carla Perry graduated from the University of Iowa Writers' Workshop with a degree in poetry. She is the founder of Writers on the Edge (www.writerson-theedge.org) and the Nye Beach Writers' Series, now in its tenth year on Oregon's coast. For her contributions to Oregon's literary life, she received the Stewart Holbrook Special Award at the Oregon Book Awards, the Oregon State Governor's Art Award, and numerous literary fellowships and residencies. She was the editor/publisher of *Wild Dog Literary Magazine* and *Talus & Scree International Literary Journal*, and owns Dancing Moon Press (www.dancingmoonpress.com). Her poetry, essays, interviews, short stories, and photos of writers have been published widely.

Francine Prose is the author of fourteen books of fiction, including, most recently, *A Changed Man* and *Blue Angel*, which was a finalist for the National Book Award. She has taught literature and writing for more than twenty years at major universities such as Harvard, Iowa, Columbia, Arizona, and the New School. She is a distinguished critic and essayist. Prose lives in New York City.

Rachel Resnick, the author of *Go West Young F*cked-Up Chick* (St. Martin's), is writing a memoir, *Love Junkie*, forthcoming from Bloomsbury. She also runs Writers on Fire (*www.writersonfire.com*), a series of luxury writing retreats.

Marilynne Robinson is the author of the novels *Gilead*, which won the Pulitzer Prize and the National Book Critics Circle Award, and *Housekeeping*, which won the PEN/Hemingway Award. She is also the author of two books of nonfiction, *Mother Country* and *The Death of Adam*. She teaches at the University of Iowa Writers' Workshop.

Barney Rosset is former publisher/editor of Grove Press, which published writers such as Samuel Beckett, Jean Genet, Eugène Ionesco, Harold Pinter, William Burroughs, Tom Stoppard, Kenzaburo Oe, and Jack Kerouac. He was awarded the French title of Commandeur de l'Ordre des Arts et des Lettres in 1999. Now publisher of the *Evergreen Review* (*www.evergreenreview.com*), he lives in New York City.

James Salter's novels include *Light Years*, *A Sport and a Pastime*, and *Solo Faces*, and his titles have been in Modern Library and Penguin Classics. He won the PEN/Faulkner Award in 1989 and was a finalist in 2006. He lives in Colorado and on Long Island.

Marjane Satrapi was born in Rasht, Iran, and grew up in Tehran. Her commentary and comics appear in newspapers and magazines around the world, including the *New Yorker* and the *New York Times*. She lives in Paris.

George Saunders is the author of the short story collections *CivilWarLand in Bad Decline*, *Pastoralia*, and *In Persuasion Nation*; the children's book *The Very Persistent Gappers of Frip*; and the novella *The Brief and Frightening Reign of Phil*. He teaches at Syracuse University.

Elissa Schappell is the author of *Use Me*, a finalist for the PEN/Hemingway award, and coeditor with Jenny Offill of two anthologies, *The Friend Who Got Away* and *Money Changes Everything*. She is currently a contributing editor at *Vanity Fair*, a cofounder and now editor-at-large of *Tin House*, a regular contributor to the *New York Times Book Review*, and formerly senior editor of the *Paris Review*. Her fiction/essays/articles have appeared in *The Bitch in the House*, *The Mrs. Dalloway Reader*, *The KGB Bar Reader*, *SPIN*, and *Vogue*, among other places. She teaches in the low-residency MFA program at Queens University in North Carolina.

James Schiff teaches American literature and creative writing at the University of Cincinnati. He is the author of several books on contemporary American fiction, including, most recently, *Updike in Cincinnati*. His work has appeared in *Southern Review*, *Missouri Review*, *Boulevard*, *American Literature*, *Tin House*, *Critique*, and elsewhere. He reviews fiction regularly for newspapers and magazines.

Wallace Shawn is a playwright and actor. As a playwright, he has won three Obies, and his plays include *The Hotel Play*, *Our Late Night*, *A Thought in Three Parts*, *Marie and Bruce*, *Aunt Dan and Lemon*, *The Fever*, and *The Designated Mourner*. He recently translated *The Threepenny Opera* by Brecht. His numerous film credits include *My Dinner with André*, which he wrote and starred in with André Gregory.

Jim Shepard is the author of six novels, most recently *Project X*, and three story collections, most recently *Like You'd Understand, Anyway*, which appeared in September 2007. He lives in Williamstown, Massachusetts.

Rob Spillman is the editor of *Tin House* magazine and the main roadie for the band Care Bears on Fire.

Mark Strand has published twelve books of poetry, the most recent of which is *New Selected Poems*, and received numerous awards, including a MacArthur Fellowship in 1987 and the Pulitzer Prize in 1999 for *A Blizzard of One*. He currently teaches at Columbia University.

Anderson Tepper is on the staff of *Vanity Fair* and is a contributing editor to *Words Without Borders: The Online Magazine for International Literature*. His essay on García Lorca in Harlem appeared in *Tin House* no. 8.

Gus Van Sant is an Academy-Award nominated director whose films include *Mala Noche*, *Drugstore Cowboy*, *My Own Private Idaho*, *Even Cowgirls Get the Blues*, *To Die For*, *Good Will Hunting*, *Psycho*, *Finding Forrester*, *Gerry*, *Elephant*, *Last Days*, and *Paranoid Park*. His awards include the Palme D'Or at Cannes and many nominations and selections in the Toronto, Venice, Cesar, Berlin, and Sundance film festivals. He lives in Portland, Oregon.

Copyright Notes